THE ORIGIN OF GERMAN TRAGIC DRAMA

Walter Benjamin

Introduced by George Steiner

Translated by John Osborne

VERSO

London • New York

This edition first published by Verso 2023
Previously published by Verso 1998, 2003, 2009
First published as *Ursprung des deutschen Trauerspiels*
© Suhrkamp Verlag 1963

1 3 5 7 9 10 8 6 4 2

Verso
UK: 6 Meard Street, London W1F 0EG
US: 388 Atlantic Ave, Brooklyn, NY 11217
versobooks.com

Verso is the imprint of New Left Books

ISBN-13: 978-1-80429-046-0
ISBN-13: 978-1-78960-472-6 (US EBK)
ISBN-13: 978-1-78960-473-3 (UK EBK)

British Library Cataloguing in Publication Data
A catalogue record for this book is available from the British Library

Library of Congress Cataloging-in-Publication Data
A catalog record for this book is available from the Library of Congress

Printed and bound by CPI Group (UK) Ltd, Croydon, CRO 4YY

Contents

Allegory and *Trauerspiel*

Translator's Note

Ursprung des deutschen Trauerspiels, Benjamin's most extensive, most complex, and most esoteric work, is a book which makes considerable demands on the reader, the printer, and the translator. The translator's difficulties begin with the word *Trauerspiel* (literally = mourning-play), which is used to refer to modern, baroque tragedy as distinct from classical tragedy (*Tragödie*). In the following version the German word *Trauerspiel* has been preserved throughout.

The text used is as printed in: Walter Benjamin, *Gesammelte Schriften*. Unter Mitwirkung von Theodor W. Adorno und Gershom Scholem, herausgegeben von Rolf Tiedemann und Hermann Schweppenhäuser, I, 1, Abhandlungen, Frankfurt a.M., 1974, pp. 203–430. The editorial principles of this edition (see vol. I, 3, pp. 955–961) have, as far as possible, been respected. Here, as in the edition of 1928, footnotes do not appear as page-notes but are placed at the end of the work; and quotations, even verse-quotations, are not formally separated, but are printed as an integral part of the continuous text, ensuring that a pause for breath occurs only between the separate, and intensely concentrated sections that make up the 'mosaic' which is Benjamin's text. The need both to quote Benjamin's source-material in the original, and to provide English translations – printed as page-notes – has necessitated some departure from this latter principle. To avoid ambiguity, a vertical stroke (|) is used to separate lines of verse in quotations, the diagonal stroke (/) being used as a punctuation mark (*Virgel*) in certain baroque texts.

My task in preparing this English version was rendered considerably easier than it might have been by the substantial preliminary work of Ben Brewster to whom I am deeply grateful.

I should also like to thank the friends and colleagues who generously gave their help, in particular Michael Wadsworth for his translations from the Latin, Rosemarie Ashe for her assistance in preparing the typescript, and my wife for her help with all aspects of the work. Responsibility for any failure to do justice to Benjamin's remarkable book rests, of course, with me.

J.O. University of Sussex January 1977

Introduction

George Steiner

Walter Benjamin (1892–1940) wrote the *Ursprung des deutschen Trauer-spiels* in the period between May 1924 and late March or early April 1925. A short excerpt appeared in the *Neue Deutsche Beiträge*, II, 3, for August 1927. The book itself was published in Berlin in January 1928. Up to 1931 it received six brief notices, at least three of which were abruptly negative. After 1931, the *Ursprung* (it is best to keep the German title until its main terms can be looked at closely) was literally an extinct work – one of a fascinating group of writings and works of art assigned to oblivion by the rise of National Socialism and the consequent dispersal or destruction of the German-Jewish community. Single copies survived in the custody and recollection of Benjamin's friends or of a handful of interested refugees – Gershon Scholem, T. W. Adorno, Siegfried Kracauer, Hannah Arendt. The text became available again in the 1955 two-volume edition of Benjamin's *Schriften*. Since then it has become recognized as one of the most original books of literary and philosophical criticism of the twentieth century.

Whoever engages this difficult text seriously, will rely on the variorum version issued in the Frankfurt edition of the collected works, *Gesammelte Schriften*, I, 1 (1974) by Rolf Tiedemann and Hermann Schweppen-häuser; and more particularly on the textual-biographical material which the editors have assembled in volume I, 3, pp. 868–981. Surprisingly, a great number of Benjamin's letters and notebooks, together with academic and journalistic documents relevant to the *Ursprung*, survived personal and public catastrophe. They now form part of the Benjamin archive. With their aid, the editors can give an almost continuous account of the sources, composition and publication of the work, and of Walter Benjamin's inner history at the time. It is the most fragile of evidence – notes, provisional outlines, an unpublished preface to a monograph which academic contempt and political barbarism had consigned to silence – which has proved the most durable. What follows draws throughout on Tiedemann's and Schweppenhäuser's detailed findings.

The dedication of the *Ursprung* is marked 'sketched' or 'conceived' *(entworfen)* 1916 and 'written' 1925. Both statements are factually erroneous and characteristic of Benjamin's casualness or arcane tomfoolery. But the earlier date has its pertinence, for it was in 1916 that Benjamin wrote three unpublished essays in which a number of the crucial ideas and techniques of the *Ursprung* are first set out. 'Trauerspiel und Tragödie' argues a distinction which will be fundamental to the book; 'Die Bedeutung der Sprache in Trauerspiel und Tragödie' and the sovereignly entitled 'Ueber Sprache überhaupt und über die Sprache der Menschen' – now available in volume II of the Frankfurt edition – are a first trial of the philosophy of language and poetic logic that determine both the method and style of the *Ursprung*. Between 1916 and 1924, Benjamin wrote his doctoral dissertation on the concept of art-criticism in the German romantic movement (1920) and his famous analysis of Goethe's *Elective Affinities* published, under the enthusiastic patronage of the poet and dramatist Hugo von Hofmannsthal in the April 1924 and January 1925 numbers of the *Neue Deutsche Beiträge*. Both the dissertation and the essay enter into the intellectual fabric and idiom of the study of baroque drama.

In the German system, a doctoral thesis is only a first and local step towards higher academic qualification. The latter depends on a *Habilitationsschrift*, which is a full-scale text, ready for impression, and submitted to the appropriate faculty of a university for public examination and judgement. If the work is found acceptable, the author receives the *venia legendi*, which is the invitation and right to lecture in the university as a *Privatdozent*. It is from this body that the university system as a whole recruits its extraordinary and ordinary professors.

This bit of titular heraldry is necessary if one is to grasp Benjamin's purpose in writing the *Ursprung* as well as certain features of the book.

Though born into comfortable Jewish-Berlin circumstances, Benjamin, now married and entering his thirties, had no professional endowments or means of support. He and his wife lived in his father's house and benefited from parental financial help. There were tensions between father and son, and inflation raged. As early as 1919, Benjamin had resolved to 'habilitate himself' and thus obtain an academic berth. Neither of his alternative projects, a career as a free-lance man of letters or as an antiquarian bookseller (Benjamin was a rapacious, expert bibliophile) looked at all realistic. At first Benjamin thought of the university in Berne, where he had spent a part of the war years. But the German financial crisis made residence in Switzerland prohibitive. So in December 1922, Benjamin went to Heidelberg to reconnoitre. His conclusions are a graphic witness to the situation then prevailing in Weimar academic spheres. As Benjamin wrote to Scholem on December 30th, the professor he called on had not asked him back, and the fact that one Karl Mannheim was proposing to do his 'habilitation' under the aegis of Alfred Weber almost ruled out prospects for any other Jewish aspirant. By March 1923, Benjamin had fixed on Frankfurt where his grand-uncle had held a chair of mathematics and where the *Ordinarius* for *Germanistik* (we would now say 'the Chairman of the Department of German language and literature') seemed well disposed.

By the late summer of 1923, Benjamin, back in Berlin, had chosen his theme and had begun to give rough outline to his argument. A letter to Professor Schultz, the *Ordinarius* in question, suggests that it was he who had directed Benjamin towards the Baroque tragedians, mainly of the Silesian school, of the mid-seventeenth century. But as we shall see, the grounds of sensibility and craft from which the *Ursprung* derives are specific to Benjamin. By the autumn of the year, Benjamin's research was in progress. He was a library-cormorant and devourer of ancient print quite in the manner of a Coleridge or a Marx. He had collected baroque poetry and emblem-books for his personal delight. Now he could ferret with intent among the folios, broadsheets and in-octavos of the Berlin *Staatsbibliothek*. He made some six-hundred excerpts from long-dormant baroque plays, from theological tracts of that tormented period, and from secondary sources.

This burrowing took place against a darkening domestic and political backdrop. During the winter of 1923-4, Benjamin conceived the notion of completing his labours abroad, under less stringent pressures. In a letter to his intimate, Christian Florens Rang, Benjamin, immersed in the grey of archival scholarship, hit on an arresting image: the requisite research and discipline of scholarly form makes of 'every completed work the death-mask of its intention'. To Scholem, who had emigrated to Palestine, Benjamin reported in March of 1924 that his library-quarrying was essentially complete and that the structure of the book as a whole was now clear in his mind. The letter dated March 5th is key: in it Benjamin relates his ideas on the emblematic-allegorical temper of the baroque spirit to the esoteric sides of German romanticism – notably in Johann Wilhelm Ritter and Novalis. Here was the necessary continuity with Benjamin's preceding studies.

May found Walter Benjamin on Capri, steeped in the actual composition of the *Ursprung*. Letters to Scholem of June 13th and the 16th of September tell of progress, and of the ever-increasing density and complication of Benjamin's treatment. The arcane material exercises 'its dizzying force of attraction'. The very act of writing is generating its own singular methodology and philosophic bias. There are, moreover, counter-currents at work. On July 7th, Benjamin reports to Scholem that he has met a woman-revolutionary from Riga, and that this meeting has raised in his mind the possibilities of 'a radical communism'. Asja Lacis was to play a still obscure but important role in Benjamin's existence and political thought. Simultaneously, Benjamin was reading Lukács's *History and Class Consciousness*; it was striking and, in a sense, validating (*bestätigend*), observed Benjamin, that Lukács, operating from wholly political premises, should have reached epistemological conclusions very similar to those he himself was now expounding. After a Rome visit in the fall, Benjamin returned to Berlin. The death of Rang, in October, signified that his ideal reader, and perhaps the only reader fully capable of judging the *Ursprung*, was gone. The reflections on baroque melancholy and on the triumphs of desolation in baroque fantasy and speech took on a private edge. By April 6th, 1925, the monograph was completed.

The next episode is one of predictable rout. In the process of working on the *Ursprung*, Benjamin had felt dubious as to the academic flavour of his theories and style. Nor was he convinced that the routine of teaching demanded of a *Privatdozent* would suit the labyrinthine involutions and meditative ease of his person. But now the manuscript lay ready, its scholarly apparatus prominent and extensive. Benjamin's confidence returned. Lesser men had achieved their *Habilitation* for a shallow fraction of the work *he* had done. In February, nearing the end of his efforts, Benjamin had judged the Frankfurt situation to be 'not unfavourable'. Soon he knew better.

Professor Schultz found the *Ursprung* inappropriate to *Germanistik*. He passed it on to the department of aesthetics or philosophy of art. Formal submission took place on May 12th. On July 27th, 1925, Schultz wrote to Benjamin urging him to withdraw his application and thus avoid the unpleasantness of public refusal. Professor Hans Cornelis (and it is from such episodes that academics sometimes garner their mite of immortality), the local aesthetician, had found the *Ursprung* to be an incomprehensible morass. By late September, Benjamin's tenuous links with the university world were broken. Long after Benjamin's death the affair was to have its epitaph: 'Geist kann man nicht habilitieren', said a professor of post-war vintage. 'One cannot habilitate *Geist*'. The word, of course, means both 'spirit' and 'wit', and carries those connotations of 'knowledge', of 'masterly knowing' which 'wit' or *wissen* derive from Anglo-Saxon and Old German roots. Benjamin's editors castigate this bit of repartee as heartless and impertinent. But is it?

What remains certain is the fact that Benjamin's failure to obtain an academic toehold compelled him to a free-lance life, to the precarious, errant practices of a critic, translator, reviewer and script-writer for radio. Whether his achievements were lamed or incited by this condition is, even today, an awkward question. The *Ursprung des deutschen Trauerspiels* is Walter Benjamin's only completed book. The rest of his writings, which will comprise eight sizeable tomes, was produced in the guise of essays, translations, fragments, short notices, scripts. And the reader he envisaged for the serious part of his work was, literally, posthumous.

* * *

What sort of book is the *Ursprung*? No simple answer will do, because Benjamin's text is multiple in its voice and intentions. The first point to make is one of general background. Any *Geisteswissenschaftler* – that notoriously elusive but essential term which aims to distinguish the intuitions, the disciplines of analysis in the philosophic-spiritual sphere from those in the purely historical, sociological or exact sciences – working in Germany in the 1920s, would relate to two exemplary precedents. Hegel's *Phenomenology* had dramatized the experience and the exposition of abstract thought. It had made of philosophic discourse a self-unfolding, dramatic process inseparable from the characteristics of individual style. To this dramatization and dynamic reciprocity of matter and tone, the dialectic, Nietzsche's *The Birth of Tragedy* had added a seductive amalgam of lyricism and professional philology.

In agreeing to play the academic game, in striving to become a participant in it, Benjamin will have had in mind, as did Adorno when he composed his *Habilitationsschrift* on Kierkegaard, that Hegel had spent his life as a pedagogue, that Nietzsche had begun as a young professor in the most mandarin of faculties, that of classical studies. The launching of radical, sharply idiosyncratic books from an official scholastic base seemed to guarantee that one could at once satisfy and ironically transcend the demands of the university (Kierkegaard's own *Magister* dissertation on the nature of Socratic irony, a masterpiece of indirection, would have served as a further example of subversion from within). By virtue of its title and numerous textual echoes, the *Ursprung* aligns itself immediately with Nietzsche's famous monograph. In its motion of spirit, in the way in which idiom and organization enact the formal case, Benjamin's treatise is Hegelian.

But although its stance is ambiguous, Benjamin's work does aim resolutely at fulfilling academic conventions. The resigned or playful tone of Benjamin's letters only half conceals the pride of a scholarly initiate, bibliographer, philological critic and pioneer iconographer. The fields of reference are rich and hermetic: an *Ars heraldica* of 1688, a Rosicrucian tract of 1679, a Latin lexicon of mottoes and devices, dated 1683, pamphlets and pasquinades in defense of the antique dignity of the German tongue issued in Nuremberg during the 1640s and 50s, Salmasius on regicide, the posthumous writings of J. W. Ritter, the romantic illuminist (at which point Dr. Benjamin draws attention to a forged title-page). The secondary sources are also duly recondite: Conrad Höfer on the Rudolfstädter *Festspiel* of 1665–7; Lukács's early *Die Seele und die Formen* (then scarcely known); Werner Weisbach on the Italian *trionfi*; Yeats's essays on theatre; Panofsky and Saxl on Dürer's *Melencolia*.

In a way that is symptomatic of the man of letters advancing on academic ground, Benjamin becomes entranced by the props and rituals of the exercise. The obscurity of his primary texts, the very fact that Opitz, Gryphius, Lohenstein and their fellow-playwrights had lain so long neglected, excites the commentator. Like philologists and professors throughout the guild, Benjamin found himself praising works just because they were opaque and rebarbative. Perhaps unconsciously, he mimed the tricks of the trade: the magisterial footnote, the allusive digression, the qualifying yet copious resort to examples and citations where a point is to be scored. At several marked levels, the *Ursprung is a Habilitationsschrift* aiming to enlist and instruct the faculties of German and/or Aesthetics at the esteemed University of Frankfurt a. Main.

At other points it is a poetic-metaphysical meditation unique to Walter Benjamin's intellectual world and private feelings. The Jewish facets make this obvious. Franz Rosenzweig's *Der Stern der Erlösung* had appeared in 1921. It seemed to articulate, as no other book had, the unstable glories of the German-Jewish connection and of the bearing of that connection on the Jewish past and on the enigma of the messianic future. It also contained one of the three models of a theory of tragedy which Benjamin drew on – the two others being Nietzsche's and that of the phenomenologist and Husserl-follower Max Scheler. And what of the Kabbalah? The question is relevant to the *Erkenntniskritische Vorrede* (the 'Epistemo-Critical Prologue' as our translator puts it) to the *Ursprung*. This is, together with Heidegger's work of whose beginnings Benjamin was uneasily aware, one of the more impenetrable pieces of prose in German or, for that matter, in any modern language. In his exquisite memoir of his friend, *Walter Benjamin – die Geschichte einer Freundschaft* (1975), Gershom Scholem reports that Benjamin had said of this prologue, to the scholar-critic Max Rychner and to Adorno, that it could be understood only by a reader who also knew the Kabbalah. Scholem's own work on the Kabbalah had hardly begun at that point, and it was certainly not esoteric Judaica that the two men had discussed during their years of intimacy first in Berne and then in Germany. Did Benjamin mean no more than to say that there were vital texts even darker, more riddling than his? Or had he already caught some intimation of the kabbalistic paradigm of the hidden word, of the forty-nine levels of meaning in and beneath the written letter which Scholem was later to expound? Whatever its overt intention, Benjamin's analogy is in fact penetrating. Steeped in the ambience of Lutheran and counter-Reformation art and drama, with their decisive bias towards allegory, the *Ursprung*, and not merely the problematic first section, does reflect a Jewish hallowing of the word, an almost tactile sense of the mystery of saying. This makes Benjamin's critique contemporary, in more than date, of Kafka and the earlier Wittgenstein (indeed how profound and curious are the affinities between technical philosophy and literary criticism, between fiction and the new music, across the entire spectrum of European Judaism in the 1920s).

To Asja Lacis, *if* the recollections she published in 1971 are to be trusted, Benjamin said nothing of Kabbalah. Challenged on the unworldly, owlish nature of his research, Benjamin replied as follows. He was bringing a new, presumably more exact terminology into aesthetics. In particular, he was mapping the hitherto blurred distinction between 'tragedy' and *Trauerspiel*. A clear demarcation between these two terms was essential not only to a grasp of baroque drama and the baroque world-view, but also to that of certain aspects of German literature in the eighteenth and nineteenth centuries. Benjamin went further. His examination of the baroque theatre and of the devices of figuration and allegory which are its predominant attribute, had its contemporary pertinence. It would throw light on parallel elements in Expressionism. And now, according to Asja Lacis, Benjamin was involved in the study of Lukács and was beginning to take an active interest in the possibilities of a materialist aesthetic.

So far as they can be reconstructed, the facts are these: Benjamin had come to Capri with Ernst Bloch, the Marxist millenarian. Asja Lacis certainly exercised a real influence. Benjamin may have started his reading of *History and Class Consciousness* before going on to Rome (the point is not clear). In later years Benjamin himself said of the *Ursprung* that it was a 'dialectical' work though in no way an example of dialectical materialism. The weight Benjamin attached to this remark is uncertain. The dialectical strain in the *Ursprung* is, at best, that of certain schemes of argument in Hegel – for instance, in the Hegelian discussions of the *Antigone* – or in Nietzsche's scenario of a clash and fusion between Dionysian and Apollonian forces. Scholem's conclusion is irrefutable: the 'dialectical' stylization of the *Trauerspiel* phenomenon in Benjamin's representation stems from and stays wholly within a metaphysical framework. 'There is not the slightest evidence of Marxist categories.' The book and its academic mishap mark the close of an essentially romantic-metaphysical period in Benjamin's thought. His highly ambiguous contacts with Marxism came immediately after.

What we find in front of us, therefore, is an uncomfortable hybrid. Benjamin laboured to reconcile the technical demands and tonal manners of a *Habilitationsschrift* with those of an uncompromisingly personal, even lyric statement. From the academic point of view, the German baroque horror-dramas and emblem-books were the object of dispassionate investigation. From an epistemological-formal point of view, and the two terms must be seen as interwoven, these cobwebbed texts were the occasion for a chain of reflections on the nature of aesthetic objects, on the metaphysical presumptions of allegory, on language in general, and on the problem, obsessive to Benjamin, of the relations between a work of art and the descriptive-analytic discourse of which it is the target. To these must be added the very nearly private status of the *Erkenntniskritische Vorrede*, probably written last, but almost certainly conceived first. The product of these intentional and methodological disparities is, undoubtedly, a major work. But it is also a work which is flawed and difficult to place in focus.

* * *

For Benjamin, as for every German thinker after Herder, the word *Ursprung* is resonant. It signifies not only 'source', 'fount', 'origin', but also that primal leap *(Sprung)* into being which at once reveals and determines the unfolding structure, the central dynamics of form in an organic or spiritual phenomenon. Benjamin is at pains to show that the Aristotelian and neo-classical elements in the baroque theatre of Lutheran and Counter-Reformation Germany are deceptive, indeed immaterial. The true *Ursprung* is to be found in the intricate energies, visionary habits and political-doctrinal emblem-code of the baroque. German literary theory and scholarship, with its strong classicizing bias, has misread or simply neglected this compaction. From this oversight and misinterpretation derives the attempt to make of the baroque *Trauerspiel* a bastard or ancillary version of eighteenth-century tragedy. Nothing, according to Benjamin, could be more erroneous.

Tragödie and *Trauerspiel* are radically distinct, in metaphysical foundation and executive genre. Tragedy is grounded in myth. It acts out a rite of heroic sacrifice. In its fulfilment of this sacrificial-transcendent design, tragedy endows the hero with the realization that he is ethically in advance of the gods, that his sufferance of good and evil, of fortune and desolation, has projected him into a category beyond the comprehension of the essentially 'innocent' though materially omnipotent deities (Artemis' flight from the dying Hippolytus, Dionysus' myopia exceeding the blindness of Pentheus). This realization compels the tragic hero to silence, and here Benjamin is strongly influenced by Rosenzweig's concept of the 'meta-ethical' condition of tragic man.

The *Trauerspiel*, on the contrary, is not rooted in myth but in history. Historicity, with every implication of political-social texture and reference, generates both content and style. Feeling himself dragged towards the abyss of damnation, a damnation registered in a profoundly carnal sense, the baroque dramatist, allegorist, historiographer, and the personages he animates, cling fervently to the world. The *Trauerspiel* is counter-transcendental; it celebrates the immanence of existence even where this existence is passed in torment. It is emphatically 'mundane', earth-bound, corporeal. It is not the tragic hero who occupies the centre of the stage, but the Janus-faced composite of tyrant and martyr, of the Sovereign who incarnates the mystery of absolute will and of its victim (so often himself). Royal purple and the carmine of blood mingle in the same emblematic persona.

Behind this fusion stands the *exemplum* of Christ's kingship and crucifixion. Baroque drama is inherently emblematic-allegoric, as Greek tragedy never is, precisely because it postulates the dual presence, the twofold organizing pivot of Christ's nature – part god, part man, and overwhelmingly of this world. If the German baroque theatre has antecedents, these must be located not in the classics, but in the medieval misreading of classical-Senecan fragments and in the obsessive 'physicality' of the mystery cycles. It is in the Senecan obsession with loud agony and in the medieval-Christological insistence on the mortification of the flesh, especially where the flesh is merely the momentary husk of divine or sanctified spirit, that baroque stagecraft has its roots.

Drawing on Nietzsche's critique of Socrates, Benjamin differentiates the silences of tragedy from the torrential prolixity of the *Trauerspiel*. The Socratic dialogue, with its ironies and pathos, with its agonistic play of stroke and parry, with, above all, its declared trust in the capacity of language to image, elucidate and preserve reality, is the very opposite of tragic silence. As the end of the *Symposium* demonstrates, the discourse of the Socratic dialectic operates beyond the confines of either tragedy or comedy. It is purely dramatic. And it is from this dramatization of the word, says Benjamin, that stems the teeming, figurative, polarized rhetoric of the baroque playwrights.

These antinomies of transcendence and immanence of myth and history, of heroism and tyranny or martyrdom, of silence and loquacity, lead Benjamin to his fundamental distinction between tragedy and *Trauer*. Tragic feelings, in the sense assigned to them by Aristotle's *Poetics* and Nietzsche's *Birth of Tragedy*, are experienced by the spectator. They refine, enrich and bring into tensed equilibrium the inchoate muddle or incipience of the spectator's emotions. But fundamentally, tragedy does not require an audience. Its space is inwardness and the viewer aimed at is 'the hidden god'. *Trauer*, on the other hand, signifies sorrow, lament, the ceremonies and memorabilia of grief. Lament and ceremonial demand audience. Literally and in spirit, the *Trauerspiel* is a 'play of sorrow', a 'playing at and displaying of human wretchedness'. *Spiel* compounds, as it does in its English equivalent, the two meanings: game and stage-performance, the ludic and the mimetic-histrionic. Tragedy posits an aesthetic of reticence; the 'sorrow-play' is emphatically ostentatious, gestural, and hyperbolic. It identifies the earth with the stage in the notion of the *theatrum mundi* (a conceit to which Shakespeare gives local stress when he plays on the word 'globe'). It sees in historical events, in architecture, in the collateral edifice of the human body and of the body politick, properties for a grievous pageant. The Dance of Death depicted in sixteenth and seventeenth-century art and ritual, is the crowning episode of the game or play of lamentation. Hence the striking affinities between the *Trauerspiel* of the German baroque and the puppet-theatre, a relation which the much greater finesse and visionary elegance of Spanish baroque drama internalizes (the puppet-play shown on the actual stage as an ironic or pathetic simulacrum of the main plot). Prince and puppet are impelled by the same frozen violence.

Having expounded this cardinal distinction between the tragic and the sorrowful, Benjamin proceeds to dependent topics. But his advance is oblique and digressive. It entails a running polemic against idealist and academic underestimates of the baroque. It considers, in passing, the affinities and contrasts between the *Trauerspiel*, various modes of authentic tragedy, and such specifically German genres as the eighteenth and nineteenth-century *Schicksalsdrama* or 'melodrama of fate'. Throughout his treatise, moreover, Benjamin wants to demonstrate the epistemological categories and methods of analysis which he has postulated in the philosophic prologue. As a result, the process of argument is sometimes elusive. But there are, at the same time, developments of great brilliance.

Relating the immanence of the baroque, its tortured worldliness, to the microcosm of the court, Benjamin elaborates the dominant role of the *Intrigant*, the courtier whose intimacy with the tyrant or royal victim makes of him the key witness and also the weaver of murderous plots. In baroque drama, more than in any other, 'plot' is both the cat's-cradle of incidents and the conspiracy that breeds disaster. Cain was the first courtier, because fratricide had made him homeless. All 'intriguers' after him have been the rootless creatures of their own devices. Via a series of acute comparisons, Benjamin measures the limitations of the German achievement: it can neither add to the *Intrigant* the compassionate magic of comedy which produces a Polonius and even, to a certain extent, an Iago; nor can it rival the poetry, the delicacy of felt motive which characterize the court and martyr-plays of Lope de Vega and Calderón. The dramas of Gryphius, of Lohenstein, of Martin Opitz, remain trapped in their special vortex of brutal sadness and allegory.

This vortex is best understood when one looks at the tropes, rhetorical and pictorial figures, and emblem-literature of the period. Among these 'Melencolia' and her attributes are essential. Working outward from Dürer's famous engraving, Benjamin offers an inspired diagnosis of the theory and embodiments of saturnine melancholy in the baroque world. He points to the cultivation of private and public *tristesse* so symptomatic of political and philosophic postures in the seventeenth-century. He relates it to the physiology of humours. He traces the irrational but perfectly congruent network which knits blackness in the individual soul or complexion to planetary maleficence, to bile and, above all, to that proximity of literal hell which haunts baroque reflexes. Benjamin shows how it is in its figuration of 'world-sadness', of *acedia* – that final boredom of the spirit – that baroque thought and art achieve their truest depths.

Allegory and emblem had begun to be studied seriously before Benjamin. Nevertheless, his contribution is at once solid and original. It draws on, it is exactly contemporaneous with Erwin Panofsky's and Fritz Saxl's monograph on Dürer's 'Melencolia, I' published in 1923. Benjamin was among the very first to recognize the seminal power of what was to become the Warburg Institute approach to renaissance and baroque art and symbolism. He sought personal contact with the Warburg group, but Panofsky's response to the *Ursprung* (did he read it?) was dismissive. This marks, I think, the most ominous moment in Walter Benjamin's career. It is the Aby Warburg group, first in Germany and later at the Warburg Institute in London, which would have afforded Benjamin a genuine intellectual, psychological home, not the Horkheimer-Adorno Institute for Research in the Social Sciences with which his relations were to prove so ambivalent and, during his life time, sterile. Panofsky could have rescued Benjamin from isolation; an invitation to London might have averted his early death.

Having sketched the history of allegory and the inner conventions of

the allegoric code (with frequent reference to his own previous dissertation on romantic typologies of art), Benjamin proceeds to the emblematic
devices, sayings, mottoes, *sententiae* and stock metaphors in baroque
drama. These provide a natural transition to baroque language-theory.
It is as a philosopher of language (a *Sprachphilosoph*), a species entirely
different from, in fact antithetical to what Anglo-American usage identifies as 'linguistic philosophers', as a metaphysician of metaphor and
translation as was Coleridge, that Benjamin accomplished his best work.
Already by 1924, as the essay on *The Elective Affinities* shows, Benjamin
had few rivals in degree of linguistic penetration and none who could
mediate more subtly between a text and the speculative instruments of
interpretation. His reflexions on the differences between the baroque
concept of the written word (the 'hieroglyph') and the spoken are, therefore, profoundly instructive. Benjamin connects the strong cesura in the
seventeenth-century alexandrine with the baroque instinct towards a
segmented yet also equilibrated structure of statement. His hints towards
a linguistic analysis of baroque theatrical utterance, of the way in which
a pronouncement exercises an immediate, palpable fatality over speaker
and hearer – almost every locution being, in essence, either curse or invo-
cation – are pioneering. Here, more than anywhere else in the book,
Benjamin is master of his ground.

The *Ursprung* closes with an almost mystically-intense apprehension
of the ubiquity of evil in baroque sensibility. It suggests, in a vein which
is unmistakably personal, that only allegory, in that it makes substance
totally significant, totally representative of ulterior meanings and, therefore, 'unreal' in itself, can render bearable an authentic perception of the
infernal. Through allegory, the Angel, who in Paul Klee's depiction,
Angelus Novus, plays so obsessive a part in Benjamin's inner existence,
can look into the deeps.

There remains the gnomic foreword. It can best be conceived of as in
three movements. The first is methodological. Benjamin is working consciously in the current of Schleiermacher and Dilthey, though he seeks
to add something specifically private (the 'kabbalistic'). He is trying to
determine and to instance, at precisely the same moment, the modes of
intellection and argument proper to aesthetic-historical discourse. It is

from this simultaneity that the difficulty springs: to determine by more or less normal types of definitional and sequential usage, and to exemplify, to act out at the same time that which is being determined. It is not only that Benjamin is trapped in the hermeneutic circle – the use of the part to define the whole whose own definition governs the status of the part – but, like Heidegger, he welcomes this circularity, perceiving in it the characteristic intimacy which binds object to interpretation and interpretation to object in the humanities. What Benjamin polemicizes against is the unworried dissociation between scholarly-critical styles of analysis and the privileged, irreducibly autonomous objects of such analysis, a dissociation that is particularly damaging in respect of works of art and letters. Category will locate and classify form, but form generates category. Being itself composed of language, the poem or play must elicit from its interpreter, who is working in and with words, a co-active, formally and substantively cognate, indeed mirroring response. Benjamin is striving to make clear, in what he says and in the manner of his saying, in just what ways the critical text, the translation of the life of the meditated object into the secondary 'meta-life' of the commentary, is a profoundly responsive and therefore responsible, mimetic act. The true critic-understander, the reader whose reading underwrites the continued life of the page before him, enacts his perceptions, creating an elucidatory, enhancing counter-statement to the primary text ('counter-statement' is Kenneth Burke's word, and there is in English-language literary theory and criticism no one closer to Benjamin's model).

In the case of German baroque drama, with its singular fabric of emblem and hyperbole, with its inauthentic relations to antique tragedy and the later neo-classical ideal, such reflective re-enactment demands a very particular, highly self-conscious idiom and argumentative proceeding (cf. Coleridge on *Venus and Adonis* in the *Biographia Literaria*). It will detour: 'Methode ist Umweg. Darstellung als Umweg . . .'. It will examine but also embody the authority of quotation, the many ways in which a quotation energizes or subverts the analytic context. And it is at this point that Benjamin refers most cogently to theology, to the pluralistic relations between canonic quote and commentary in the Hebraic and Christian traditions. But Benjamin's hermeneutic of and by citation also has its contemporary flavour: it is very obviously akin to the collage and montage-aesthetic in the poetry of Ezra Pound and T. S. Eliot, and in the prose of Joyce – all of whom are producing major works at exactly the same date as Benjamin's *Ursprung*.

The commentary will, moreover, have a fragmentary, possibly aphoristic tenor. It will not flinch from a built-in incompletion and abruptness of statement. Benjamin is reacting against the orotund inflation and magisterial, often bullying comprehensiveness of German academic-official rhetoric. It may be that he had in mind, though largely at a hearsay level, the riddling concision, the deliberate inadequacy of certain Talmudic exegetes. But again, the implicit notion is one that was in vogue: following on Lichtenberg and Nietzsche, Wittgenstein too was finding an aphoristic, 'leaping' style of philosophic discourse, whereas Kafka, yet another precise contemporary, was composing laconic, mysteriously unfinished parables.

Thirdly, Benjamin pleads, though in a voice muted by concurrent hopes of academic acceptance, for the rights of the esoteric. It is not only his material – the neglected plays and emblem-collections of the German seventeenth century – that is esoteric; it is his critical task. How could it be otherwise? How could the empathic decipherment of many-layered texts in an idiom long-forgot, pretend to perfect clarity? In this context opaqueness and inwardness of semantic arrangement are a manifest of honesty. No doubt, this plea reflects very strong traits in Benjamin's personality, traits which find expression in his love of the arcane, in his pretense to kabbalism, in the condensations and bracketings that mark his own prose. But once more, we are also dealing with a motif of the moment. The esoteric is a decisive symptom throughout the modernist movement, whether in Yeats's mature poetry, in *Ulysses*, in the *Tractatus* or in the abstract art and music of the 1920s. Benjamin's hermeticism represents a bias in himself and in the atmosphere of the day.

The second movement of the foreword is epistemological, and loses most readers. Benjamin was not, in any technical sense, a philosopher. Like other lyric thinkers, he chose from philosophy those metaphors, dramas of argument and intimations of systematic totality – whether Platonic, Leibnizian or Crocean – which best served, or rather which most suggestively dignified and complicated his own purpose. (Later on, in the 'Historical-Philosophical Theses', he was to use Marx in just this innocently-exploitative way.)

In the proem to the *Ursprung*, this source for a source, it is Plato, Leibniz and Croce who are enlisted. The questions posed by Benjamin are more or less traditional and lucid. How can there be a general and generalizing treatment of artistic-literary objects which are, by definition, unique? Is it possible to escape historical relativism or the vacant dogmatics of historicism while, at the same time, being faithful to the temporal specificity, even unrecapturability of one's documents? Can the interpreter interpret 'outside' his own self and moment? Affirmative answers depend on 'the rescue of phenomena' (the Kantian echo is explicit) and on 'the representation of Ideas' – in which term the capital letter is standard German usage but also figurative of Benjamin's purpose.

Combining a Platonic metaphor or mythography of 'Ideas' with a language-realism which does, for once, carry genuine kabbalistic overtones, Benjamin affirms that 'an Idea' is that moment in the substance and being of a word (*im Wesen des Wortes*, a phrase which is uncannily Heideggerian), in which this word has become, and performs as, a symbol. It is this capacity, this existentially potentialized capacity of language to symbolize as well as to become itself symbolic, which enables a critical-philosophic discourse to uncover 'Ideas'. Why 'Ideas'? Because it is 'ideally-ideationally' that discrete, fully autonomous objects – like baroque plays or renaissance paintings – enter into mutual compaction, into significant fusion without thereby losing their identity. The relevant paradigm is that of Leibniz's monads – independent, perfectly separate units which nevertheless and, indeed, necessarily enter into combinatorial, harmonic groupings and interactions. Thus the singular 'finds salvation', i.e. realizes its potential of full meaning, in the monadic plurality or, more precisely, in the representative manifold – the symbol, the icon, the declarative emblem – of 'Ideas'.

Such rescue and salvation, says Benjamin, is Platonic. The 'Idea' 'contains a picture of the world' specific to yet wholly transcending the particulars that have found lodging in it. It is in Croce's theory of the 'universal singularity' of linked cultural phenomena, of historical crystallizations such as the baroque, that Benjamin finds an application of his Platonic-Leibnizian scheme to actual cultural-textual material. But the allusions to Croce are only fleeting, and do little to clarify what is, so evidently, an acutely suggestive (consider the aphorism: 'Truth is the death of purpose'), but also incomplete and esoteric blueprint. The irate bafflement of the first academic readers is not surprising, and could not really have surprised Benjamin whose pride in difficulty was poignant.

Part three of the introduction is straightforward. Benjamin makes ritual, though perfectly valid, gestures towards the intrinsic interest of his chosen topic, and towards the neglect and misconceptions it has long endured. The time is ripe for revaluation: Franz Werfel's version of the *Trojan Women* (1915) and the Expressionist movement throughout the arts, give to the baroque theatre a fresh immediacy. As during the crises of the Thirty Years' War and its aftermath, so in Weimar Germany the extremities of political tension and economic misère are reflected in art and critical discussion. Having drawn the analogy, Benjamin closes with hints towards a recursive theory of culture: eras of decline resemble each other not only in their vices but also in their strange climate of rhetorical and aesthetic vehemence (the ambience of the *Ursprung* is sometimes that of Spengler). Thus a study of the baroque is no mere antiquarian, archival hobby: it mirrors, it anticipates and helps grasp the dark present.

The publication of this monograph in English, in 1977, under this imprint, is pregnant with ironies. What English-speaking reader has ever glanced at the plays and allegories which Benjamin would, though indirectly, resuscitate? Where could he find them? The mandarins and aestheticians with whom Benjamin seeks his quarrels are long forgotten. The German-Jewish community of which he was a late ornament lies in cinders. Benjamin himself died a hunted fugitive. Had he lived, Walter Benjamin would doubtless have been sceptical of any 'New Left'. Like every man committed to abstruse thought and scholarship, he knew that not only the humanities, but humane and critical intelligence itself, resides in the always-threatened keeping of the very few. *Trauerspiel* is beautifully apt: a presentment of man's suffering and cruelty, made bearable through stately, even absurd form. A play of sorrow.

Conceived 1916   Written 1925

Then, as now, dedicated to my Wife

Epistemo-Critical Prologue

Neither in knowledge nor in reflection can anything whole be put together, since in the former the internal is missing and in the latter the external; and so we must necessarily think of science as art if we expect to derive any kind of wholeness from it. Nor should we look for this in the general, the excessive, but, since art is always wholly represented in every individual work of art, so science ought to reveal itself completely in every individual object treated.

Johann Wolfgang von Goethe: *Materialien zur Geschichte der Farbenlehre*

It is characteristic of philosophical writing that it must continually confront the question of representation. In its finished form philosophy will, it is true, assume the quality of doctrine, but it does not lie within the power of mere thought to confer such a form. Philosophical doctrine is based on historical codification. It cannot therefore be evoked *more geometrico*. The more clearly mathematics demonstrate that the total elimination of the problem of representation – which is boasted by every proper didactic system – is the sign of genuine knowledge, the more conclusively does it reveal its renunciation of that area of truth towards which language is directed. The methodological element in philosophical projects is not simply part of their didactic mechanism. This means quite simply that they possess a certain esoteric quality which they are unable to discard, forbidden to deny, and which they vaunt at their own peril. The alternative philosophical forms represented by the concepts of the doctrine and the esoteric essay are precisely those things which were ignored by the nineteenth century, with its concept of system. Inasmuch as it is determined by this concept of system, philosophy is in danger of accommodating itself to a syncretism which weaves a spider's web between separate kinds of knowledge in an attempt to ensnare the truth as if it were something which came flying in from outside. But the universalism acquired by such philosophy falls far short of the didactic authority of doctrine. If philosophy is to remain true to the law of its own form, as the representation of truth and not as a guide to the acquisition of knowledge, then the exercise of this form – rather than its anticipation in the system – must be accorded due importance. This exercise has imposed itself upon all those epochs which have recognized the uncircumscribable essentiality of truth in the form of a propaedeutic, which can be designated by the scholastic term treatise because this term refers, albeit implicitly, to those objects of theology without which truth is inconceivable. Treatises may be didactic in tone, but essentially they lack the conclusiveness of an instruction which could be asserted, like doctrine, by virtue of its own authority. The treatise dispenses also with the coercive proof of mathematics. In the canonic form of the treatise the only element of an intention – and it is an educative rather than a didactic intention – is the authoritative quotation. Its method is essentially representation. Method is a digression. Representation as digression – such is the methodological nature of the treatise. The absence of an uninterrupted purposeful structure is its primary characteristic. Tirelessly the process of thinking makes new beginnings, returning in a roundabout way to its original object. This continual pausing for breath is the mode most proper to the process of contemplation. For by pursuing different levels of meaning in its examination of one single object it receives both the incentive to begin again and the justification for its irregular rhythm. Just as mosaics preserve their majesty despite their fragmentation into capricious particles, so philosophical contemplation is not lacking in momentum. Both are made up of the distinct and the disparate; and nothing could bear more powerful testimony to the transcendent force of the sacred image and the truth itself. The value of fragments of thought is all the greater the less direct their relationship to the underlying idea, and the brilliance of the representation depends as much on this value as the brilliance of the mosaic does on the quality of the glass paste. The relationship between the minute precision of the work and the proportions of the sculptural or intellectual whole demonstrates that truth-content is only to be grasped through immersion in the most minute details of subject-matter. In their supreme, western, form the mosaic and the treatise are products of the Middle Ages; it is their very real affinity which makes comparison possible.

The difficulty inherent in this kind of representation proves only its peculiar quality as a prose form. Whereas the speaker uses voice and gesture to support individual sentences, even where they cannot really stand up on their own, constructing out of them – often vaguely and precariously – a sequence of ideas, as if producing a bold sketch in a single attempt, the writer must stop and restart with every new sentence. And this applies to the contemplative mode of representation more than any other, for its aim is not to carry the reader away and inspire him with enthusiasm. This form can be counted successful only when it forces the reader to pause and reflect. The more significant its object, the more detached the reflexion must be. Short of the didactic precept, such sober prose is the only style suited to philosophical investigation. Ideas are the object of this investigation. If representation is to stake its claim as the real methodology of the philosophical treatise, then it must be the representation of ideas. Truth, bodied forth in the dance of represented ideas, resists being projected, by whatever means, into the realm of knowledge. Knowledge is possession. Its very object is determined by the fact that it must be taken possession of – even if in a transcendental sense – in the consciousness. The quality of possession remains. For the thing possessed, representation is secondary; it does not have prior existence as something representing itself. But the opposite holds good of truth. For knowledge, method is a way of acquiring its object – even by creating it in the consciousness; for truth it is self-representation, and is therefore immanent in it as form. Unlike the methodology of knowledge, this form does not derive from a coherence established in the consciousness, but from an essence. Again and again the statement that the object of knowledge is not identical with the truth will prove itself to be one of the profoundest intentions of philosophy in its original form, the Platonic theory of ideas. Knowledge is open to question, but truth is not. Knowledge is concerned with individual phenomena, but not directly with their unity. The unity of knowledge – if indeed it exists – would consist rather in a coherence which can be established only on the basis of individual insights and, to a certain extent, their modification of each other; whereas unity is present in truth as a direct and essential attribute, and as such it is not open to question. For if the integral unity in the essence of truth were open to question, then the question would have to be: how far is the answer to the question already given in any conceivable reply which truth might give to questions? And the answer to this question would necessarily provoke the same question again, so that the unity of truth would defy all questioning. As a unity of essence rather than a conceptual unity, truth is beyond all question. Whereas the concept is a spontaneous product of the intellect, ideas are simply given to be reflected upon. Ideas are pre-existent. The distinction between truth and the coherence provided by knowledge thus defines the idea as essence. Such is the implication of the theory of ideas for the concept of truth. As essences, truth and idea acquire that supreme metaphysical significance expressly attributed to them in the Platonic system.

This is evident above all in the *Symposium*, which contains two pronouncements of decisive importance in the present context. It presents truth – the realm of ideas – as the essential content of beauty. It declares truth to be beautiful. An understanding of the Platonic view of the relationship of truth and beauty is not just a primary aim in every investigation into the philosophy of art, but it is indispensable to the definition of truth itself. To interpret these sentences in terms of the logic of their system, as no more than part of a time-honoured panegyric to philosophy, would inevitably mean leaving the sphere of the theory of ideas; which is where – and perhaps nowhere more clearly than in the statements to which we have referred – the mode of existence of ideas is illuminated. The second of these pronouncements needs some amplification. If truth is described as beautiful, this must be understood in the context of the *Symposium* with its description of the stages of erotic desires. Eros – it should be understood – does not betray his basic impulse by directing his longings towards the truth; for truth is beautiful: not so much in itself, as for Eros. And so it is with human love; a person is beautiful in the eyes of his lover, but not in himself, because his body belongs in a higher order of things than that of the beautiful. Likewise truth; it is not so much beautiful in itself, as for whomsoever seeks it. If there is a hint of relativism here, the beauty which is said to be a characteristic of truth is nevertheless far from becoming simply a metaphor. The essence of truth as the self-respecting realm of ideas guarantees rather that the assertion of the beauty of truth can never be devalued. This representational impulse in truth is the refuge of beauty as such, for beauty remains brilliant and palpable as long as it freely admits to being so. Its brilliance – seductive as long as it wishes only to shine forth – provokes pursuit by the intellect, and it reveals its innocence only by taking refuge on the altar of truth. Eros follows it in is flight, but as its lover, not as its pursuer; so that for the sake of its outward appearance beauty will always flee: in dread before the intellect, in fear before the lover. And only the latter can bear witness to the fact that truth is not a process of exposure which destroys the secret, but a revelation which does justice to it. But can truth do justice to beauty? That is the innermost question of the *Symposium*. Plato's answer is to make truth the guarantor of the existence of beauty. This is the sense in which he argues that truth is the content of beauty. This content, however, does not appear by being exposed; rather it is revealed in a process which might be described metaphorically as the burning up of the husk as it enters the realm of ideas, that is to say a destruction of the work in which its external form achieves its most brilliant degree of illumination. This relationship between truth and beauty shows more clearly than anything else the great difference between truth and the object of knowledge, with which it has customarily been equated, and at the same time it provides an explanation of that simple and yet unpopular fact that even those philosophical systems whose cognitional element has long since lost any claim to scientific truth still possess contemporary relevance. In the great philosophies the world is seen in terms of the order of ideas. But the conceptual frameworks within which this took place have, for the most part, long since become fragile. Nevertheless these systems, such as Plato's theory of ideas, Leibniz's Monadology, or Hegel's dialectic, still remain valid as attempts at a description of the world. It is peculiar to all these attempts that they still preserve their meaning, indeed they often reveal it more fully, even when they are applied to the world of ideas instead of empirical reality. For it was as descriptions of an order of ideas that these systems of thought originated. The more intensely the respective thinkers strove to outline the image of reality, the more were they bound to develop a conceptual order which, for the later interpreter, would be seen as serving that original depiction of the world of ideas which was really intended. If it is the task of the philosopher to practise the kind of description of the world of ideas which automatically includes and absorbs the empirical world, then he occupies an elevated position between that of the scientist and the artist. The latter sketches a restricted image of the world of ideas, which, because it is conceived as a metaphor, is at all times definitive. The scientist arranges the world with a view to its dispersal in the realm of ideas, by dividing it from within into concepts. He shares the philosopher's interest in the elimination of the merely empirical; while the artist shares with the philosopher the task of representation. There has been a tendency to place the philosopher too close to the scientist, and frequently the lesser kind of scientist; as if representation had nothing to do with the task of the philosopher. The concept of philosophical style is free of paradox. It has its postulates. These are as follows: the art of the interruption in contrast to the chain of deduction; the tenacity of the essay in contrast to the single gesture of the fragment; the repetition of themes in contrast to shallow universalism; the fullness of concentrated positivity in contrast to the negation of polemic.

The demand for flawless coherence in scientific deduction is not made in order that truth shall be represented in its unity and singularity; and yet this very flawlessness is the only way in which the logic of the system is related to the notion of truth. Such systematic completeness has no more in common with truth than any other form of representation which attempts to ascertain the truth in mere cognitions and cognitional patterns. The more scrupulously the theory of scientific knowledge investigates the various disciplines, the more unmistakably their methodological inconsistency is revealed. In each single scientific discipline new assumptions are introduced without any deductive basis, and in each discipline previous problems are declared solved as emphatically as the impossibility of solving them in any other context is asserted.[1] It is one of the most unphilosophical traits of that theory of science which, instead of the single disciplines, takes as the point of departure for its investigations certain supposedly philosophical postulates, that it considers this inconsistency as coincidental. However, far from characterizing an inferior and provisional stage of knowledge, this discontinuity in scientific method could positively advance the theory of knowledge, were it not for the ambition to grasp the truth – which remains an indivisible unity – in an encyclopaedic accumulation of items of knowledge. Systems have no validity except where they are inspired in their basic outline by the constitution of the world of ideas. The great categories which determine not only the shape of the systems, but also philosophical terminology – logic, ethics, and aesthetics, to mention the most general – do not acquire their significance as the names of special disciplines, but as monuments in the discontinuous structure of the world of ideas. Phenomena do not, however, enter into the realm of ideas whole, in their crude empirical state, adulterated by appearances, but only in their basic elements, redeemed. They are divested of their false unity so that, thus divided, they might partake of the genuine unity of truth. In this their division, phenomena are subordinate to concepts, for it is the latter which effect the resolution of objects into their constituent elements. Conceptual distinctions are above all suspicion of destructive sophistry only when their purpose is the salvation of phenomena in ideas, the Platonic τὰ φαινόμενα σώζειν.

Through their mediating role concepts enable phenomena to participate in the existence of ideas. It is this same mediating role which fits them for the other equally basic task of philosophy, the representation of ideas. As the salvation of phenomena by means of ideas takes place, so too does the representation of ideas through the medium of empirical reality. For ideas are not represented in themselves, but solely and exclusively in an arrangement of concrete elements in the concept: as the configuration of these elements.

The set of concepts which assist in the representation of an idea lend it actuality as such a configuration. For phenomena are not incorporated in ideas. They are not contained in them. Ideas are, rather, their objective, virtual arrangement, their objective interpretation. If ideas do not incorporate phenomena, and if they do not become functions of the law of phenomena, the 'hypothesis', then the question of how they are related to phenomena arises. The answer to this is: in the representation of phenomena. The idea thus belongs to a fundamentally different world from that which it apprehends. The question of whether it comprehends that which it apprehends, in the way in which the concept genus includes the species, cannot be regarded as a criterion of its existence. That is not the task of the idea. Its significance can be illustrated with an analogy. Ideas are to objects as constellations are to stars. This means, in the first place, that they are neither their concepts nor their laws. They do not contribute to the knowledge of phenomena, and in no way can the latter be criteria with which to judge the existence of ideas. The significance of phenomena for ideas is confined to their conceptual elements. Whereas phenomena determine the scope and content of the concepts which encompass them, by their existence, by what they have in common, and by their differences, their relationship to ideas is the opposite of this inasmuch as the idea, the objective interpretation of phenomena – or rather their elements – determines their relationship to each other. Ideas are timeless constellations, and by virtue of the elements' being seen as points in such constellations, phenomena are subdivided and at the same time redeemed;

so that those elements which it is the function of the concept to elicit from phenomena are most clearly evident at the extremes. The idea is best explained as the representation of the context within which the unique and extreme stands alongside its counterpart. It is therefore erroneous to understand the most general references which language makes as concepts, instead of recognizing them as ideas. It is absurd to attempt to explain the general as an average. The general is the idea. The empirical, on the other hand, can be all the more profoundly understood the more clearly it is seen as an extreme. The concept has its roots in the extreme. Just as a mother is seen to begin to live in the fullness of her power only when the circle of her children, inspired by the feeling of her proximity, closes around her, so do ideas come to life only when extremes are assembled around them. Ideas – or, to use Goethe's term, ideals – are the Faustian 'Mothers'. They remain obscure so long as phenomena do not declare their faith to them and gather round them. It is the function of concepts to groups phenomena together, and the division which is brought about within them thanks to the distinguishing power of the intellect is all the more significant in that it brings about two things at a single stroke: the salvation of phenomena and the representation of ideas.

Ideas are not among the given elements of the world of phenomena. This gives rise to the question of the manner in which they are in fact given, and whether it is necessary to hand over the task of accounting for the structure of the world of ideas to a much-cited intellectual vision. The weakness which esotericism invariably imparts to philosophy is nowhere more overwhelmingly apparent than in that particular way of looking at things which is the philosophical approach required of the adepts of all the theories of neo-Platonic paganism. The being of ideas simply cannot be conceived of as the object of vision, even intellectual vision. For even in its most paradoxical periphrasis, as *intellectus archetypus*, vision does not enter into the form of existence which is peculiar to truth, which is devoid of all intention, and certainly does not itself appear as intention. Truth does not enter into relationships, particularly intentional ones.

The object of knowledge, determined as it is by the intention inherent in the concept, is not the truth. Truth is an intentionless state of being, made up of ideas. The proper approach to it is not therefore one of intention and knowledge, but rather a total immersion and absorption in it. Truth is the death of intention. This, indeed, is just what could be meant by the story of the veiled image of Saïs, the unveiling of which was fatal for whomsoever thought thereby to learn the truth. It is not some enigmatic cruelty in actual meaning which brings this about, but the very nature of truth, in the face of which even the purest fire of the spirit of inquiry is quenched. The mode of being in the world of appearances is quite different from the being of truth, which is something ideal. The structure of truth, then, demands a mode of being which in its lack of intentionality resembles the simple existence of things, but which is superior in its permanence. Truth is not an intent which realizes itself in empirical reality; it is the power which determines the essence of this empirical reality. The state of being, beyond all phenomenality, to which alone this power belongs, is that of the name. This determines the manner in which ideas are given. But they are not so much given in a primordial language as in a primordial form of perception, in which words possess their own nobility as names, unimpaired by cognitive meaning. 'It is to some extent doubtful whether Plato's theory of "Ideas" would have been possible if the very meaning of the word had not suggested to the philosopher, familiar only with his mother tongue, a deification of the verbal concept, a deification of words: Plato's "Ideas" are – if, for once, they might be considered from this one-sided viewpoint – nothing but deified words and verbal concepts'[2]. The idea is something linguistic, it is that element of the symbolic in the essence of any word. In empirical perception, in which words have become fragmented, they possess, in addition to their more or less hidden, symbolic aspect, an obvious, profane meaning. It is the task of the philosopher to restore, by representation, the primacy of the symbolic character of the word, in which the idea is given self-consciousness, and that is the opposite of all outwardly-directed communication. Since philosophy may not presume to speak in the tones of revelation, this can only be achieved by recalling in memory the primordial form of perception. Platonic anamnesis is, perhaps, not far removed from this kind of remembering; except that here it is not a question of the actualization of images in visual terms; but rather, in philosophical contemplation, the idea is released from the heart of reality as the word, reclaiming its name-giving rights. Ultimately, however, this is not the attitude of Plato, but the attitude of Adam, the father of the human race and the father of philosophy. Adam's action of naming things is so far removed from play or caprice that it actually confirms the state of paradise as a state in which there is as yet no need to struggle with the communicative significance of words. Ideas are displayed, without intention, in the act of naming, and they have to be renewed in philosophical contemplation. In this renewal the primordial mode of apprehending words is restored. And so, in the course of its history, which has so often been an object of scorn, philosophy is – and rightly so – a struggle for the representation of a limited number of words which always remain the same – a struggle for the representation of ideas. In philosophy, therefore, it is a dubious undertaking to introduce new terminologies which are not strictly confined to the conceptual field, but are directed towards the ultimate objects of consideration. Such terminologies – abortive denominative processes in which intention plays a greater part than language – lack that objectivity with which history has endowed the principal formulations of philosophical reflections. These latter can stand up on their own in perfect isolation, as mere words never can. And so ideas subscribe to the law which states: all essences exist in complete and immaculate independence, not only from phenomena, but, especially, from each other. Just as the harmony of the spheres depends on the orbits of stars which do not come into contact with each other, so the existence of the *mundus intelligibilis* depends on the unbridgeable distance between pure essences. Every idea is a sun and is related to other ideas just as suns are related to each other. The harmonious relationship between such essences is what constitutes truth. Its oft-cited multiplicity is finite; for discontinuity is a characteristic of the 'essences . . . which lead a life that differs utterly from that of objects and their conditions; and which cannot be forced dialectically into existence by our selecting and adding some . . . complex of properties which we happen to encounter in an object; but whose number is, by the same token, limited, and every single one of which must be searched for laboriously at the appropriate place in its world, until it is found, as a *rocher de bronze*, or until the hope that it exists is shown to be illusory.[3] Ignorance of this, its discontinuous finitude, has, not infrequently, frustrated energetic attempts to renew the theory of ideas, most recently those undertaken by the older generation of the romantics. In their speculations truth assumed the character of a reflective consciousness in place of its linguistic character.

In the sense in which it is treated in the philosophy of art the *Trauerspiel* is an idea. Such a treatment differs most significantly from a literary-historical treatment in its assumption of unity, whereas the latter is concerned to demonstrate variety. In literary-historical analysis differences and extremes are bought together in order that they might be relativized in evolutionary terms; in a conceptual treatment they acquire the status of complementary forces, and history is seen as no more than the coloured border to their crystalline simultaneity. From the point of view of the philosophy of art the extremes are necessary; the historical process is merely virtual. Conversely the idea is the extreme example of a form or genre, and as such does not enter into the history of literature. *Trauerspiel*, as a concept, could, without the slightest problem, be added to the list of aesthetic classifications. But not as an idea, for it defines no class and does not contain that generality on which the respective conceptual levels in the system of classification depend: the average. The consequent inadequacies of inductive reasoning in artistic theory could not long remain concealed; hence the critical bewilderment of modern scholars. With reference to his study 'Zum Phänomen des Tragischen', Scheler asks: 'how . . . are we . . . to proceed? Are we to assemble all manner of examples of the tragic, that is to say occurrences and events which are said to create the impression of the tragic, and then analyse inductively what it is that they all have "in common"? That would be a kind of inductive method which could be supported by experiment. This would not, however, lead us any further than self-observation at those moments when we are affected by the tragic. For how justified are we in accepting that what people describe as tragic *is* tragic?'[4] The attempt to define ideas inductively – according to their range – on the basis of popular linguistic usage, in order then to proceed to the investigation of the essence of what has been thus defined, can lead nowhere. Invaluable though common linguistic usage may be to the philosopher as a pointer to ideas, it is dangerous to be misled by loose speech or thinking into accepting it, in interpretation, as the formal basis of a concept. Indeed, this permits us to say that it is only with the greatest reservation that the philosopher may adopt the habitual tendency of ordinary thinking, which is to make words into concepts embracing whole species in order to be more sure of them. And the philosophy of art has not infrequently succumbed to this temptation. When Volkelt's *Ästhetik des Tragischen* – to take one striking example from many – includes in its analyses plays by Holz or Halbe alongside dramas by Aeschylus or Euripides, without so much as asking whether the tragic is a form which can be realized at all at the present time, or whether it is not a historically limited form, then, as far as the tragic is concerned, the effect of such widely divergent material is not one of tension, but of sheer incongruity. When facts are amassed in this way so that the less obvious original qualities are soon obscured by the chaos of more immediately appealing modern ones, the investigation in which this accumulation was undertaken – with a view to examining what these things have 'in common' – is left with nothing but some psychological data which, on the slender basis of an identity in the subjective reaction of the investigator or, at least, the ordinary contemporary citizen, are held to establish the similarity of things which are in fact quite different. In terms of the concepts of psychology it is perhaps possible to reproduce a variety of impressions, regardless of whether these impressions have been evoked by works of art; but it is not possible to express the essence of a field of artistic endeavour. This can only be done in a comprehensive explanation of the underlying concept of its form, the metaphysical substance of which should not simply be found within, but should appear in action, like the blood coursing through the body.

The reasons for the uncritical use of inductive methods have always been the same: on the one hand the love of variety and, on the other hand, indifference to intellectual rigour. Again and again it is a question of that aversion to constitutive ideas – *universalia in re* – which Burdach explains with such clarity. 'I have promised to speak of the origin of Humanism as if it were a living being which came as a single whole into the world at one particular time and in one particular place, and then grew as a whole . . . To do so is to proceed in the manner of the so-called Realists of mediaeval scholasticism, who attributed reality to general concepts, or "universals". In the same way – hypostatizing after the fashion of primitive mythologies – we posit a being of uniform substance and complete reality and call it Humanism, just as if it were a living individual. But in this and countless other cases like it . . . we ought to be clear that we are doing no more than inventing an abstract concept in order to help us come to grips with an infinite series of varied spiritual manifestations and widely differing personalities. It is a fundamental principle of human perception and cognition that we can do such a thing only if, as a consequence of our innate need for systematization, we see in these varied series certain properties, which appear to be similar or identical, more distinctly, and emphasize these similarities more strongly than the differences. . . . Such kinds of Humanism or Renaissance are arbitrary, indeed they are false because they give life, with its multiplicity of sources, forms, and spirits, the false appearance of a real unity of essence. Every bit as arbitrary and misleading is the term "Renaissance man", which has been so popular since the time of Burckhardt and Nietzsche.'[5] A footnote to this passage runs as follows: 'An unfortunate counterpart to the ubiquitous "Renaissance man" is "Gothic man", currently a source of much confusion, who haunts even the intellectual world of important and respected historians (E. Troeltsch!). And he has been joined by "Baroque man", a guise in which Shakespeare, for instance, has been presented.'[6] The correctness of such an attitude is evident, inasmuch as it is opposed to the hypostatization of general concepts – although this does not include universals in all their forms. But it is a quite inadequate response to a Platonic theory of science, whose aim is the representation of essences, for it fails to appreciate its necessity. Such a theory is, indeed, the only means of preserving the language of scientific exposition, as it functions outside the sphere of mathematics, from the boundless scepticism which ultimately engulfs every inductive methodology, however subtle, and to which the arguments of Burdach provide no answer. For these arguments constitute a private *reservatio mentalis*, not a methodological defence. As far as historical types and epochs in particular are concerned, it can, of course, never be assumed that the subject matter in question might be grasped conceptually with the aid of ideas such as that of the renaissance or the baroque, and to adopt the view that a modern insight into the different periods of history can be validated in, for instance, polemic confrontations in which, as at great historical turning points, the epochs faced each other eyeball to eyeball, so to speak, would be to misunderstand the nature of one's sources, which is usually determined by considerations of contemporary interest rather than the ideas of historiography. As ideas, however, such names perform a service they are not able to perform as concepts: they do not make the similar identical, but they effect a synthesis between extremes. Although it should be stated that conceptual analysis, too, does not invariably encounter totally heterogeneous phenomena, and it can occasionally reveal the outlines of a synthesis, even if it is not able to confirm it. Thus Strich has rightly observed of baroque literature, in which the German *Trauerspiel* had its origins, 'that the principles of composition remained unchanged throughout the entire century.'[7]

Burdach's critical reflection is inspired not so much by the desire for a positive revolution in method as by the fear of material errors of detail. But in the last analysis a methodology must not be presented in negative terms, as something determined by the simple fear of inadequacy on a factual level, a set of warnings. It must rather proceed from convictions of a higher order than are provided by the point of view of scientific verism. Such verism must then, in its treatment of the individual problem, necessarily be confronted by the genuine questions of methodology which are ignored in its scientific credo. The solution of these problems will generally lead to the reformulation of the whole mode of questioning along the following lines: how is the question, 'What was it really like?'

susceptible, not just of being scientifically answered, but of actually being put. Only with this consideration, which has been prepared for by what precedes and will be concluded in what follows, can it be decided whether the idea is an undesirable abbreviation, or whether, in its linguistic expression, it establishes the true scientific content. A science in conflict with the language of its own investigations is an absurdity. Words, along with mathematical signs, are the only means of expression available to science, and they are not signs. For in the concept, to which the sign would, of course, correspond, the very word which realizes its essence as idea, is depotentiated. The verism, which is served by the inductive method of the theory of art, is not improved by the fact that the discursive and inductive questions ultimately converge in a 'view' [*Anschauung*][8] which according to R. M. Meyer and many others, is capable of assuming the form of a syncretism of the most varied methods. And this, like all naively realistic paraphrases of the problem of methodology, brings us back to our point of departure. Because it is precisely the view which must be interpreted. Thus the image of the inductive method of aesthetic investigation reveals its customary murky colouring here too, for the view in question is not the view of the object, resolved in the idea, but that of subjective states of the recipient projected into the work; that is what the empathy, which R. M. Meyer regards as the keystone of his method, amounts to. This method, which is the opposite of the one to be used in the course of the current investigation, 'sees the art-form of the drama, the forms of tragedy or comedy of character or situation, as given factors with which it has to reckon. And its aim is to abstract, by means of a comparison of the outstanding representatives of each genre, rules and laws with which to judge the individual product. And by means of a comparison of the genres it seeks to discover general principles which apply to every work of art.'[9] In such a philosophy of art the 'deduction' of the genre would be based on a combination of induction and abstraction, and it would not be so much a question of establishing a series of these genres and species by deduction, as of simply presenting them in the deductive scheme.

Whereas induction reduces ideas to concepts by failing to arrange and order them, deduction does the same by projecting them into a pseudo-logical continuum. The world of philosophical thought does not, however, evolve out of the continuum of conceptual deductions, but in a description of the world of ideas. To execute this description it is necessary to treat every idea as an original one. For ideas exist in irreducible multiplicity. As an enumerated – or rather a denominated – multiplicity, ideas are rendered up for contemplation. This it is which prompted Benedetto Croce's fierce criticism of the deductive concept of genre in the philosophy of art. He rightly sees in classification, the framework of speculative deductions, the basis of a superficially schematic criticism. And whereas the nominalism of Burdach, which is based on the concept of the historical epoch, and his resistance to the slightest loss of contact with the factual, are to be attributed to the fear of departing from what is correct, Croce's totally analogous nominalism, which is based on the concept of the aesthetic genre, and his analogous devotion to the particular, are to be attributed to the concern that departure from it might mean the complete loss of the essential. More than anything else, this interest in the essential is precisely what is calculated to show the aesthetic genres in their true meaning and in the right perspective. *The Essence of Aesthetic* criticizes prejudice in favour 'of the possibility of distinguishing a greater or lesser number of particular artistic forms, each of which is definable within its own limits as a particular concept, and each of which is furnished with its own rules . . . There are still many aestheticians who write about the aesthetics of the tragic or the comic, or of lyric or humour, and the aesthetics of painting, or music, or poetry . . .; but what is worse, . . . in judging works of art, critics have not entirely renounced te habit of measuring them against the genre or the particular art-form to which, in the critic's opinion, they belong.'[10] 'Any conceivable theory of the division of the arts is untenable. The genre or the class is, in this case, a single one: art itself, or the intuition; the individual works of art, on the other hand, are infinite in number: all are original, and none can be translated into another . . . Considered philosophically, nothing is interposed between the universal and the individual, no sequence of genres or species, no *generalia*.'[11] This statement is perfectly valid in respect of the aesthetic genres. But it does not go far enough. For although it is clearly futile to assemble a series of works of art with certain features in common, if the intention is to establish their essential quality rather than to produce a collection of historical or stylistic examples, it is equally inconceivable that the philosophy of art will ever divest itself of some of its most fruitful ideas, such as the tragic or the comic. For these ideas are not simply the sum total of certain sets of rules; they are themselves structures, at the very least equal in consistency and substance to any and every drama, without being in any way commensurable. They therefore make no claim to embrace a number of given works of literature on the basis of certain features that are common to them. For even if there were no such things as the pure tragedy or the pure comic drama which could be named after them, these ideas can still survive. And their survival can be helped by an investigation which does not, from the very outset, commit itself to the inclusion of everything which has ever been described as tragic or comic, but looks for that which is exemplary, even if this exemplary character can be admitted only in respect of the merest fragment. Such an investigation does not therefore contribute to the development of standards for the reviewer. Neither criticism nor the criteria of a terminology – the test of the philosophical theory of ideas in art – evolves in response to external comparison, but they take shape immanently, in a development of the formal language of the work itself, which brings out its content at the expense of its effect. It is, moreover, precisely the more significant works, inasmuch as they are not the original and, so to speak, ideal embodiments of the genre, which fall outside the limits of genre. A major work will either establish the genre or abolish it; and the perfect work will do both.

The impossibility of the deductive elaboration of artistic forms and the consequent invalidation of the rule as a critical authority – it will always preserve its validity in the field of artistic instruction – provide the spur to a productive scepticism. This can be likened to a pause for breath, after which thought can be totally and unhurriedly concentrated even on the very minutest object without the slightest inhibition. For the very minutest things will be discussed wherever the work of art and its form are considered with a view to judging their content. To snatch hastily, as if stealing the property of others, is the style of the *routinier*, and is no better than the heartiness of the philistine. In the act of true contemplation, on the other hand, the abandoning of deductive methods is combined with an ever wider-ranging, an ever more intense reappraisal of phenomena, which are, however, never in danger of remaining the objects of vague wonder, as long as the representation of them is also a representation of ideas, for it is here that their individuality is preserved. It goes without saying that the radicalism which would deprive the terminology of aesthetics of many of its best formulations and would reduce the philosophy of art to silence is, even for Croce, not the last word. Rather he states: 'To deny the theoretical value of the abstract classification is not to deny the theoretical value of that genetic and concrete classification which is not, in fact, "classification" at all, but is what we call History.'[12] In this obscure sentence the writer touches – alas, all too fleetingly – on the core of the theory of ideas. But the psychologizing tendency, thanks to which his definition of art as 'expression' is undermined and replaced by that of art as 'intuition', prevents him from perceiving this. He fails to see how the contemplation which he described as 'genetic classification' can be reconciled with an idealist theory of art forms in the problem of origin. Origin [*Ursprung*], although an entirely historical category, has, nevertheless, nothing to do with genesis [*Entstehung*]. The term origin is not intended to describe the process by which the existent came into being, but rather to describe that which emerges from the process of becoming and disappearance. Origin is an eddy in the stream of becoming, and in its current it swallows the material involved in the process of genesis. That which is original is never revealed in the naked and manifest existence of the factual; its rhythm is apparent only to a dual insight. On the one hand it needs to be recognized as a process of restoration and reestablishment, but, on the other hand, and precisely because of this, as something imperfect and incomplete. There takes place in every original phenomenon a determination of the form in which an idea will constantly confront the historical world, until it is revealed fulfilled, in the totality of its history. Origin is not, therefore, discovered by the examination of actual findings, but it is related to their history and their subsequent development. The principles of philosophical contemplation are recorded in the dialectic which is inherent in origin. This dialectic shows singularity and repetition to be conditioned by one another in all essentials. The category of origin is not therefore, as Cohen holds,[13] a purely logical one, but a historical one. Hegel's 'So much the worse for the facts', is a well-known statement. Basically what it means is: insight into the relationship between essences is the prerogative of the philosopher, and these relationships remain unaltered even if they do not take on their purest form in the world of fact. This genuinely idealist attitude pays for its confidence by abandoning the central feature of the idea of origin. For every proof of origin must be prepared to face up to the question of its authenticity. If it cannot establish this, then it does not merit the name. This consideration would seem to do away with the distinction between the *quaestio juris* and the *quaestio facti* as far as the highest objects of philosophy are concerned. This much is indisputable and inevitable. It does not, however, follow that every primitive 'fact' should straightaway be considered a constitutive determinant. Indeed this is where the task of the investigator begins, for he cannot regard such a fact as certain until its innermost structure appears to be so essential as to reveal it as an origin. The authentic – the hallmark of origin in phenomena – is the object of discovery, a discovery which is connected in a unique way with the process of recognition. And the act of discovery can reveal it in the most singular and eccentric of phenomena, in both the weakest and clumsiest experiments and in the overripe fruits of a period of decadence. When the idea absorbs a sequence of historical formulations, it does not do so in order to construct a unity out of them, let alone to abstract something common to them all. There is no analogy between the relationship of the individual to the idea, and its relationship to the concept; in the latter case it falls under the aegis of the concept and remains what it was: an individuality; in the former it stands in the idea, and becomes something different: a totality. That is its Platonic 'redemption'.

Philosophical history, the science of the origin, is the form which, in the remotest extremes and the apparent excesses of the process of development, reveals the configuration of the idea – the sum total of all possible meaningful juxtapositions of such opposites. The representation of an idea can under no circumstances be considered successful unless the whole range of possible extremes it contains has been virtually explored. Virtually, because that which is comprehended in the idea of origin still has history, in the sense of content, but not in the sense of a set of occurrences which have befallen it. Its history is inward in character and is not to be understood as something boundless, but as something related to essential being, and it can therefore be described as the past and subsequent history of this being. The past and the subsequent history of such essences is – as a token of their having been redeemed or gathered into the world of ideas – not pure history, but natural history. The life of the works and forms which need such protection in order to unfold clearly and unclouded by human life is a natural life.[14] Once this redeemed state of being in the idea is established, then the presence of the inauthentic – that is to say natural-historical – past and subsequent history is virtual. It is no longer pragmatically real, but, as natural history, is to be inferred from the state of completion and rest, from the essence. The tendency of all philosophical conceptualization is thus redefined in the old sense: to establish the becoming of phenomena in their being. For in the science of philosophy the concept of being is not satisfied by the phenomenon until it has absorbed all its history. In such investigations this historical perspective can be extended, into the past or the future, without being subject to any limits of principle. This gives the idea its total scope. And its structure is a monadological one, imposed by totality in contrast to its own inalienable isolation. The idea is a monad. The being that enters into it, with its past and subsequent history, brings – concealed in its own form – an indistinct abbreviation of the rest of the world of ideas, just as, according to Leibniz's *Discourse on Metaphysics* (1686), every single monad contains, in an indistinct way, all the others. The idea is a monad – the pre-stabilized representation of phenomena resides within it, as in their objective interpretation. The higher the order of the ideas, the more perfect the representation contained within them. And so the real world could well constitute a task, in the sense that it would be a question of penetrating so deeply into everything real as to reveal thereby an objective interpretation of the world. In the light of such a task of penetration it is not surprising that the philosopher of the *Monadology* was also the founder of infinitesimal calculus. The idea is a monad – that means briefly: every idea contains the image of the world. The purpose of the representation of the idea is nothing less than an abbreviated outline of this image of the world.

Given the previous history of the German literary baroque there is an apparent paradox in an analysis of one of its principal forms – an analysis which sees its task not in establishing rules and tendencies, but in concerning itself with the metaphysics of this form, understood concretely and in all its fullness. One of the most significant of the many and varied obstacles which have militated against our appreciation of the literature of this epoch is unmistakably to be found in the – for all its importance – awkward form which is especially characteristic of the baroque drama. The drama, more than any other literary form, needs a resonance in history. Baroque drama has been denied this resonance. The renewal of the literary heritage of Germany, which began with romanticism, has, even today, hardly touched baroque literature. It was above all Shakespeare's drama, with its richness and its freedom, which, for the romantic writers, overshadowed contemporaneous German efforts, whose gravity was, in any case, alien to the practical theatre. While the emergent science of German philology looked on the totally non-popular efforts of an educated bureaucracy with suspicion. Notwithstanding the genuine importance of what these men did for the language and the national heritage, and notwithstanding their conscious participation in the development of a national literature – their work too obviously bore the imprint of the absolutist maxim: everything for the people, nothing by the people themselves, to be able to win over philologists of the school of Grimm and Lachmann. A spirit, which prevented them – although they were labouring on the construction of a German drama – from ever using the material of German popular culture, contributes in no small way to the agonizing violence of their style. Neither German legend nor German history plays any role in baroque drama. But even the widening, indeed the undiscriminating historicism of German literary studies in the last third of the century did not do anything for the study of the baroque *Trauerspiel*. Its difficult form remained inaccessible to a science in which stylistic criticism and formal analysis were the most humble auxiliary disciplines, and the obscure physiognomy of the authors peering out through uncomprehended works did little to inspire historical-bio-graphical sketches. Though in any case there can be no question of the free or playful unfolding of poetic genius in these dramas. Rather did the dramatists of this age feel constrained by force to apply themselves to the task of actually creating the form of a secular drama. And however many times, between Gryphius and Hallmann, they applied themselves to this task – all too frequently in schematic repetition – the German drama of the Counter-Reformation never achieved that suppleness of form which bends to every virtuoso touch, such as Calderón gave the Spanish drama. It took shape – precisely because it was of necessity a product of this its age – in an extremely violent effort, and this alone would suggest that no sovereign genius imprinted his personality on this form. And yet here is the centre of gravity of every baroque *Trauerspiel*. The individual poet is supremely indebted to it for his achievement within it, and his individual limitation does not detract from its depth. This needs to be understood if the form is to be investigated. Even then, of course, it remains essential to adopt the kind of approach which, in order to contemplate a form at all, is capable of elevating itself, in the sense of recognizing in it something other than an abstraction from the body of literature. Indeed, in compari-son with some of the efforts of the baroque, the form of the *Trauerspiel* is much the richer. And just as every speech-form, even the unusual or isolated, can be seen not only as a testimony to the man who coined it, but also as a document in the life of the language, and evidence of its possi-bilities at a given time, so too does any art-form – and far more genuinely than any individual work – contain the index of a particular, objectively necessary artistic structure. Older research remained unaware of this because it never paid attention to the analysis and history of forms. But that was not the only reason. An extremely uncritical adherence to baroque theory of drama also played a part. This is the theory of Aristotle, adapted to the tendencies of the time. In most of the plays this adaptation amounted to a coarsening of the model. Commentators were all too ready to speak of distortion and misunderstanding, without first trying to discover the substantial reasons for this variation, and from here it was not far to the opinion that the dramatists of the period had basically done no more than apply respected precepts in an uncomprehending way. The *Trauerspiel* of the German baroque appeared to be a caricature of classical tragedy. There was no difficulty in reconciling with this scheme of things everything about these works which was offensive or even barbaric to refined taste. The theme of their *Haupt- und Staatsaktionen* was seen as a distortion of the ancient royal drama, the bombast as a distortion of the dignified pathos of the Greeks, and the bloody finale as a distortion of the tragic catastrophe. The *Trauerspiel* thus took on the appearance of an incompetent renaissance of tragedy. And herewith arose a new classification, which necessarily thwarted any appreciation of the form in question: viewed as renaissance-drama the *Trauerspiel* stands condemned, its most characteristic features denounced as so many stylistic shortcomings. For a long time, thanks to the authority of the historical catalogues of subject-matter, this assessment remained uncorrected. In consequence Stachel's meritorious *Seneca und das deutsche Renaissancedrama*, the basic work on the subject, is rendered quite devoid of any noteworthy insight into the essence of the *Trauerspiel*, to which it does not necessarily aspire. In his work on the lyric style of the seventeenth century, Strich has revealed this equivocation, which inhibited research for a long time. 'German poetry of the seventeenth century is customarily described as being renaissance in style. But if this form is understood to mean more than the superficial imitation of the devices of antiquity, then it is misleading, and merely shows the lack of understanding of the history of styles in literary studies, for this century possessed no trace of the classical spirit of the renaissance. The style of its poetry is, rather, baroque, even if one does not think only of bombast and excess, but considers also the profounder principles of composition.'[15] A further and remarkably persistent error in the literary history of this period is bound up with the prejudice of stylistic criticism: the assumption that its drama is unsuited to the stage. This is not perhaps the first time that perplexity in the face of an unusual scene has given rise to the thought that such a thing was never realized, that works of this kind would not have been effective, that the theatre ignored them. In the interpretation of Seneca, for instance, there occur controversies which, in this respect, are similar to the earlier discussions about baroque drama. Be that as it may – as far as the baroque is concerned, the century-old fable, handed down from A. W. Schlegel[16] to Lamprecht,[17] that the baroque drama was something to be read rather than performed, has been disproved. Indeed the quality of *theatre* speaks with particular emphasis in those violent actions with their eminently visual appeal. Even the theory does, on occasion, stress the scenic effect. The dictum of Horace: 'Et prodesse volunt et delectare poetae', forces the poetics of Buchner to face up to the question of how the *Trauerspiel* can conceivably be a source of delight; the answer is: not in its subject matter, but most certainly in its theatrical representation.[18]

Burdened down by so many prejudices, literary scholarship necessarily failed in its attempts to arrive at an objective appreciation of baroque drama, and has moreover only intensified the confusions with which any reflection on the subject must now grapple from the outset. One would hardly believe it possible, but it has even been argued that the baroque *Trauerspiel* represents a genuine form of *Tragedy* because its effects are the same as those which Aristotle attributes to tragedy, namely pity and fear – although it never occurred to Aristotle to declare that only tragedies could arouse pity and fear. One of the older authors has made the quite ridiculous observation: 'Through his studies Lohenstein became so attuned to a past world, that he forgot the contemporary world and, in expression, thought, and feeling, would have been more comprehensible to a public of antiquity than to the public of his own day.'[19] Rather than refuting such extravagances, it should be pointed out that an artistic form can never be determined by its effect. 'That a work of art should be perfect and complete in itself is the eternal and essential requirement! Aristotle, who had before him the height of perfection, was thinking of the effect? How absurd!'[20] Thus Goethe. No matter whether Aristotle is completely above the suspicion against which Goethe defends him – it is nevertheless crucial to the method of the philosophy of art that the psychological effect which Aristotle defined should have no place whatever in the debate about drama. Hence Wilamowitz-Moellendorff declares: 'it must be realized that *catharsis* cannot exercise a determining influence on drama as a genre, and even if one did wish to regard the emotions by which drama achieves its effects as generically determinative, then the unfortunate pair, fear and pity, would still be quite inadequate.'[21] Even more unfortunate and more widespread than the attempt to vindicate the *Trauerspiel* with the help of Aristotle is that sort of 'appreciation' which claims, in a few trivial *aperçus*, to have proved the 'necessity' of this kind of drama and, in so doing, to have proved either the positive worth or the futility of all value judgments – it is seldom clear which. The question of the necessity of historical phenomena is always a manifestly *a priori* question. The ill-conceived predicate 'necessity', with which the baroque *Trauerspiel* has frequently been adorned, is prone to change colour. It does not only mean historical necessity, superfluously contrasted to mere chance, but it also means the subjective necessity of sincerity in contrast to virtuosity. It is, however, obvious that we learn nothing from establishing that a work of art is necessarily prompted by a subjective disposition on the part of its author. The same is true of the 'necessity' which sees works or forms as preliminary stages of a subsequent development in a problematic context. 'The concept of nature and the view of art current in the seventeenth century may well have been irrevocably demolished; the innovations then made in respect of artistic technique continue to flourish, unfading, incorruptible, and imperishable.'[22] So it is that the most recent account vindicates the literature of this age, but merely as a means. The 'necessity'[23] of appreciations resides in a realm of equivocations and derives plausibility from the only concept of necessity which is relevant to aesthetics. That is to say the concept which Novalis had in mind when describing the *a priori* character of works of art as their immanent necessity *to be there*. It is clear that this necessity can be grasped only in an analysis which penetrates to its metaphysical substance. It will slip through the net of any moderantist 'appreciation'. And, in the last resort, Cysarz's new attempt is no more than this. Whereas in earlier studies it was the case that the principal features of a completely different way of looking at things simply passed unnoticed, in this latest one it is surprising that valuable ideas and precise observations fail to realize their potential because of the conscious attempt to relate them to the system of neo-classical poetics. Ultimately the tone is not so much that of a vindication in classical terms as of an apologetic excuse. In older works the Thirty Years War is normally mentioned in this context. It appears to bear the responsibility for all the lapses for which this form has been criticized. 'It has often been said that these were plays written by brutes for brutes. But this is what was wanted by the people of that time. Living as they did in an atmosphere of war and bloody conflict, they found such scenes quite natural; they were being presented with a picture of their own way of life. They delighted naively and brutally in the pleasure offered them.'[24]

At the end of the last century research had strayed hopelessly far from critical examination of the form of the *Trauerspiel*. The attempt to find a substitute for reflection on the philosophy of art in a syncretism of cultural-historical, literary-historical, and biographical approaches has a rather less innocuous parallel in the most recent research. Just as a man lying sick with fever transforms all the words which he hears into the extravagant images of delirium, so it is that the spirit of the present age seizes on the manifestations of past or distant spiritual worlds, in order to take possession of them and unfeelingly incorporate them into its own self-absorbed fantasizing. This is characteristic of our age: there is no new style, no unknown popular heritage to be discovered which would not straight away appeal with the utmost clarity to the feelings of contemporaries. This fatal, pathological suggestibility, by means of which the historian seeks through 'substitution',[25] to insinuate himself into the place of the creator – as if the creator were, just because he created it, also the best interpreter of his work – this has been called 'empathy', in an attempt to provide a disguise under which idle curiosity masquerades as method. In this adventure the lack of autonomy manifest in the present generation has for the most part been overwhelmed by the compelling force it encountered in the baroque. Hitherto there have been no more than a few isolated cases where the revaluation which began with the emergence of expressionism – and which was, perhaps, affected by the poetics of the school of Stefan George[26] – has led to a genuine insight which reveals new relationships within the material itself and not just between the modern critic and his material.[27] But the authority of the old prejudices is beginning to wane. Remarkable analogies to present-day German literature have given increased grounds for an interest in the baroque which, although it is for the most part sentimental in quality, is nonetheless positive in tendency. As early as 1904 a literary historian declared of this period: 'It seems to me . . . that not for two centuries has there been a period in which artistic feeling has been closer than it is now to the baroque literature of the seventeenth century in its search for its own style. Inwardly empty or profoundly disturbed, outwardly pre-occupied with technical problems of form which seemed at first to have very little to do with the existential problems of the age – this is what most of the baroque writers were like, and, so far as one can see, the same is true of at least those present-day poets who impress their personality upon their work.'[28] In the meantime this opinion, expressed here all too diffidently and guardedly, has been substantiated in a very much wider sense. 1915 saw the publication of Werfel's *Die Troerinnen*, a herald of the expressionist drama. It is not entirely fortuitous that the same subject is to be encountered in the work of Opitz in the early days of the baroque drama. In both works the poet was concerned with the instrument of lamentation and its resonance. In both cases what was therefore required was not ambitious artificial developments, but a verse-form modelled on dramatic recitative. The analogy between the endeavours of the baroque and those of the present and the recent past is most apparent in the use of language. Exaggeration is characteristic of both. The creations of these two literary styles do not emerge from any sense of communal existence; the violence of their manner is, rather, designed to conceal the absence of widely accepted works of literature. For like expressionism, the baroque is not so much an age of genuine artistic achievement as an age possessed of an unremitting artistic will. This is true of all periods of so-called decadence. The supreme reality in art is the isolated, self-contained work. But there are times when the well-wrought work is only within reach of the epigone. These are the periods of 'decadence' in the arts, the periods of artistic 'will'. Thus it was that Riegl devised this term with specific reference to the art of the final period of the Roman Empire. The form as such is within the reach of this will, a well-made individual work is not. The reason for the relevance of the baroque after the collapse of German classical culture lies in this will. To this should be added the desire for a vigorous style of language, which would make it seem equal to the violence of world-events. The practice of contracting adjectives, which have no adverbial usage, and substantives into a single block, is not a modern invention. *'Grosstanz'*, *'Grossgedicht'* (i.e. epic), are baroque words. Neologisms abound. Now, as then, many of them are an expression of a desire for new pathos. Writers were attempting personally to gain a mastery of that innermost formative power from which the precise but delicate language of metaphor derives. Glory was sought in devising figurative words rather than figurative speeches, as if linguistic creation were the immediate concern of poetic verbal invention. Baroque translators delighted in the most arbitrary coinings such as are encountered among contemporaries, especially in the form of archaisms, in which it is believed one can reassure oneself of the wellsprings of linguistic life. Such arbitrariness is always the sign of a production in which a formed expression of real content can scarcely be extracted from the conflict of the forces which have been unleashed. In this state of disruption the present age reflects certain aspects of the spiritual constitution of the baroque, even down to the details of its artistic practice. Just as the pastoral play formed a contrast to the political novel, which then, as now, attracted the interest of respected authors, so, nowadays, do the pacifist avowals of faith in the 'simple life' and the natural goodness of man. Men of letters, who today, as always, live their lives in a sphere cut off from the active national feeling of the people, are once again consumed by an ambition in the satisfaction of which the writers of the baroque period were, of course, and in spite of everything, more successful than the writers of today. For Opitz, Gryphius, and Lohenstein were occasionally able to perform gratefully rewarded political duties. And here our parallel reaches its limits. The baroque writer felt bound in every particular to the ideal of an absolutist constitution, as was upheld by the Church of both confessions. The attitude of their present-day heirs, if not actually hostile to the state, that is revolutionary, is characterized by the absence of any idea of the state. And finally, so many analogies should not lead us to forget this great difference: in seventeenth-century Germany, literature, however little account the nation took of it, underwent a significant rebirth. The twenty years of German literature which have been referred to here in order to explain the renewal of interest in the earlier epoch, represent a decline, even though it may be a decline of a fruitful and preparatory kind.

All the more powerful, therefore, is the impact which can be made at this very moment by the expression of related tendencies in the eccentric artistic medium of the German baroque. Confronted with a literature which sought, in a sense, to reduce both its contemporaries and posterity to silence through the extravagance of its technique, the unfailing richness of its creations, and the vehemence of its claims to value, one should emphasize the necessity of that sovereign attitude which the representation of the idea of a form demands. Even then the danger of allowing oneself to plunge from the heights of knowledge into the profoundest depths of the baroque state of mind, is not a negligible one. That characteristic feeling of dizziness which is induced by the spectacle of the spiritual contradictions of this epoch is a recurrent feature in the improvized attempts to capture its meaning. 'Even the most intimate idioms of the baroque, even its details – indeed, perhaps they more than anything else – are antithetical.'[29] Only by approaching the subject from some distance and, initially, foregoing any view of the whole, can the mind be led, through a more or less ascetic apprenticeship, to the position of strength from which it is possible to take in the whole panorama and yet remain in control of oneself. The course of this apprenticeship is what had to be described here.

Trauerspiel and Tragedy

Der ersten Handlung. Erster Eintritt. Heinrich. Isabelle. Der Schauplatz ist der Königl. Saal. *Heinrich.* Ich bin König. *Isabelle.* Ich bin Königin. *Heinrich.* Ich kan und will. *Isabelle.* Ihr könt nicht und must nicht wollen. *Heinrich.* Wer will mirs wehren? *Isabelle.* Mein Verboth. *Heinrich.* Ich bin König. *Isabelle.* Ihr seyd mein Sohn. *Heinrich.* Ehre ich euch schon als Mutter/ so müsset ihr doch wissen/ das ihr nur Stiefmutter seyd. Ich will sie haben. *Isabelle.* Ihr sollt sie nicht haben. *Heinrich.* Ich sage: Ich will sie haben/ die Ernelinde.

Filidor: *Ernelinde Oder Die Viermahl Braut**

The necessary tendency towards the extreme which, in philosophical investigations, constitutes the norm in the formation of concepts, means two things as far as the representation of the origin of the German baroque *Trauerspiel* is concerned. Firstly it serves as a reminder that the whole range of subject matter should be disinterestedly observed. Given the by

---

* First act. First scene. Heinrich. Isabelle. The setting is the throne-room. *Heinrich:* I am King. *Isabelle:* I am Queen. *Heinrich:* I can and wish to. *Isabelle:* You cannot and should not wish to. *Heinrich:* Who shall prevent me? *Isabelle:* I forbid it. *Heinrich:* I am King. *Isabelle:* You are my son. *Heinrich:* If I honour you as a mother, you must know that you are only my stepmother. I want her. *Isabelle:* You shall not have her. *Heinrich:* I say, I want her, Ernelinde.

Filidor: *Ernelinde or the fourfold betrothed.*

no means excessive quantity of dramatic production, the task of such research must not look for schools of poets, epochs of the *oeuvre*, or strata of individual works, as the literary historian quite properly might. Rather will it be guided by the assumption that what seems diffuse and disparate will be found to be linked in the adequate concepts as elements of a synthesis. And so the production of lesser writers, whose works frequently contain the most eccentric features, will be valued no less than those of the great writer. It is one thing to incarnate a form; it is quite a different thing to give its characteristic expression. Whereas the former is the business of the poetic elect, the latter is often done incomparably more distinctly in the laborious efforts of minor writers. The life of the form is not identical with that of the works which are determined by it, indeed the clarity with which it is expressed can sometimes be in inverse proportion to the perfection of a literary work; and the form itself becomes evident precisely in the lean body of the inferior work, as its skeleton so to speak. Secondly the study of extremes means taking account of the baroque theory of drama. The straightforwardness with which the theoreticians enunciate their prescriptions is a particularly attractive feature of this literature, and their rules are extreme for the simple reason that they are presented as more or less binding. Thus the eccentrics of this drama can, for the most part, be traced back to the poetics, and since even the limited number of clichés which constitute its plots are derived from theorems, the writers' manuals prove to be indispensable source materials for analysis. If they were critical, in the modern sense, they would be much less important. It is not only the subject itself which demands that they should be referred to, but as this is also manifestly justified by the current state of research. Until very recently this has been inhibited by prejudices of stylistic classification and aesthetic judgement. The discovery of the literary baroque took place at such a late date and under such an ambiguous aspect because of a predilection for a convenient periodization based on the characteristics and the data contained he treatises of past epochs. Since, in Germany, a literary 'baroque' did not anywhere become conspicuous – even with reference to the plastic arts the expression does not occur before the eighteenth century – and since writers who aspired to a courtly tone were not disposed to indulge in

clear, loud, aggressive proclamations, there was subsequently no desire
to grant this particular chapter in the history of German literature its own
particular heading. 'The non-polemic attitude is a decisive characteristic
of the whole of the baroque. Everyone attempts as far as possible – even
when following his own inclination – to maintain the appearance that he
is treading in the footsteps of respected teachers and established authori-
ties.'[1] The growth of interest in the poetic dispute, which emerged at the
same time as the corresponding passions of the artistic academies in
Rome,[2] should not be allowed to conceal this fact. Thus poetics took the
form of variations on the *Poetices libri septem* of Julius Caesar Scaliger,
which had appeared in 1561. Classicistic schemes are predominant:
'Gryphius is the undisputed master, the German Sophocles, and behind
him Lohenstein, the German Seneca, takes secondary place; only with
certain reservations can Hallmann, the German Aeschylus, be placed
alongside them.'[3] And there is in the dramas undeniably something
which corresponds to the Renaissance-façade of the poetics. Their
stylistic originality – this much may be said in advance – is comparably
greater in the details than in the whole. This, as Lamprecht has emphasized,[4] possesses a certain ponderousness and yet a simplicity of
action which is distantly reminiscent of the bourgeois drama of the German Renaissance. However, in the light of serious stylistic criticism,
which may not consider the whole without regard to its determination by
the detail, the non-renaissance, not to say baroque features appear everywhere, from the language and behaviour of the participants, to the theatrical
machinery and choice of subject. At the same time it is particularly
illuminating, that, as will be shown, certain emphases can be given to the
traditional texts of poetics, which permit the baroque interpretation,
indeed that adherence to them served baroque intentions better than
revolt. In a literature which saw itself directly confronted with formal tasks
for which it was quite unprepared, the will to classicism is practically the
only feature genuinely characteristic of the renaissance – though this
latter is far surpassed in wildness and recklessness. Notwithstanding what
was ahieved in individual cases, every attempt to approach antique form
necessarily exposed the undertaking to highly baroque elaboration, by its
very violence. The failure of literary scholarship to indulge in the

stylistic analysis of such attempts is explained by its own verdict on the age of bombast, linguistic corruption, and academic poetry. Insofar as it sought to qualify this verdict by the consideration that the school of Aristotelian dramaturgy was a necessary transitional stage for renaissance-literature in Germany, it was merely countering one prejudice with another. Both are interdependent, because the thesis of the renaissance-form of German drama in the seventeenth century is supported by reference to the Aristotelianism of the theoreticians. We have already noted now inhibiting the Aristotelian definitions were to any appreciation of the value of the dramas. We should now emphasize that the term 'renaissance-tragedy' implies an overestimation of the influence of the Aristotelian doctrine on the drama of the baroque.

The insignificance of the influence of Aristotle

The history of modern German drama has known no period in which the themes of the ancient tragedians have been less influential. This alone testifies against the dominance of Aristotle. All the preconditions for an understanding of his work were lacking, not least the will. For obvious reasons no-one looked to the Greek author for the serious instruction in matters of technique and subject-matter which, from the time of Gryphius, had been derived from Dutch classicism and from the Jesuit theatre. First and foremost it was a question of establishing a connection with the poetics of Scaliger by recognizing the authority of Aristotle, and so asserting the validity of the indigenous efforts. Moreover, in the middle of the seventeenth century Aristotelian poetics had not yet become that simple and imposing structure of dogma with which Lessing came to grips. Trissino, the first commentator on the *Poetics*, introduces unity of action as a complement to unity of time: unity of time is regarded as aesthetic only if it is accompanied by unity of action. Gryphius and Lohenstein adhered to these unities – although in the case of *Papinian* the unity of action is questionable. This solitary fact completes the list of those features derived from Aristotle. The theory of the period does not give a precise definition of unity of time. That of Harsdörffer, which in other respects does not depart from tradition, declares that even an action lasting four to five days is permissible. Unity of place, which was only introduced into the discussion by Castelvetro, is irrelevant to the baroque *Trauerspiel*; it does not occur even in Jesuit theatre. Even more conclusive is the indifference towards the Aristotelian theory of tragic effect which is evident in the manuals. Although this particular part of the *Poetics*, in which the influence of the cultic character of the Greek theatre is more conspicuous than elsewhere, cannot have been very accessible to the seventeenth-century mind. However, the greater the difficulty of fathoming this doctrine, in which the theory of purification by the mysteries was at work, the more room there was for interpretation. And this is every bit as slight in its thought-content as it is striking in its distortion of the original antique intention. Fear and pity are not seen as participation in the integral whole of the action, but as participation in the fate of the most outstanding characters. Fear is aroused by the death of the villain, pity by that of the pious hero. For Birken even this definition is too classical, and he replaces fear and pity with the glorification of God and the edification of one's fellow-men as the purpose of the *Trauerspiel*. 'Wir Christen sollen / gleichwie in allen unsren Verrichtungen / also auch im Schauspiel-schreiben und Schauspielen das einige Absehen haben / dass Gott damit geehret / und der Neben-Mensch zum Guten möge belehrt werden.'[5]* The *Trauerspiel* should fortify the virtue of its audience. And if there was a particular virtue which was indispensable in its heroes, and edifying for its public, then this was the old virtue of ἀπάθεια. The association of the stoic ethic with the theory of modern tragedy was effected in Holland; and I¦psius had remarked that the Aristotelian ἔλεος should be understood exclusively as an active impulse to alleviate the physical and mental suffering of others, and not as a pathological collapse at the sight of a terrifying fate, not as *pusillanimitas* but as *misericordia*.[6] Without any doubt such glosses are quite alien to Aristotle's description of the contemplation of tragedy. Thus, again and again, it is the single fact of the royal hero which prompted the critics to relate the new *Trauerspiel* to the ancient tragedy of the Greeks. And so

---

* We Christians should, in all our actions and therefore also in writing and performing plays, have as our sole aim that God be therein glorified and our fellow-men thereby improved.

there can be no more appropriate place to begin an investigation into the peculiar character of the *Trauerspiel* than in the famous definition of Opitz, couched in the language of the *Trauerspiel* itself.

'Die Tragödie ist an der majestet dem Heroischen gedichte gemesse / ohne das sie selten leidet / das man geringen standes personen und schlechte sachen einführe: weil sie nur von königlichem willen / todschlägen / verzweiffelungen / kinder und vätermörden / brande / blutschanden / kriege und auffruhr / klagen / heulen / seuffzten und dergleichen handelt.'[7]* It may be that the modern aesthetician will not value this definition too highly, because it appears to be no more than a description of the subject-matter of tragedy. And indeed it never has been regarded as significant. This appearance is, however, deceptive. Opitz does not actually say so – for in his day it was self-evident – but the incidents listed are not so much the subject-matter as the artistic core of the *Trauerspiel*. Historical life, as it was conceived at that time, is its content, its true object. In this it is different from tragedy. For the object of the latter is not history, but myth, and the tragic stature of the *dramatis personae* does not derive from rank – the absolute monarchy – but from the pre-historic epoch of their existence – the past age of heroes. For Opitz it is not the conflict with God and Fate, the representation of a primordial past, which is the key to a living sense of national community, but the confirmation of princely virtues, the depiction of princely vices, the insight into diplomacy and the manipulation of all the political schemes, which makes the monarch the main character in the *Trauerspiel*. The sovereign, the principal exponent of history, almost serves as its incarnation. In a crude way, the participation in contemporary events of world-history is frequently referred to in the poetics. In the *Alleredelster Belustigung* Rist states: 'Wer Tragödien schreiben wil muss in Historien oder Geschicht-

---

* Tragedy is equal in majesty to heroic poetry, except that it seldom suffers from the introduction of characters of lowly estate and ignorable matters: because it deals only with the commands of kings, killings, despair, infanticide and patricide, conflagrations, incest, war and commotion, lamentation, weeping, sighing, and suchlike.

Büchern so wol der Alten / als Neuen / trefflich seyn beschlagen / er muss die Welt- und Staats-Händel / als worinn die eigentliche Politica bestehet / gründlich wissen . . . wissen / wie einem Könige oder Fürsten zu muthe sey / so wol zu Krieges- als Friedens-Zeiten / wie man Land und Leute regieren / bey dem Regiment sich erhalten / allen schädlichen Rath-schlägen steuren / was man für Griffe müsse gebrauchen / wann man sich ins Regiment dringen / andere verjagen / ja wol gar auss dem Wege räumen wolle. In Summa / die Regier-Kunst muss er so fertig / als seine Mutter-Sprache verstehen.'⁸* The *Trauerspiel*, it was believed, could be directly grasped in the events of history itself; it was only a question of finding the right words. And there was no desire to feel free even in this latter procedure. Haugwitz may well have been the least talented among the authors of baroque *Trauerspiele*, indeed quite simply the only really untalented one, but to attribute one particular statement in the notes to *Maria Stuarda* to a lack of skill would be to misunderstand the technique of the *Trauerspiel*. Here he complains that in writing this work he had only one source available – the *Hoher Trauersaal* by Franziscus Erasmus – so that he 'had to restrict himself excessively to the words of the translator of Franziscus.'⁹ In the case of Lohenstein this same attitude gives rise to the corpus of notes which rivals the dramas in length; and also to the words with which the notes conclude in *Papinian* by Gryphius, here too the more inventive and incisive writer: 'Und so viel vor diesesmal. Warum aber so viel? Gelehreten wird dieses umsonst geschrieben, ungelehrten ist es noch zu wenig.'¹⁰† Like the term 'tragic' in present-day usage – and with greater justification – the word *Trauerspiel* was applied in the seventeenth century to dramas and to historical events alike. Even the style gives an indication of how close to each other the two things were in the contemporary mind. What is customarily condemned

---

* Whoever will write tragedies must be excellently well-versed in chronicles and history books, both ancient and modern, he must know thoroughly the affairs of the world and the state, in which politics truly consist . . . must know what is the state of mind of a king or prince, both in time of peace and in time of war, how countries and people are governed, how power is maintained, how harmful counsel is avoided, what skills are needed in order to seize power, to expel others, even to clear them from one's way. In short, he must understand the art of government as thoroughly as his mother-tongue.

† So much, then, this time. But why so much? For the learned it is all written in vain; for the unlearned it is not enough.

as bombast in the stage-works can, in many cases, scarcely be described better than in the words which Erdmannsdörffer uses to characterize the tone of the historical sources in those decades: 'In all the texts which speak of war and the disasters of war one notices an extravagant tone of plaintive lamentation, which a :quires the character of a fixed mannerism; an incessant hand-wringing mode of expression, so to speak, becomes general usage. Whereas the misery, however great it was, differed nevertheless in degree, in describing it, the writing of the time is completely lacking in nuances.'[11] The radical consequence of assimilating the theatrical and the historical scene would have been that the agent of historical execution himself would have been called upon before all others for the writing of literature. Thus it is that Opitz begins the preface to his *Troerinnen*: 'Trawerspiele tichten ist vorzeiten Keyser / Fürsten / grosser Helden wnd Weltweiser Leute thun gewesen. Aus dieser zahl haben Julius Cesar in seiner jugend den Oedipus / Augustus den Achilles wnd Ajax / Mecenas den Prometheus / Cassius Serverus Parmensis, Pomponius Secundus / Nero wnd anders sonsten was dergleichen vor sich genommen.'[12]* Following Opitz, Klai declares: 'es sei unschwer zu erweisen, wie selbst das Trauerspieldichten nur der Kaiser, Fürsten, grosser Helden und Weltweisen, nicht aber schlechter Leute Thun gewesen'.[13]† Without going quite as far as his friend and pupil, Klai, Harsdörffer devises a rather vague scheme of correspondences between estate and form – which can be applied just as easily to the subject as to the reader, the actor as to the author – according to which the pastoral is allotted to the peasantry, the comedy to the middle classes, and the *Trauerspiel*, along with the novel, to the princely estate. These theories, however, had a converse consequence which was even more farcical. Political intrigue took a hand in literary conflict; Hunold and Wernicke denounced each other to the kings of Spain and England respectively.

---

* Writing tragedies was formerly the task of emperors, princes, great heroes and sages. Among them Julius Caesar, in his youth, took up the *Oedipus*, Augustus the *Achilles* and *Ajax*, Maecenas the *Prometheus*, while Cassius Serverus Parmensis, Pomponius Secundus, Nero, and others did things of the same kind.

† it is not difficult to show that actually writing tragedies is the business of emperors, princes, great heroes and sages, but not of humble people.

The sovereign is the representative of history. He holds the course of history in his hand like a sceptre. This view is by no means peculiar to the dramatists. It is based on certain constitutional notions. A new concept of sovereignty emerged in the seventeenth century from a final discussion of the juridical doctrines of the middle ages. The old exemplary problem of tyrannicide became the focal point in this debate. Among the various kinds of tyrant defined in earlier constitutional doctrine, the usurper had always been the subject of particular controversy. The Church had abandoned him, but beyond that it was a question of whether the people, the anti-king, or the Curia alone could give the signal to depose him. The attitude of the Church had not lost its relevance; for in this century of religious conflicts the clergy clung firmly to a doctrine which armed them against hostile princes. Protestantism rejected the theocratic claims of this doctrine; and in the assassination of Henry IV of France its consequences were exposed. The publication of the Gallican articles in 1682 marked the final collapse of the theocratic doctrine of the state: the absolute right of the monarch had been established before the Curia. Despite the alignment of the respective parties, this extreme doctrine of princely power had its origins in the counter-reformation, and was more intelligent and more profound than its modern version. Whereas the modern concept of sovereignty amounts to a supreme executive power on the part of the prince, the baroque concept emerges from a discussion of the state of emergency, and makes it the most important function of the prince to avert this.[14] The ruler is designated from the outset as the holder of dictatorial power if war, revolt, or other catastrophes should lead to a state of emergency. This is typical of the Counter-Reformation. With the release of the worldly and despotic aspects of the rich feeling for life which is characteristic of the Renaissance, the ideal of a complete stabilization, an ecclesiastical and political restoration, unfolds in all its consequences. And one of these consequences is the demand for a prince-dom whose constitutional position guarantees the continuity of the community, flourishing in feats of arms and in the sciences, in the arts and in its Church. The theological-juridical mode of thought, which is so characteristic of the century,[15] is an expression of the retarding effect of

the over-strained transcendental impulse, which underlies all the provo-
catively worldly accents of the baroque. For as an antithesis to the historical ideal of restoration it is haunted by the idea of catastrophe. And it is in
response to this antithesis that the theory of the state of emergency is
devised. If one wishes to explain how 'the lively awareness of the significance of the state of emergency, which is dominant in the natural law of
the seventeenth century'[16] disappears in the following century, it is not
therefore enough simply to refer to the greater political stability of the
eighteenth century. If it is true, that 'for Kant . . . emergency law was no
longer any law at all',[17] that is a consequence of his theological rationalism.
The religious man of the baroque era clings so tightly to the world
because of the feeling that he is being driven along to a cataract with it.
The baroque knows no eschatology; and for that very reason it possesses
no mechanism by which all earthly things are gathered in together and
exalted before being consigned to their end. The hereafter is emptied of
everything which contains the slightest breath of this world, and from it
the baroque extracts a profusion of things which customarily escaped the
grasp of artistic formulation and, at its high point, brings them violently
into the light of day, in order to clear an ultimate heaven, enabling it, as a
vacuum, one day to destroy the world with catastrophic violence. A
variation of the same idea is touched on by the insight that the naturalism
of the baroque is 'the art of least distances . . . In every case naturalistic
means are used to reduce distances . . . The most vivid and concrete
actuality is sought as a contraposition from which to revert all the more
surely into formal elevation and the forecourts of the metaphysical.'[18]
Nor do the exaggerated forms of baroque Byzantinism testify against the
tension between immanence and transcendence. They have a disturbed
quality, and contented radiance is foreign to them. The preface to the
Heldenbriefe states: 'Wie ich denn der tröstlichen Zuversicht lebe / es
werde meine Kühnheit / dass ich etlicher erlauchten Häuser / die ich
unterhänigst ehre / auch dafern es nicht wieder Gott were / anzubeten
bereit bin, längst-verrauchte Liebes Regungen zuerfrischen mich
unterstanden / nicht allzufeindseelig angesehen werden.'[19]* Birken is

---

* So, then, I live in the consoling trust that my boldness in daring to rekindle the long-
extinguished flames of love of certain illustrious houses which I most humbly honour and am
ready to worship, so far as it would not be offensive to God, will not be viewed with too great
disfavour.

unsurpassed: the more elevated the persons, the better it is to praise them, 'als welches fürnehmlich Gott und frommen ErdGöttern gebühret'.[20]* Is this not a petty bourgeois counterpart to the royal processions of Rubens? 'The prince appears here not only as the hero of an antique triumph but he is at the same time directly associated with divine beings, served and celebrated by them: thus he is himself deified. Earthly and heavenly figures mingle in his train and contribute to the same idea of glorification.' This, however, is still a pagan glorification. In the *Trauerspiel* monarch and martyr do not shake off their immanence. The theological hyperbole is accompanied by a very popular cosmological argumentation. The comparison of the prince with the sun is repeated countless times in the literature of the epoch. The purpose of this is to stress the exclusiveness of this ultimate authority. 'Wer iemand auf den thron | An seine seiten setzt, ist würdig, dass man cron | Und purpur ihm entzieh. Ein fürst und eine sonnen | Sind vor die welt und reich.'[21]†
'Der Himmel kan nur eine Sonne leiden / | Zwey können nicht im Thron' und Eh-Bett weiden',[22]‡ says 'Ambition' in Hallmann's *Mariamne*. In the *Abris Eines Christlich-Politischen Printzens | In CI Sinn-Bildern*, by Saavedra Fajardos, there is a quite remarkable statement which showed how easily the extension of these metaphors led from the juridical establishment of the ruler's internal position to the extravagant ideal of world dominance, which corresponded as closely to the theocratic passion of the baroque as it was incompatible with its political wisdom. An allegorical engraving, which depicts an eclipse of the sun with the inscription: 'Praesentia nocet' (sc. lunae), is accompanied by the explanation that princes should keep well away from each other. 'Die Fürsten die erhalten vntereinander gute freundtschafft / vermittelst deroselbigen bedienten vnd brieffen; wo sie sich aber wollen wegen einiger sachen selbsten vnter einander bereden / alsobaldt entstehen nur auss dem angesicht allerhand verdacht vnd wiederwillen / dan es findet einer in dem anderen das jenige nit / was er ihm eingebildet / auch niemandt auss ihnen ermist sich selbsten / weil gemeiniglich keiner auss ihnen nit ist / welcher nit mehr /

---

* as is the due above all of God and pious earthly Gods.
† Whoever sets anyone beside him on the throne deserves to be stripped of crown and purple. There is one sun for the world and one prince for the kingdom.
‡ The heavens can tolerate only one sun. Two men may not enjoy the same throne or the same marriage bed.

als ihm von rechts wegen zukombt / seyn will. Die Fürstliche zusammen-
kunfft vnd gegenwart ist ein immerwehrender krieg / in welchem man
nur vmb die gepreng streitet / vnd wil ein jeder den vorzug haben / vnd
streitet mit dem anderen vmb den Sieg.'[23]*

The favourite source of subject matter was the history of the Orient,
where absolute imperial power was to be encountered to a degree unknown in the West. Thus in *Catharina* Gryphius takes the Shah of Persia,
while Lohenstein, in his first and last dramas, uses the Sultanate. But it is
the theocratic Empire of Byzantium which figures most prominently.
This is the age which saw the beginnings of 'the systematic discovery and
investigation of Byzantine . . . literature . . . in the great editions of the
Byzantine historians which . . . were undertaken under the auspices of
Louis XIV by French scholars such as Du Cange, Combefis, Maltrait
etc.'[24] These historians, above all Cedrenus and Zonaras, were read
widely, and perhaps not only for the bloodthirsty accounts which they
gave of the fate of the Eastern Empire, but also because of the attraction
of the exotic images. The influence of these sources increased throughout
the seventeenth and into the eighteenth century. For as, towards the end
of the baroque era, the tyrant of the *Trauerspiel* tended increasingly to
become that role which found a by no means inglorious end in the
Viennese farces of Stranitzky, so did the chronicles of the Eastern Empire,
crammed as they were with misdeeds, prove more and more useful. For
instance: 'Man hänge brenne, man rädere, es trieffe in bluth und ersauffe
im Styx wer Uns beleidiget.'[25]† Or again: 'Es blühe die gerechtigkeit, es
hersche die grausambkeit, es triumphire Mord und tyranney, damit

---

* Princes, by the benefit of their Ministers and Letters, maintain and uphold mutual
Correspondence with each other: But if they should Conferr Personally with one another,
their Interview would create shadows of Suspicion and Jealousie, which would put all their
States in Confusion, for that they never find in one another what they promis'd to themselves,
and that neither measures himself by his own Rule, but pretends always to much more than
his Due. An Interview of two Princes, is almost like a Duel, in which they fight with Ceremonies, each endeavouring to conquer t'other.'

† If anyone offend us let him be hanged, burned, broken on the wheel, let him drip blood
and drown in the Styx.

Wenceslaus auf bluthschaumenden leichen statt der stuffen auf seinen Sieghafften thron steigen könne.'[26]* In the north the *Haupt- und Staatsaktionen* eventually merged into the opera; in Vienna they ended up as parody. 'Eine neue Tragoedie, Betitult: Bernadon Die Getreue Prinzessin Pumphia, Und Hanns-Wurst Der tyrannische Tartar-Kulikan, Eine Parodie in lächerlichen Versen'[27]†; with its cowardly tyrant, and the theme of chastity taking refuge in marriage, reduces the motifs of the great *Trauerspiel* to absurdity. It could almost carry a motto from Gracián, which shows just how closely the role of the prince in the *Trauerspiel* had to conform to the stereotype and the extreme. 'Könige misst man nach keinem Mittelmasse. Man rechnet sie entweder unter die gar guten / oder die gar bösen.'[28]‡

For the 'very bad' there was the drama of the tyrant, and there was fear; for the 'very good' there was the martyr-drama and pity. This juxtaposition of forms appears strange only as long as one neglects to consider the legal aspect of baroque princedom. Seen in ideological terms they are strictly complementary. In the baroque the tyrant and the martyr are but the two faces of the monarch. They are the necessarily extreme incarnations of the princely essence. As far as the tyrant is concerned, this is clear enough. The theory of sovereignty which takes as its example the special case in which dictatorial powers are unfolded, positively demands the completion of the image of the sovereign, as tyrant. The drama makes a special point of endowing the ruler with the gesture of executive power as his characteristic gesture, and having him take part in the action with the words and behaviour of a tyrant even where the situation does not require it; in the same way it was probably unusual for full robes, crown and sceptre to be wanting when the ruler appeared on the stage.[29] Not even

---

* Let righteousness flourish, terror reign, murder and tyranny triumph, so that Wenceslaus might ascend his victorious throne on bleeding corpses instead of steps.

† A new tragedy, entitled: Bernadon, the constant Princess Pumphia, and Hans Wurst, the tyrannical Tartar-Kulikan, a parody in comic verse.

‡ Kings are never moderate. They are judged to be either very good or very bad.

the most dreadful corruption of the person of the prince – and that is the baroque aspect of the whole business – can really disturb this norm of sovereignty. The solemn speeches with their ceaseless variations on the maxim: 'Der purpur muss es decken'[30]* are, it is true, meant to be provocative, but they evoke sympathetic wonder even when they refer to fratricide, as in Gryphius' *Papinian*, incest, as in Lohenstein's *Agrippina*, infidelity, as in his *Sophonisbe*, or wife-murder, as in Hallmann's *Mariamne*. Above all it is the figure of Herod, as he was presented throughout the European theatre at this time,[31] which is characteristic of the idea of the tyrant. It was his story which lent the depiction of the *hubris* of kings its most powerful features. Even before this period a terrifying mystery had been woven around this king. Before being seen as a mad autocrat and a symbol of disordered creation, he had appeared in an even crueller guise to early Christianity, as the Antichrist. Tertullian – and in this he is not alone – speaks of a sect of Herodians, who worshipped Herod as the Messiah. The story of his life did not provide material for drama alone. The Latin juvenilia of Gryphius, the Herodian epics, show clearly what fascinated these people: the seventeenth-century ruler, the summit of creation, erupting into madness like a volcano and destroying himself and his entire court. Artists took great delight in painting the picture of him falling into insanity, holding two babes in his hands in order to batter out their brains. The spirit of the drama of princes manifests itself clearly in that the features of the martyr-drama are interwoven in this typical version of the end of the Jewish king. At the moment when the ruler indulges in the most violent display of power, both history and the higher power, which checks its vicissitudes, are recognized as manifest in him. And so there is this one thing to be said in favour of the Caesar as he loses himself in the ecstasy of power: he falls victim to the disproportion between the unlimited hierarchical dignity, with which he is divinely invested and the humble estate of his humanity.

The antithesis between the power of the ruler and his capacity to rule led

---

* The purple must cover it.

to a feature peculiar to the *Trauerspiel* which is, however, only apparently a generic feature and which can be illuminated only against the background of the theory of sovereignty. This is the indecisiveness of the tyrant. The prince, who is responsible for making the decision to proclaim the state of emergency, reveals, at the first opportunity, that he is almost incapable of making a decision. Just as compositions with restful lighting are virtually unknown in mannerist painting, so it is that the theatrical figures of this epoch always appear in the harsh light of their changing resolve. What is conspicuous about them is not so much the sovereignty evident in the stoic turns of phrase, as the sheer arbitrariness of a constantly shifting emotional storm in which the figures of Lohenstein especially sway about like torn and flapping banners. And they also bear a certain resemblance to the figures of El Greco in the smallness of their heads,[32] if we understand this in a metaphorical sense. For their actions are not determined by thought, but by changing physical impulses. It is consistent with such a style 'that the literature of the period, even the less formal narrative genre, is frequently successful in rendering even the most fleeting expressions, but remains helpless when confronted with the human face'.[33] Through the messenger, Disalces, Masinissa sends Sophonisbe poison to save her from imprisonment by the Romans: 'Disalces geh / und wirff mir mehr kein Wort nicht ein. | Jedoch / halt! Ich vergeh / ich zitter / ich erstarre! | Geh immer! es ist nicht mehr Zeit zu zweiffeln. Harre! | Verzieh! Ach! schaue / wie mir Aug' und Hertze bricht! | Fort! immer fort! der Schluss ist mehr zu ändern nicht.'[34]* At the corresponding place in *Catharina* Chach Abas despatches the Imam Kuli with the order to execute Catharina, concluding: 'Lass dich nicht eher schauen | Als nach volbrachtem werck! Ach was beklämmt vor grauen | Die abgekränckte brust! Verzeuch! geh hin! ach nein! | Halt inn! komm her! ja geh! es muss doch endlich seyn.'[35]† Indecision, the complement of bloody terror, occurs in the Viennese farce too: 'Pelifonte:

---

* Disalces, go without another word. But no, stay! I die, I tremble, I am struck with horror. Yet go! There is no time for doubt. Wait! Be gone! Alas! Look how the tears flow and how my heart is breaking! Away, away! It cannot be altered now.

† Do not show yourself again until the work is done. Alas, what terrors weigh upon my tortured heart! Away! Be gone! But no! Stay. Come back! Yes, go! It must be done at last.

Nu! so lebe sie dann, sie lebe, – doch nein, – – ia, ia, sie lebe . . . Nein, nein, sie sterbe, sie vergehe, man entseele sie . . . Gehe dann, sie soll leben.'[36]* Thus speaks the tyrant, briefly interrupted by others.

The enduring fascination of the downfall of the tyrant is rooted in the conflict between the impotence and depravity of his person, on the one hand, and, on the other, the extent to which the age was convinced of the sacrosanct power of his role. It was therefore quite impossible to derive an easy moral satisfaction, in the manner of the dramas of Hans Sachs, from the tyrant's end. For if the tyrant falls, not simply in his own name, as an individual, but as a ruler and in the name of mankind and history, then his fall has the quality of a judgment, in which the subject too is implicated. That which emerges from a close examination of the Herodian drama is immediately obvious in works such as *Leo Armenius*, *Carolus Stuardus*, and *Papinian*, which in any case either resemble martyr-dramas or are to be reckoned among them. Indeed, it is not too much to say that, basically, a description of the martyr-drama can be seen in all the definitions of drama in the poetic manuals. They are not so much concerned with the deeds of the hero as with his suffering, and frequently not so much with his spiritual torment as with the agony of the physical adversity which befalls him. And yet the martyr-drama was never explicitly proposed, except in one sentence of Harsdörffer's: 'Der Held . . . sol ein Exempel seyn aller vollkomenen Tugenden / und von der Untreue seiner Freunde / und Feinde betrübet werden; jedoch dergestalt / dass er sich in allen Begebenheiten grossmütig erweise und den Schmertzen / welcher mit Seufftzen / Erhebung der Stimm und vielen Klagworten hervorbricht / mit Tapferkeit überwinde.'[37]† The words: 'afflicted by the faithlessness of friends and enemies' could be used with reference to the Passion of

---

* Pelifonte: Well, then let her live, let her live, – but no, – yes, yes, she shall live . . . No, no, she shall die, she shall perish, let her be killed . . . Go, then, she shall live.

† The hero . . . must be the perfect embodiment of all virtues, and must be afflicted by the faithlessness of friends and enemies; and yet in such a way that he shows magnanimity in all circumstances and courageously overcomes the pain which causes sighing, loud cries, and much lamentation.

Christ. Just as Christ, the King, suffered in the name of mankind, so, in the eyes of the writers of the baroque, does royalty in general. 'Tollat qui te non noverit'* runs the heading to sheet LXXI of Zincgref's *Emblematum ethico-politicorum centuria*. It depicts a mighty crown in the foreground of a landscape. Beneath are the lines: 'Ce fardeau paroist autre à celuy qui le porte, | Qu'à ceux qu'il esblouyt de son lustre trompeur, | Ceuxcy n'en ont jamais conneu la pesanteur, Mais l'autre sçait expert quel tourment il apporte.'[38]* And so there was, on occasion, no hesitation in explicitly endowing princes with the title of martyr. 'Carolus der Märtyrer', 'Carolus Martyr'[39] is written beneath the engraving on the title-page of the *Königliche Verthätigung für Carl I* [A royal defence for Charles I]. In Gryphius' first *Trauerspiel* these antitheses interact in a manner which is both unsurpassed and confusing. The sublime status of the Emperor on the one hand, and the infamous futility of his conduct on the other, create a fundamental uncertainty as to whether this is a drama of tyranny or a history of martyrdom. Gryphius would certainly have asserted the former; Stachel seems to regard the latter as self-evident.[40] In these dramas the structure undermines the formal stereotype associated with the subject. Nowhere more so than in *Leo Armenius*, to the detriment of any clearly delineated ethical profile. Deeper examination is not therefore necessary in order to ascertain that an element of martyr-drama lies hidden in every drama of tyranny. It is much less easy to trace the element of the drama of tyranny in the martyr-drama. A precondition of this is familiarity with that strange image of the martyr which was traditional in the baroque – at least in the literary baroque. It has nothing to do with religious conceptions; the perfect martyr is no more released from the sphere of immanence than is the ideal image of the monarch. In the drama of the baroque he is a radical stoic, for whom the occasion to prove himself is a struggle for the crown or a religious dispute ending in torture and death. A peculiarity is the introduction of a woman as the

---

* This burden appears different to him who bears it than to those who are dazzled by its deceptive brilliance. The latter have never known its weight, but the former knows full well what torment it brings.

victim in many of these dramas: in *Catharina von Georgien* by Gryphius, *Sophia* and *Mariamne* by Hallmann, *Maria Stuarda* by Haugwitz. This is of decisive importance for the correct appreciation of the martyr-drama. The function of the tyrant is the restoration of order in the state of emergency: a dictatorship whose utopian goal will always be to replace the unpredictability of historical accident with the iron constitution of the laws of nature. But the stoic technique also aims to establish a corresponding fortification against a state of emergency in the soul, the rule of the emotions. It too seeks to set up a new, anti-historical creation – in woman the assertion of chastity – which is no less far removed from the innocent state of primal creation than the dictatorial constitution of the tyrant. The hallmark of domestic devotion is replaced by physical asceticism. Thus it is that in the martyr-drama the chaste princess takes pride of place.

Whereas the theoretical discussion of the term drama of tyranny, even in the face of its most extreme forms, has never begun, the discussion of the martyr-drama belongs, as is well known, to the staple diet of German dramaturgy. All the reservations customarily voiced about the *Trauerspiel* of this period, whether they were based on Aristotle, on the despised atrociousness of the plots, or, not least, on linguistic considerations, pale into insignificance before the complacency with which authors have, for a century and a half, rejected it in the concept of the martyr-drama. The reason for this unanimity need not be looked for in the subject itself, but in the authority of Lessing.[41] Given the tenacity with which histories of literature have always connected the critical discussion of works to long-dead controversies, the influence of Lessing is not surprising. And this could not be corrected by a psychological approach which, instead of beginning with the object itself, considers its effect on the ordinary contemporary citizen, whose relationship to theatre and public has dwindled to a certain rudimentary avidity for action. For the performance of the martyr-drama does not provide enough of the trivial emotion of suspense which is the only evidence of theatricality still acknowledged by such a spectator. The consequent disappointment has therefore assumed the language of scholarly protest, and the value of these dramas has, supposedly, been definitively settled in the conclusion that they are deficient in inner conflict and tragic guilt. To this can be added the evaluation of the plot. It differs from the so-called antithetical plot of classical tragedy by virtue of the isolation of motives, scenes, and types. Just as in the Passion-play tyrants, devils, or Jews appear on stage in the profoundest viciousness and wickedness, without being permitted to explain themselves or to develop, or indeed to display, anything other than their base schemes, so too does the drama of the baroque like to show the antagonists in crudely illuminated separate scenes, where motivation usually plays an insignificant part. It could be said that baroque intrigue takes place like a change of scenery on the open stage, so minimal is the illusionistic intention, so obtrusive the economy of the counter-plot. Nothing is more instructive than the nonchalance with which decisive motives in the intrigue may be relegated to the notes. For instance, in Hallmann's *Mariamne*, Herod concedes: 'Wahr ists: Wir hatten ihm / die Fürstin zu entleiben / | Im Fall uns ja Anton möcht' unverseh'ns auffreiben / | Höchstheimlich anbefohl'n.'[42]* And the note explains: 'Nehmlich aus allzugrosser Liebe gegen sie / damit sie keinem nach seinem Tode zu theil würde.'[43]† Reference might also be made to *Leo Armenius*, not so much as an example of a loosely constructed plot, as of careless composition. The Empress Theodosia herself prevails upon the prince to postpone the execution of the rebel, Balbus, and it is this which leads to the death of the Emperor Leo. But in the course of her long lament for her husband she makes no mention whatever of her own earlier remonstrances. A decisive motive is passed over. The 'unity' of a simply historical plot required that the drama follow an unequivocal line of development, and thereby jeopardized its quality. For just as surely as such a line of development is the basis for any pragmatic representation of history, so too does the dramatic genre, by its very nature, demand closed form, in order to achieve that totality which is denied to all external temporal

---

* It is true: we did order him in the utmost secrecy to murder the princess if Antony should suddenly slay us.

† For too great love of her lest she should fall into the hands of another after his death.

progression. The subsidiary plot, either as a parallel or as a contrast to the main plot, guarantees this totality. But Lohenstein is the only dramatist to make frequent use of it; generally it was excluded in the belief that this was the better way of making history visible as such. The Nuremberg-School proposes the simple notion, that the plays were called *Trauer-spiele*, 'Weil vorzeiten in der Heidenschaft meistteils Tyrannen das Regiment geführet / und darum gewönlich auch ein grausames Ende genommen'.[44]* Gervinus makes the following judgment of the dramatic structures of Gryphius: 'the progression of the scenes is designed only to explain and continue the actions; dramatic effectiveness is never the aim',[45] and with certain reservations, at least as far as *Cardenio und Celinde* is concerned, it is basically correct. Nevertheless it needs to be borne in mind that such isolated observations, however well-founded, will not serve as the basic principles of criticism. The fact that the dramatic form employed by Gryphius and his contemporaries does not possess the same dramatic quality as later forms does not make it inferior to them. Its value is determined in a context which is autonomous.

In this context we need to bear in mind the affinity between the baroque drama and the religious drama of the Middle Ages, which is evident in the extent to which both share the character of the Passion-play. But given the kind of insights that are current in a critical literature dominated by empathy, this reference needs to be cleared of the suspicion that it is an example of that futile analogy-mongering which hinders rather than advances the task of stylistic analysis. Here it might be observed that the representation of the mediaeval elements in the drama of the baroque and its theory is to be seen as a preliminary to further confrontations of the spiritual worlds of the baroque and the middle ages, which will be encountered elsewhere. The resurrection of mediaeval theories in the age of the wars of religion,[46] the continued dominance of the middle ages in

---

* Because in pagan times government was generally in the hands of tyrants who usually came to a dreadful end.

'politics and economics, art and science',[47] the fact that the middle ages were not overcome, indeed, were not given their name, until during the seventeenth century,[48] all this has long since been stated. A glance at certain details will reveal a surprising mass of evidence. Even a purely statistical compilation from the poetics of the epoch leads to the conclusion that the essence of the definitions of tragedy is 'exactly the same as in the grammatical and lexicographical works of the Middle Ages'.[49] Nor is the striking similarity between Opitz's definition and the standard mediaeval definitions of Boethius or Placidus in any way affected by the fact that Scaliger, who in other respects is consistent with them, produced examples which speak against their distinction between tragic and comic poetry.[50] In the text of Vincent de Beauvais this distinction runs: 'Est autem Comoedia poesis, exordium triste laeto fine commutans. Tragoedia vero poesis, a laeto principio in tristem finem desinens.'[51]* It seems to be regarded as an almost irrelevant distinction whether this sad occurrence is presented in the form of dramatic dialogue or in continuous prose. Accordingly Franz Joseph Mone has convincingly demonstrated the connection between the mediaeval drama and the mediaeval chronicle. It appears 'that world history [was] seen by the chroniclers as a great *Trauerspiel*, and the chronicles of world history were related to the old German plays. In so far as the chronicles conclude with the Day of Judgment, that is to say the end of the drama of the world, Christian historiography is, of course, related to the Christian drama; and here it is important to note the statements of those chroniclers who clearly indicate this relationship. Otto von Freisingen says (*praefat ad. Frid. imp.* [Preface to the Emperor Frederick]): cognoscas, nos hanc historiam ex amaritudine animi scripsisse, ac ob hoc non tam rerum gestarum seriem quam earundem miseriam in modum tragoediae texuisse.† He repeats this in the *praefat. ad Singrimum* [Preface to Singrimus]: in quibus (libris) non tam historias quam aerumnosas mortalium calamitatum tragoedias

---

* A comedy is a poem which transforms a sad beginning into a happy end. A tragedy however is a poem that leads from a happy beginning to a sad end.

† You should know that we wrote this history from the bitterness of our heart, and that we have therefore not so much woven a sequence of events, as the wretchedness of the same in the manner of a tragedy.

prudens lector invenire poterit.* For Otto, then, world history was a tragedy, not in its form but in its content.[52] Five hundred years later we encounter the same view in Salmasius: 'Ce qui restoit de la Tragedie iusques à la conclusion a esté le personnage des Independans, mais on a veu les Presbyteriens iusques au quatriesme acte et au delà, occuper auec pompe tout le theatre. Le seul cinquiesme et dernier acte est demeure pour le partage des Independans; qui ont paru en cette scene, apres auoir sifflé et chassé les premiers acteurs. Peut estre que ceux-là n'auroient pas fermé la scene par vne si tragique et sanglante catastrophe.'[53]† It is here, far from the confines of Lessing's *Hamburg Dramaturgy*, not to mention post-classical dramaturgy, in the 'tragedy', which the middle ages probably read into what little they knew of the subject matter of ancient drama, rather than seeing it realized in their own mystery-plays, that the formal world of the baroque *Trauerspiel* is revealed.

Nevertheless: whereas the Christian mystery-play and the Christian chronicle present the entire course of world history as a story of redemption, the *Haupt- und Staatsaktion* deals with only a part of pragmatic events. Christendom or Europe is divided into a number of European Christian provinces whose historical actions no longer claim to be integrated in the process of redemption. The relationship of the *Trauerspiel* to the mystery-play is called into question by the insuperable despair which seems necessarily to be the last word of the secularized Christian drama. For no one will regard the stoic morality, to which the martyrdom of the hero leads, or the justice, which transforms the tyrant's rage to madness, as an adequate foundation for the tension of an independent dramatic structure. A massive ornamental layer of truly baroque stucco

---

* in these books the prudent reader will be able to find not so much histories as harsh tragedies of mortal calamities.

† The Independents were the tragic element which remained right up to the conclusion, although the Presbyterians were seen to occupy the whole theatre in pomp until the fourth act and beyond. The fifth and final act alone was left for the Independents, who appeared after howling down and chasing off the previous actors. It is possible that the latter would not have brought the drama to a close with such a tragic and bloody catastrophe.

conceals the keystone, and only the closest investigation can locate it. The tension derives from a question concerning the redemption of mankind, which was allowed to expand to immeasurable proportions by the secularization of the mystery-play, which did not only occur among the Protestants of the Silesian and Nuremberg schools, but equally so among the Jesuits and with Calderón. For all that the increasing worldliness of the Counter-Reformation prevailed in both confessions, religious aspirations did not lose their importance: it was just that this century denied them a religious fulfilment, demanding of them, or imposing upon them, a secular solution instead. These generations enacted their conflicts under the yoke of this compulsion or the spur of this demand. Of all the profoundly disturbed and divided periods of European history, the baroque is the only one which occurred at a time when the authority of Christianity was unshaken. Heresy, the mediaeval road of revolt, was barred; in part precisely because of the vigour with which Christianity asserted its authority, but primarily because the ardour of a new secular will could not come anywhere near to expressing itself in the heterodox nuances of doctrine and conduct. Since therefore neither rebellion nor submission was practicable in religious terms, all the energy of the age was concentrated on a complete revolution of the content of life, while orthodox ecclesiastical forms were preserved. The only consequence could be that men were denied all real means of direct expression. For this would have led to the unambiguous manifestation of the will of the age and so to that very conflict with the Christian life to which romanticism was later to succumb. And this was avoided in both a positive and a negative sense. For the dominant spiritual disposition, however eccentrically it might elevate acts of ecstasy, did not so much transfigure the world in them as cast a cloudy sky over its surface. Whereas the painters of the Renaissance know how to keep their skies high, in the paintings of the baroque the cloud moves, darkly or radiantly, down towards the earth. In contrast to the baroque the Renaissance does not appear as a godless and heathen period, but as an epoch of profane freedom for the life of the faith, while the Counter-Reformation sees the hierarchical strain of the middle ages assume authority in a world which was denied direct access to a beyond. Burdach's new definition of Renaissance and Reformation, which is directed against the prejudices derived from Burckhardt, first reveals, *per contrarium*, these decisive features of the Counter-Reformation in their true light. Nothing was more foreign to it than the expectation of the end of the world, or even a revolution, such as has been shown by Burdach to inform the Renaissance movement. In philosophical-historical terms its ideal was the acme : a golden age of peace and culture, free of any apocalyptic features, constituted and guaranteed *in aeternum* by the authority of the Church. The influence of this attitude extends even over the surviving religious drama. Thus the Jesuits 'no longer [take] the whole of the life of Christ as their theme, and more and more infrequently do they take the Passion ; instead they prefer subjects from the Old Testament, expressing their proselytizing intentions more adequately in the legends of the martyrs'.[54] The effect of the restoration philosophy of history on the secular drama was necessarily more evident. It had to deal with historical subject matter – the initiative of writers who took up contemporary events, like Gryphius, or the *Haupt- und Staatsaktionen* of the orient, like Lohenstein and Hallmann, was immense. But from the outset these efforts remained confined to a context of strict immanence, without any access to the beyond of the mystery plays and so, for all their technical ingenuity, limited to the representation of ghostly apparitions and the apotheoses of rulers. It was under such restrictions that the German baroque drama grew up. Small wonder that this occurred in an eccentric and so all the more intense way. Hardly any trace of the German drama of the renaissance survives ; with the *Troerinnen* of Opitz the restrained gaiety and the simple moralism of these plays had already been renounced. Gryphius and Lohenstein would have been all the more energetic in proclaiming the artistic value and the metaphysical significance of their dramas if it had been permissible to emphasize craftsmanship anywhere other than in dedications and panegyrics.

The developing formal language of the *Trauerspiel* can very well be seen as the emergence of the contemplative necessities which are implicit in the contemporary theological situation. One of these, and it is consequent upon the total disappearance of eschatology, is the attempt to find, in a reversion to a bare state of creation, consolation for the renunciation of a state of grace. Here, as in other spheres of baroque life, what is vital is the transposition of the originally temporal data into a figurative spatial simultaneity. This leads deep into the structure of the dramatic form. Whereas the middle ages present the futility of world events and the transience of the creature as stations on the road to salvation, the German *Trauerspiel* is taken up entirely with the hopelessness of the earthly condition. Such redemption as it knows resides in the depths of this destiny itself rather than in the fulfilment of a divine plan of salvation. The rejection of the eschatology of the religious dramas is characteristic of the new drama throughout Europe; nevertheless the rash flight into a nature deprived of grace, is specifically German. For in the supreme form of this European theatre, the drama of Spain, a land of Catholic culture in which the baroque features unfold much more brilliantly, clearly, and successfully, the conflicts of a state of creation without grace are resolved, by a kind of playful reduction, within the sphere of the court, whose king proves to be a secularized redemptive power. The *stretta* of the third act, with its indirect inclusion of transcendence – as it were mirrored, crystallized, or in marionette-form – guarantees the drama of Calderón a conclusion which is superior to that of the German *Trauerspiel*. It cannot renounce its claim to touch on the substance of existence. But if the secular drama must stop short on the borders of transcendence, it seeks, nevertheless, to assure itself of this indirectly, in play. Nowhere is this clearer than in *La vida es sueño*, where we have a totality worthy of the mystery-play, in which the dream stands over waking life like the vault of heaven, Morality is valid within it: 'But, waking or sleeping, one thing only | Matters: to act rightly; If awake, because acts are real, | If dreaming, to win friends for the time of awaking.'[55] Nowhere but in Calderón could the perfect form of the baroque *Trauerspiel* be studied. The very precision with which the 'mourning' [*Trauer*] and the 'play' [*Spiel*] can harmonize with one another gives it its exemplary validity – the validity of the word and of the thing alike. There are three periods in the history of the concept 'play' in German aesthetics: the baroque, classicism and romanticism. The first is concerned predominantly with the product, the second with production, and the third with both. The view which sees life itself as a game and which, *a fortiori*, must designate the work of art as such, is foreign to classicism. Schiller's theory of the play-impulse reflected his interest in the genesis and effect of art, not in the structure of works of art. They may be 'cheerful' where life is 'serious', but they may take a playful form only when life too, in the face of an intense pre-occupation with the absolute, has lost its ultimate seriousness. This was true, whatever the differences, of both the baroque and romanticism. And in both cases such that this intense preoccupation had to find its expression in the forms and the subject-matter of secular art. In the drama the play-element was demonstratively emphasized, and transcendence was allowed its final word in the worldly disguise of a play within a play. The technique is not always transparent, as when the stage itself is set up on the stage, or the auditorium is extended onto the stage-area. And yet for the theatre of profane society – and this is what makes it 'romantic' – the power of salvation and redemption only ever lies in a paradoxical reflection of play and appearance. In the ideal romantic *Trauerspiel* of Calderón the mourning [*Trauer*] is dispersed by that intentionality which, according to Goethe, emanates from every work of art. The new theatre has artifice as its god. It is characteristic that in the German baroque *Trauerspiel* this element of play is not unfolded with the brilliance of the Spanish drama, nor with the artfulness of the later romantic works. It does however have the motif which found its most powerful formulations in the lyric of Andreas Gryphius. A variation of it is to be found in the dedication of Lohenstein's *Sophonisbe*. 'Wie nun der Sterblichen ihr gantzer Lebens-Lauf | Sich in der Kindheit pflegt mit Spielen anzufangen / | So hört das Leben auch mit eitel Spielen auf. | Wie Rom denselben Tag mit Spielen hat begangen / | An dem August gebohrn; so wird mit Spiel und Pracht | Auch der Entleibten Leib in sein Begräbnüs bracht / | . . . Der blinde Simson bringt sich spielend in das Grab; | Und unsre kurtze Zeit ist nichts als ein Getichte. | Ein Spiel / in dem bald der tritt auf / bald jener ab; | Mit Thränen fängt es an / mit Weinen wirds zu nichte. | Ja nach dem Tode pflegt mit uns die Zeit zu spielen / | Wenn

Fäule / Mad' und Wurm in unsern Leichen wühln.'[56]* In its very monstrosity the plot of *Sophonisbe* anticipates the subsequent development of the play-element, which leads through the highly important medium of the puppet-theatre to the grotesque on the one hand, and to the subtle on the other. The dramatist is fully aware of the fantastic twists: 'Die für den Ehmann itzt aus Liebe sterben wil, | Hat in zwey Stunden sein' und ihrer Hold vergessen. | Und Masinissens Brunst ist nur ein Gaukelspiel, | Wenn er der, die er früh für Liebe meint zu fressen, | Den Abend tödlich Gift als ein Geschencke schickt, | Und, der erst Buhler war, als Hencker sie erdrückt. | So spielet die Begierd und Ehrgeitz in der Welt!'[57]† Such play need not be thought of as accidental, it might just as easily be planned and calculated and might therefore be seen as a puppet-play, with ambition and desire holding the strings. It remains indisputable, however, that the German drama of the seventeenth century had not yet mastered that exemplary artistic means which enabled the romantic drama from Calderón to Tieck to employ the techniques of enclosure by a framework, and miniaturization: reflection. This latter comes into its own not only as one of the principal artistic means of romantic comedy, but also in the so-called tragedy of romanticism, the drama of fate [*Schicksalsdrama*]. In the drama of Calderón it corresponds to the volute in the architecture of the time. It repeats itself infinitely, and reduces to immeasurability the circle which it encloses. Both these aspects of reflection are equally essential: the playful miniaturization of reality and the introduction of a reflective infinity of thought into the finite space of a profane fate. For the world of the drama of fate is – to anticipate our conclusions – a self-enclosed world. This was particularly so in Calderón, whose Herod-drama, *El major munstro del mondo*, has been described as

---

* As now of mortals the whole life's course begins in childhood with games, so does life end in vain games. As Rome celebrated the day of Augustus' birth with games, so too with play and splendour will the victim's body be brought to burial . . . The blind Samson goes playing to his grave; and our brief life is nothing but a poem. A play in which now one man enters and now another leaves; with tears it begins and with weeping it ends. Yea, after death time also plays with us, when maggot and worm burrow in our decaying bodies.

† She who now wishes to die for love of her husband has, within two hours, forgotten their mutual faith. And Masinissa's lust is mere deception if he, at evening, sends deadly poison as a gift to her whom he earlier intends to devour for love, and if he, who once was paramour, now destroys her as executioner. Thus do desire and ambition play their roles in the world!

the first drama of fate in world literature. It was the sublunary world in the strict sense, a world of the wretched or vainglorious creature, in which, to the greater glory of God and for the delight of the spectators, the rule of fate was to be confirmed, at the same time surprisingly and purposefully. It is no accident that a man like Zacharias Werner tried his hand at the drama of fate before seeking refuge in the Roman Catholic Church. The apparently pagan worldliness of this form is in fact the profane complement to the religious mystery-play. But what attracted even the theoreticians among the romantics so irresistibly to Calderón – so that he, rather than Shakespeare, might perhaps be called their dramatist, κατ᾽ ἐξοχήν – is the unparalleled virtuosity of the reflection, thanks to which his heroes are always able to turn the order of fate around like a ball in their hands, and contemplate it now from one side, now from the other. To what else did the romantics ultimately aspire than genius, decked out in the golden chains of authority, reflecting without responsibility? Yet this unparalleled Spanish perfection, which, however high it stands in terms of artistic quality, seems always to be one step higher in calculatedness, does not perhaps reveal the stature of the baroque drama, which extends beyond the limits of the purely literary, quite so clearly as the German drama, whose ambiguous nature is not so much concealed in the primacy of the artistic, as revealed in that of the moral. As its vocational ethic so emphatically proclaims, Lutheran moralism was always intent on bringing together the transcendence of the life of faith and the immanence of everyday life; it therefore never permitted the decisive confrontation between human-earthly perplexity and princely-hierarchical power on which the conclusion of so many of Calderón's dramas depends. The end of the German *Trauerspiel* is therefore both less formal and less dogmatic, it is – morally, not, of course, artistically – more responsible than that of the Spanish drama. Notwithstanding, it is inconceivable that an investigation will not come across many connections which are relevant to the weighty and equally enclosed form of Calderón. The less room there is in the following for excurses and cross-references, the more clearly must our investigation explain the fundamental relationship to the *Trauerspiel* of the Spanish dramatist, with which the Germany of that time had nothing to compare.

The level of the state of creation, the terrain on which the *Trauerspiel* is enacted, also unmistakably exercises a determining influence on the sovereign. However highly he is enthroned over subject and state, his status is confined to the world of creation; he is the lord of creatures, but he remains a creature. Let us demonstrate this with reference to Calderón. It is by no means a specifically Spanish idea that is expressed in the following words of the steadfast prince, Don Fernando. In them the motif of the name of king in nature is carried to its conclusion. 'For even 'mong brutes and beasts of prey I This name, authority so ample I Does in its wondrous way enforce, I That, by a certain law, obedience I Follows in Nature's usual course; I And thus, within his rude republics, I We read the lion-king doth reign, I Who, when his horrid front he wrinkleth, I And crowns him with his royal mane, I Feels pity, for he ne'er abuseth I Whatever prey his wrath hath slain. I So on the sea's salt foam the dolphin, I Who is the king of fish, we're told, I Worketh upon his azure shoulder, I In scales of silver and of gold, I The shapes of crowns; and we behold him, I When the wild tempest shrieks with glee, I Bear on his back the sinking seaman, I Lest he should perish in the sea . . . I If then, among beast and fishes, I Plants and stones, and birds, the august I Majesty of King, is pity – I It, my Lord, were not unjust I That men's bosoms should possess it.'[58] The attempt to find the origin of kingship in the state of creation is even encountered in legal theory. So it was that the opponents of tyrannicide demanded that the murderers of kings be brought into disrepute as *parricidi*. Claudius Salmasius, Robert Silmer, and many others derived 'the authority of the king from the dominion over the world which Adam received as lord of all creation, and which was passed on to certain heads of families, finally to become hereditary in one family, though only within certain territorial limits. Regicide therefore amounts to parricide.'[59] Even the nobility could appear to be so much a natural phenomenon that, in his *Leich-Reden* Hallmann can address death with the following lament: 'Ach dass du auch vor privilegirte Personen keine eröffnete Augen noch Ohren hast!'[60]* The simple subject, man, is

---

* Alas that even before privileged persons your eyes and ears are not open!

consequently a beast: 'das göttliche Thier' [the divine beast], 'das kluge Thier' [the wise beast],[61] 'ein fürwitzig und kitzliches Thier' [an inquisitive and delicate beast].[62] Thus the formulations of Opitz, Tscherning, and Buchner. And, on the other hand, Butschky writes: 'Was ist ... ein Tugendhafter Monarch anders / als ein Himmlisches Thier.'[63]* And then there are the beautiful lines of Gryphius: 'Ihr, die des höchsten bild verlohren, | Schaut auf das bild, das euch gebohren! | Fragt nicht, warum es in dem stall einzieh! | Er sucht uns, die mehr viehisch als ein vieh.'[64]* This latter is demonstrated by despots in their madness. When Hallmann's Antiochus is driven mad by the sudden terror awoken in him by the sight of a fish's head at table;[65] or when Hunold introduces his Nebuchadnezzar in the shape of a beast – the setting consists of 'eine wüste Einöde. Nebucadnezar an Ketten mit Adlers Federn und Klauen bewachsen unter vielen wilden Thieren ... Er geberdet sich seltsam ... Er brummet und stellt sich übel'[66]† – this reflects the conviction that in the ruler, the supreme creature, the beast can re-emerge with unsuspected power.

The Spanish theatre developed a significant motif of its own on just such a basis, which, more than anything else, enables the narrow earnestness of the German *Trauerspiel* to be recognized as a national peculiarity. It may be surprising to see that the dominant role played by honour, in the intrigues of the *comedia de capa y espada* [cloak and dagger play] and the *Trauerspiel* alike, derives from the creaturely estate of the dramatic character. But so it is. Honour is, as Hegel defined it, 'the extreme embodiment of violability'.[67] 'For the personal self-subsistency for which honour contends does not assert itself as intrepitude on behalf of a

---

* You who have lost sight of the image of the Highest: behold the image that has been born unto you! Ask not why it enters into a stable! He is seeking us, who are more like animals than the animals themselves.

† A desolate wilderness. Nebuchadnezzar in chains with the eagle's feathers and talons he has grown among wild beasts ... He makes strange gestures ... He growls and shows his ill-nature

communal weal, and the repute of thoroughness in relation to it and integrity of private life. On the contrary it contends simply for the recognition and formal inviolability of the individual subject.'[68] This abstract inviolability is, however, no more than the strictest inviolability of the physical self, the purity of flesh and blood in which even the most secondary demands of the code of honour are grounded. For this reason dishonour is caused by the shame of a relative no less than by an offence against one's own person. And the name which, in its own inviolability, claims to bear witness to the apparently abstract inviolability of the person, is in the context of the life of the creature, as opposed to religion, nothing in and for itself; it is only the shield designed to protect man's physical vulnerability. The man without honour is an outlaw: in calling for the punishment of the man who is its object, shame reveals its origin in some physical defect. The unparalleled dialectic of the concept of honour in the Spanish drama permitted a uniquely superior, indeed a conciliatory representation of the creaturely exposure of the person. The bloody torture, in which the life of the creature comes to an end in the martyr-drama, has a pendant in the calvary of honour which, however mishandled, can always be reasserted at the end of the dramas of Calderón, thanks to a royal decree or a sophistry. The Spanish drama found in honour the creaturely spirituality appropriate to the creaturely body, and in doing so discovered a cosmos of the profane unknown to the writers of the German baroque, even the later theorists. The intended similarity of motive did not, however, escape their notice. Schopenhauer writes: 'The distinction, so often discussed in our day, between *classic* and *romantic* poetry seems to me to rest ultimately on the fact that the former knows none but purely human, actual, and natural motives; the latter, on the other hand, maintains as effective also motives that are pretended, conventional, and imaginary. Among such motives are those springing from the Christian myth, then those of the chivalrous, exaggerated, extravagant, and fantastic principle of honour . . . But even in the best poets of the romantic sort, e.g., Calderón, we can see to what ridiculous distortions of human relations and human nature these motives lead. Not to speak at all of the *Autos*, I refer merely to pieces like *No siempre el peor es cierto* and *El postrero dualo en España*, and similar comedies *en capa y espada*. Associated with these elements is the scholastic subtlety that often appears in the conversation which at that time was part of the mental culture of the upper classes.'[69] Schopenhauer has failed to understand the spirit of the Spanish drama, despite the fact that – in a different context – he wished to set the Christian *Trauerspiel* far above tragedy. And one is tempted to attribute his distaste to that amorality in the Spanish outlook which is so foreign to the German he was. It was this which provided the basis for the interplay of tragedy and comedy in Spain.

Sophistic problems, indeed solutions, such as are to be found therein, do not occur in the ponderous reasoning of the German Protestant dramatists. But the contemporary understanding of history severely restricted their Lutheran moralism. The constantly repeated drama of the rise and fall of princes, the steadfastness of unshakeable virtue, appeared to the writers less as a manifestation of morality than as the natural aspect of the course of history, essential in its permanence. Any profound fusion of historical and moral concepts was almost as unknown to the pre-rationalist west as it had been to antiquity; and as far as the baroque is concerned this is particularly borne out in an intention focussed on world-history in the manner of a chronicle. Inasmuch as it became absorbed in the microscopic examination of details, it progressed no further than the painstaking analysis of the calculations of political intrigue. Baroque drama knows no other historical activity than the corrupt energy of schemers. In none of the countless rebels who confront a monarch frozen in the attitudes of the Christian martyr, is there any trace of revolutionary conviction. Discontent is the classic motive. The sovereign alone reflects any kind of moral dignity, and even here it is the totally unhistorical moral dignity of the stoic. For this, rather than the Christian hero's trust in salvation, is the attitude which is universally encountered in the principal characters of the baroque drama. The most cogent objection to the story of the martyr is certainly that it can lay no claim to historical content. But it is an objection to a false theory of this form rather than to the form itself. Moreover, in the following sentence of Wackernagel, it is as inadequate a conclusion, as the assertion which is meant to support this conclusion is relevant. 'Tragedy should not merely show that everything human is impermanent in comparison with the divine, but also that this must be so; it must not therefore conceal the frailties which are the necessary reason for the catastrophe. If it showed punishment without guilt, it would . . . contradict history, which knows no such thing, and from which tragedy must derive the manifestations of that basic tragic idea.'[70] Setting aside the dubious optimism of this view of history – in the terms of the martyr-drama it is not moral transgression but the very estate of man as creature which provides the reason for the catastrophe. This typical catastrophe, which is so different from the extraordinary catastrophe of the tragic hero, is what the dramatists had in mind when – with a word which is employed more consciously in dramaturgy than in criticism – they described a work as a *Trauerspiel*. It is therefore no accident – to take an example which is authoritative enough to excuse its remoteness from the subject in question – that *Die natürliche Tochter*, which is not in the least affected by the world-historical impact of the revolutionary happenings around which it is enacted, is designated a *Trauerspiel*. Inasmuch as he saw in the political events only the horror of a destructive will which periodically stirs in the manner of the forces of nature, Goethe resembled a seventeenth-century poet in his attitude to his subject. The classicistic tone of the work forced these events into an exposition conceived in more-or-less natural-historical terms; for this reason Goethe exaggerated, creating between style and action a tension which is as incomparably lyrical as it is dramatically restrictive. In this work by Goethe the ethos of the historical drama is every bit as alien as in any baroque *Staatsaktion*, except, of course, that here historical heroism has not given way to stoic heroism. In the baroque drama fatherland, liberty, and faith are no more than freely interchangeable causes which put private virtue to the test. Lohenstein goes furthest in this respect. No other writer approached him in his use of the technique of blunting any tendency to ethical reflection by means of metaphorical analogies between history and the cycle of nature. Apart from stoic ostentation, every ethically motivated attitude or discussion is excluded with a radicalism which, more even than the violence of any plot, makes for that harsh contrast between the content and the preciosity of the diction, which is characteristic of Lohenstein's dramas. When Johann Jacob Breitinger gave his assessment of the celebrated dramatist in his *Critische Abhandlung von der Natur, den Absichten und dem Gebrauch der Gleichnisse* of 1740, he referred to his habit of giving apparent emphasis to moral principles by examples from nature, which in fact undermine them.[71] This kind of comparison acquires its proper significance only when an ethical transgression is justified purely and simply by referring to natural conduct. 'Man weicht den Bäumen aus die auf dem Falle stehen'[72]*; with these words Sofia takes leave from Agrippina, as her end approaches. These words should not be understood as characterizing the speaker, but as a maxim derived from natural conduct and appropriate to the events of high politics. The authors had available an immense store of images by means of which they could convincingly resolve historical and ethical conflicts into the demonstrations of natural history. Breitinger observed: 'This flaunting of his knowledge of physical science is so characteristic of our Lohenstein, that he invariably reveals such a secret of nature whenever he wishes to declare that something is strange or impossible, that it will come to pass probably, improbably, or never . . . when . . . the father of Arsinoë wishes to prove that it is improper for his daughter to be betrothed to anyone less than a royal prince, he concludes as follows: 'Ich versehe mich zu Arsinoen, wenn ich sie anders für meine Tochter halten soll, sie werde nicht von der Art, des den Pöbel abbildenden Epheus seyn, welcher so bald eine Haselstaude, als einen Dattelbaum umarmet. Dann, edle Pflantzen kehren ihr Haupt gegen dem [sic] Himmel; die Rosen schliessen ihr Haupt nur der anwesenden Sonne auf; die Palmen vertragen sich mit keinem geringen Gewächse: Ja der todte Magnetstein folget keinem geringern, als dem so hochgeschäzten Angel-Sterne. Und Polemons Haus (ist der Schluss) sollte sich zu den Nachkommen des knechtischen Machors abneigen.''[73]† Like Erich Schmidt the reader

---

* one avoids trees which are about to fall

† I expect of Arsinoë, if I am to regard her as my daughter, that she will not resemble the ivy, image of the rabble, which embraces a hazel bush as readily as a palm tree. For noble plants lift their heads to the sky; roses open only in the light of the sun; palm trees tolerate the presence of no inferior plant: yea the dead lodestone follows nothing less than the esteemed pole-star. Should, then Polemon's house (he concludes) incline to the descendants of the servile Machor?

will probably be persuaded by such passages, of which there are numerous examples, especially in rhetorical writings, epithalamia, and funeral orations, that compendia were part of the tools of the trade of these writers.[74] These compendia did not only contain factual information, but poetic formulae in the manner of the mediaeval *Gradus ad Parnassum*. This much can at least be confidently concluded in respect of Hallmann's *Leich-Reden*, which have stereotyped formulae to hand for a number of unfamiliar catchwords: Genofeva,[75] Quäker,[76] etc. The use of natural-historical metaphors made the same rigorous demands on the learning of the authors as did the precise handling of historical sources. Thus the writers share the cultural ideal of the polymath which Lohenstein saw realized in Gryphius. 'Herr Gryphens . . . l Hielt für gelehrt-seyn nicht / in einem etwas missen / l In vielen etwas nur / in einem alles wissen.'[77]*

The creature is the mirror within whose frame alone the moral world was revealed to the baroque. A concave mirror; for this was not possible without distortion. Since it was the view of the age that all historical life was lacking in virtue, virtue was also of no significance for the inner constitution of the *dramatis personae* themselves. It has never taken a more uninteresting form than in the heroes of these *Trauerspiele*, in which the only response to the call of history is the physical pain of martyrdom. And just as the inner life of the person has to attain mystical fulfilment in the creaturely condition, even in mortal pain, so do the authors attempt to impose the same restriction on the events of history. The sequence of dramatic actions unfolds as in the days of the creation, when it was not history which was taking place. The nature of the creation which absorbs history back into itself, is quite different from the nature of Rousseau. It is touched upon, though not fundamentally, in the following statement: 'The tendency has always arisen from contradiction . . . How are we to understand that powerful and violent attempt by the baroque to create some kind of synthesis of the most heterogeneous elements in galant

---

* Herr Gryphius . . . held that learning meant to be deficient in no subject, to have some knowledge of many things, and to know all about one thing.

pastoral poetry. An antithetical yearning for nature in contrast to a harmonious closeness to nature certainly explains this too. But the form of life opposed to it was something else; it was the experience of the destructive effect of time, of inevitable transience, of the fall from the heights. Remote from high things, the existence of the *beatus ille* must therefore be beyond the reach of all change. And so for the baroque nature is only one way out of time; and the baroque does not know the problems of subsequent ages.'[78] On the contrary: what is peculiar about the baroque enthusiasm for landscape is particularly evident in the pastoral. For the decisive factor in the escapism of the baroque is not the antithesis of history and nature but the comprehensive secularization of the historical in the state of creation. It is not eternity that is opposed to the disconsolate chronicle of world-history, but the restoration of the timelessness of paradise. History merges into the setting. And in the pastoral plays above all, history is scattered like seeds over the ground. 'In a place where a memorable event is said to have taken place, the shepherd will leave commemorative verses in a rock, a stone, or a tree. The columns dedicated to the memory of heroes, which can be admired in the halls of fame erected everywhere by these shepherds, are all resplendent with panegyric inscriptions.'[79] The term 'panoramatic'[80] has been coined to give an excellent description of the conception of history prevalent in the seventeenth century. 'In this picturesque period the whole conception of history is determined by such a collection of everything memorable.'[81] If history is secularized in the setting, this is an expression of the same metaphysical tendency which simultaneously led, in the exact sciences, to the infinitesimal method. In both cases chronological movement is grasped and analysed in a spatial image. The image of the setting or, more precisely, of the court, becomes the key to historical understanding. For the court is the setting *par excellence*. In his *Poetischer Trichter* Harsdörffer has assembled a multitude of suggestions for the allegorical – and, indeed, critical – representation of courtly life, the form of life which is more worthy of consideration than any other.[82] While in his interesting preface to *Sophonisbe* Lohenstein actually asserts: 'Kein Leben aber stellt mehr Spiel und Schauplatz dar, | Als derer, die den Hof fürs Element erkohren.'[83]* And this, of course, remains true where heroic greatness meets its downfall, and the court is reduced to a scaffold, 'und diss, was sterblich heisst, wird auf den schauplatz gehn'.[84]† In the *Trauerspiel* the court represents the timeless, natural décor of the historical process. Following Vitruvius, it had been laid down since the renaissance that for the *Trauerspiel* 'stattliche Paläste / und Fürstliche Garten-Gebäude / die Schauplätze [sind]'.[85]‡ Whereas the German theatre usually adheres rigidly to this prescription – in the *Trauerspiele* of Gryphius there are no outdoor scenes – the Spanish theatre delights in including the whole of nature as subservient to the crown, creating thereby a veritable dialectic of setting. For on the other hand the social order, and its representation, the court, is, in the work of Calderón, a natural phenomenon of the highest order, whose first law is the honour of the ruler. With his characteristic and ever astonishing sureness of touch, A. W. Schlegel gets to the root of the matter when he says of Calderón: 'His poetry, whatever its apparent object, is a never-ending hymn of joy on the majesty of the creation; he celebrates the productions of nature and human art with an astonishment always joyful and always new, as if he saw them for the first time in an unworn festal splendour. It is the first awakening of Adam, and an eloquence withal, a skill of expression, and a thorough insight into the most mysterious affinities of nature, such as high mental culture and mature contemplation can alone bestow. When he compares the most remote objects, the greatest and the smallest, stars and flowers, the sense of all his metaphors is the mutual attraction subsisting between created things by virtue of their common origin.'[86] The dramatist loves playfully to re-arrange the order of creation: in *La vida es sueño* Segismundo is described as a 'courtier . . . of the mountain',[87] and the sea is called a 'coloured crystal beast'.[88] In the German *Trauerspiel*, too, natural setting intrudes increasingly into the dramatic action. Only in the translation of Vondel's *Gebroeders*, it is true, did Gryphius make any concession to the new style, allotting one chorus to the river Jordan and its nymphs.[89] In the third

---

* Nowhere are action and setting richer than in the life of those whose element is the court.
† and that which is mortal will enter the setting.
‡ stately palaces and princely pavilions are the setting.

act of Lohenstein's *Epicharis*, however, there are choruses of the Tiber and the seven hills.[90] In the *Agrippina* the setting intervenes in the action in the manner of the 'dumbshows' of the Jesuit-theatre, so to speak: the Empress, dispatched by Nero on a ship which, thanks to a concealed mechanism, falls apart at sea, is rescued, in the chorus, thanks to the assistance of the sea-nymphs.[91] There is a 'chorus of sirens' in *Maria Stuarda* by Haugwitz,[92] and there are a number of similar passages in the work of Hallmann. In *Mariamne* he causes Mount Zion itself to give a detailed explanation of its participation in the action. 'Hier / Sterbliche / wird euch der wahre Grund gewehrt / | Warumb auch Berg und Zungenlose Klippen | Eröffnen Mund und Lippen. | Denn / wenn der tolle Mensch sich selber nicht mehr kennt / | Und durch blinde Rasereyen auch dem Höchsten Krieg ansaget / | Werden Berge / Flüss' und Sternen zu der Rache auffgejaget / | So bald der Feuer-Zorn des grossen Gottes brennt. | Unglückliche Sion! Vorhin des Himmels Seele / | Itzt eine Folter-Höle! | Herodes! ach! ach! ach! | Dein Wütten / Blut-Hund / macht / dass Berg' auch müssen schreyen / | Und dich vermaledeyen! | Rach! Rach! Rach!'[93]* If, as such passages show, the concept of nature is the same in both the *Trauerspiel* and the pastoral, then it is hardly surprising that, in the course of a development which reaches its climax in the work of Hallmann, the two forms should have tended to converge. The antithesis between the two is only a superficial one; they have a latent impulse to combine. Thus it is that Hallmann takes 'pastoral motifs into the serious drama, for instance the stereotyped praise of the shepherd's life, the satyr-motif from Tasso in *Sophia und Alexander*, and on the other hand he transposes tragic scenes like heroic farewells, suicides, divine judgments of good and evil, ghost-scenes, into the pastoral play'.[94] Even outside dramatic histories, in poetry, there is the same expression of chronological progression in spatial terms. The collections of the Nuremberg poets, like earlier scholarly Alexandrian poetry, use 'Towers

---

* Here, mortals, will you learn the true reason why even a mountain and tongue-less cliffs open mouth and lips. For when man rages and no longer knows himself and in blind fury declares war on the Almighty, then are mountains, rivers and stars urged to vengeance as soon as the fiery anger of the great God blazes. Unhappy Zion! Once the soul of heaven, now a torture-chamber! Herod! Alas! Alas! Alas! Thy raging, bloodhound, causes even the mountains to cry aloud and curse thee! Vengeance! Vengeance! Vengeance!

... fountains, orbs, organs, lutes, hour-glasses, scales, wreaths, hearts'[95] to provide the graphic outline of their poems.

The pre-eminence of these tendencies was one factor in the dissolution of the baroque drama. Gradually – the process can be traced with particular clarity in the poetics of Hunold[96] – it was replaced by the ballet. 'Confusion' [*Verwirrung*] is already a technical term in the dramaturgical theories of the Nuremberg school. The title of Lope de Vega's drama *Der verwirrte Hof* [The court in confusion; Spanish: *El palacio confuso*] is typical. Birken states: 'Die Zier von Heldenspielen ist / wann alles ineinander verwirrt / und nicht nach der Ordnung / wie in Historien / erzehlet / die Unschuld gekränkt / die Bosheit beglückt vorgestellt / endlich aber alles wieder entwickelt und auf einen richtigen Ablauf hinausgeführt wird.'[97]* The term 'confusion' is to be understood in a pragmatic as well as in a moral sense. In contrast to the spasmodic chronological progression of tragedy, the *Trauerspiel* takes place in a spatial continuum, which one might describe as choreographic. The organizer of its plot, the precursor of the choreographer, is the intriguer. He stands as a third type alongside the despot and the martyr.[98] His corrupt calculations awaken in the spectator of the *Haupt- und Staatsaktionen* all the more interest because the latter does not recognize here simply a mastery of the workings of politics, but an anthropological, even a physiological knowledge which fascinated him. The sovereign intriguer is all intellect and will-power. And as such he corresponds to an ideal which was first outlined by Machiavelli and which was energetically elaborated in the creative and theoretical literature of the seventeenth century before it degenerated into the cliché, which the intriguer became in Viennese and domestic tragedy. 'Machiavelli saw the roots of political thought in its anthropological principles. The uniformity of human nature, the power of the animal instinct and the emotions, especially the

---

* The charm of the heroic play derives from everything being confused with everything else and not being narrated in order, as in histories; here innocence is offended and wickedness rewarded but in the end everything is unravelled and brought to a proper conclusion.

emotions of love and fear, and their limitlessness – these are the insights on which every consistent political thought or action, indeed the very science of politics must be based. The positive imagination of the statesman, capable of calculating with facts, has its basis in this knowledge, which teaches us to understand man as a force of nature and to overcome emotions in such a way that they bring other emotions into play.'[99] Human emotions as the predictable driving mechanism of the creature – that is the final item in the inventory of knowledge which had to transform the dynamism of world-history into political action. It is at the same time the source of a set of metaphors which was designed to keep this knowledge as alive in the language of poetry as Sarpi or Guicciardini were doing in historiography. This system of metaphors was not confined to the political sphere. Alongside a phrase like: 'In der Uhr der Herrschaft sind die Räthe wohl die Räder / der Fürst aber muss nichts minder der Weiser und has Gewichte . . . seyn',[100]* may be set the words of 'Life' from the second chorus of *Mariamne*: 'Mein güldnes Licht hat Gott selbst angezündet / I Als Adams Leib ein gangbar Uhrwerk ward.'[101]† And from the same play: 'Mein klopffend Hertz' entflammt / weil mir das treue Blut I Ob angebohrner Brunst an alle Adern schläget / I Und einem Uhrwerck gleich sich durch den Leib beweget.'[102]‡ And it is said of Agrippina: 'Nun liegt das stoltze Thier, das aufgeblasne Weib I Die in Gedancken stand: Ihr Uhrwerck des Gehirnes I Sey mächtig umbzudrehn den Umkreiss des Gestirnes.'[103]§ It is no accident that the image of the clock dominates these formulae. In Geulincx's celebrated clock-metaphor, in which the parallelism of the psychological and physical worlds is presented schematically in terms of two accurate and synchronized clocks, the second hand, so to speak, determines the rhythm of events in both. For a long time to come – it is still evident in the texts of Bach's cantatas – the age seems to have been fascinated by this idea. The image

---

* The councillors may be the cogs in the clock of government but the prince must nonetheless be the hand and the weight

† God himself lit my golden light when Adam's body became a workable clock.

‡ My pounding heart bursts into flame because my loyal blood courses through all my veins with inborn lust and moves like clockwork through my body.

§ There lies the proud beast now, the puffed-up woman who thought the clockwork of her brain was powerful enough to reverse the course of the stars

of the moving hand is, as Bergson has shown, essential to the representation of the non-qualitative, repeatable time of the mathematical sciences.[104] This is the context within which not only the organic life of man is enacted, but also the deeds of the courtier and the action of the sovereign who, in conformity to the occasionalist image of God, is constantly intervening directly in the workings of the state so as to arrange the data of the historical process in a regular and harmonious sequence which is, so to speak, spatially measurable. 'The prince develops all virtualities of the state by a kind of continuous creation. The prince is the Cartesian God transposed into the political world.'[105] In the course of political events intrigue beats out that rhythm of the second hand which controls and regulates these events. The disillusioned insight of the courtier is just as profound a source of woe to him as it is a potential danger to others, because of the use he can make of it at any time. In this light the image of this figure assumes its most baleful aspect. To understand the life of the courtier means to recognize completely why the court, above all else, provides the setting of the *Trauerspiel*. Antonio de Guevara's *Cortegiano* contains the following remark: 'Cain was the first courtier, because through God's curse [he had] no home of his own'.[106] In the mind of the Spanish author this is certainly not the only feature that the courtier shares with Cain; often enough the curse which God laid upon the murderer rests on him too. But whereas in the Spanish drama the primary characteristic of the court was the splendour of royal power, the German *Trauerspiel* is dominated by the gloomy tone of intrigue. In *Leo Armenius* Michael Balbus laments: 'Was ist der hof nunmehr als eine mördergruben, | Als ein verräther-platz, ein wohnhauss schlimmer buben?'[107]* In the dedication of *Ibrahim Bassa* Lohenstein presents the intriguer, Rusthan as a kind of representative of the setting and calls him 'einen Ehr-vergessenden Hof-Heuchler und Mord-stifftenden Ohrenbläser'.[108]† The court official, the privy-councillor, who has access to the prince's cabinet where the projects of high politics are conceived, is presented in these and similar descriptions, his power, knowledge, and

---

* What is the court but a den of murderers, a place of treachery, a house of rogues and villains?

† a court hypocrite, unmindful of his honour, and a bearer of tales who incites to murder.

will intensified to demonic proportions. This is what Hallmann is alluding to when, with an elegant turn of phrase, he remarks in the *Leich-Reden*: 'Allein mir / als einem Politico, wil nicht anstehen / das geheime Cabinet der Himmlischen Weissheit zu beschreiten.'[109]* The drama of the German protestants emphasizes the infernal characteristics of the councillor; in Catholic Spain, on the other hand, he is clad with the dignity of *sosiego* [tranquillity], 'which combines both the ethos of Catholicism and the *ataraxia* of antiquity in an ideal of the religious and the worldly courtier'.[110] It is, moreover, the unique ambiguity of his spiritual sovereignty which provides the basis for the thoroughly baroque dialectic of his position. Spirit – such was the thesis of the age – shows itself in power; spirit is the capacity to exercise dictatorship. This capacity requires both strict inner discipline and unscrupulous external action. Its practice brought to the course of the world an icy disillusion which is matched in intensity only by the fierce aspiration of the will to power. Such a conception of perfect conduct on the part of the man of the world awakens a mood of mourning [*Trauer*] in the creature stripped of all naive impulses. And this, his mood permits the paradoxical demand for saintliness to be made of the courtier or even, as Gracián does, actually to declare that he is a saint.[111] This quite simply figurative transformation of saintliness into the mood of mourning opens the way for the unlimited compromise with the world which is characteristic of the ideal courtier in the Spanish drama. The German dramatists did not dare to plumb the vertiginous depths of this antithesis in one character. They know the two faces of the courtier: the intriguer, as the evil genius of their despots, and the faithful servant, as the companion in suffering to innocence enthroned.

In all circumstances it was necessary for the intriguer to assume a dominant position in the economy of the drama. For according to the theory of Scaliger, which in this respect harmonized with the interests of the baroque and was accepted by it, the real purpose of drama was to com-

---

* But I, as a politician, may not presume to enter the privy cabinet of heavenly wisdom.

municate knowledge of the life of the soul, in the observation of which the intriguer is without equal. In the consciousness of the new generations the moral intention of the Renaissance poets was complemented by a scientific intention. 'Docet affectus poeta per actiones, vt bonos amplecta- mur, atque imitemur ad agendum: malos aspernemur ob abstinendum. Est igitur actio docendi modus: affectus, quem docemur ad agendum. Quare erit actio quasi exemplar, aut instrumentum in fabula, affectus vero finis. At in ciue actio erit finis, affectus erit eius forma.'[112]* This scheme, in which Scaliger wishes to see the representation of the action, the means of the dramatic performance, subordinated to the emotions, its end, can, in certain respects, provide a criterion for the establishment of the presence of baroque elements in contrast to those of an earlier poetic style. For it is characteristic of seventeenth-century trends that the representation of the emotions is emphasized increasingly at the expense of a firmly defined action, such as is never absent from the drama of the Renaissance. The tempo of the emotional life is accelerated to such an extent that calm actions, considered decisions occur more and more in- frequently. The conflict between sensibility and will in the human norm, which Riegl has demonstrated so beautifully in the discord between the attitude of head and body in the figures of Giuliano and Night on the Medici tombs,[113] is not confined to the manifestations of this norm in the plastic arts but also extends to the drama. It is particularly striking in the person of the tyrant. In the course of the action his will is increasingly undermined by his sensibility: and he ends in madness. The extent to which action, which is supposed to provide their basis, could give way to the presentation of the emotions, is shown by the *Trauerspiele* of Lohen- stein, where the passions wildly succeed each other in a furore of didacti- cism. This throws light on the tenacity with which the *Trauerspiele* of the seventeenth century restrict themselves to a narrow range of subject- matter. In certain conditions it was appropriate to measure oneself against predecessors and contemporaries and to present the exaltations

---

* The poet teaches emotion through action, so that we embrace the good and imitate it in our conduct, and reject the evil and abstain from that. Action, therefore, is a mode of teach- ing; emotion, that which we are taught. Wherefore action is, as it were, the pattern or medium in a plot, emotion its end. But in civil life action is the end, and emotion its form.'

of the passion ever more compellingly and ever more drastically. A basic stock of dramaturgical realia, such as is embodied in the political anthropology and typology of the *Trauerspiel*, is what was required in order to escape from the problems of a historicism which deals with its subject as a necessary but inessential transitional manifestation. In the context of these realia one can perceive the special significance of baroque Aristotelianism, which is likely to prove confusing to more superficial consideration. In the guise of this 'alien theory'[114] an interpretation won through, on the strength of which the new, in a gesture of submission, secured for itself the most convincing authority, that of antiquity. The baroque was able to see the power of the present in this medium. It therefore regarded its own forms as 'natural', not so much the antithesis, as the conquest and elevation of its rival. Ancient tragedy is the fettered slave on the triumphal car of the baroque *Trauerspiel*.

> Hier in dieser Zeitligkeit
> Ist bedecket meine Crohne
> Mit dem Flohr der Traurigkeit;
> Dorten / da sie mir zum Lohne
> Aus Genaden ist gestellet /
> Ist sie frey / und gantz umhellet.
>
> Johann Georg Schiebel: *Neuerbauter Schausaal**

Commentators have always wanted to recognize the elements of Greek tragedy – the tragic plot, the tragic hero, the tragic death – as the essential elements of the *Trauerspiel*, however distorted they may have been at the hands of uncomprehending imitators. On the other hand – and this would have been more significant for the critical history of the philosophy of art – tragedy, that is to say Greek tragedy, has been seen as an early form of the *Trauerspiel*, intimately related to the later form. Accordingly the

---

* Here, in this temporal world, my crown is covered with the crape of sorrow; but there, where it is set on my head by grace, as a reward, it is free and brilliant.

philosophy of tragedy has been developed as a theory of the moral order of the world, without any reference to historical content, in a system of generalized sentiments, which, it was thought, was logically supported by the concepts 'guilt' and 'atonement'. For the sake of the naturalist drama this world-order was, with astonishing naivety, approximated to the process of natural causation in the theories of the philosophical and literary epigones of the second half of the nineteenth century, and tragic fate thereby became a condition 'which is expressed in the interaction of the individual with the naturally ordered environment'.[1] Thus that *Ästhetik des Tragischen*, which is nothing less than a codification of the above-mentioned prejudices, and which rests on the assumption that the tragic can be unconditionally presented in certain arrangements of facts such as occur in everyday life. This is precisely what is meant when 'the modern world-view' is described as the element 'in which alone the tragic can develop without any restriction of its power or its consistency'.[2] 'And so the modern world-view must also judge that the tragic hero, whose destiny depends on the miraculous intervention of a transcendental power, is placed in an order of things which will not bear intelligent examination, and that the humanity, of which he is an embodiment, is restricted, oppressed, and unfree in character.'[3] This thoroughly vain attempt to present the tragic as something universally human just about explains how the analysis of it can quite deliberately be based on the impression 'which we modern men feel when we expose ourselves to the artistic effects of the forms with which ancient peoples and past ages endowed tragic fate in their literatures.'[4] Nothing is in fact more questionable than the competence of the unguided feelings of 'modern men', especially where the judgment of tragedy is concerned. This insight is substantiated not only in *The Birth of Tragedy*, which appeared forty years before the *Ästhetik des Tragischen*, it is also strongly suggested by the simple fact that the modern theatre has nothing to show which remotely resembles the tragedy of the Greeks. In denying this actual state of affairs such doctrines of the tragic betray the presumption that it must still be possible to write tragedies. That is their essential but hidden motive, and any theory of tragedy designed to overturn this axiom of cultural arrogance was regarded with suspicion for that very reason. The philosophy of history was excluded. But if the perspectives of the philosophy of history should prove to be an essential part of a theory of tragedy, then it is clear that the latter can only be expected from research which shows some understanding of its own age. And this is the Archimedean point which more recent thinkers, particularly Franz Rosenzweig and Georg Lukács, have found in Nietzsche's early work. 'In vain did our democratic age wish to establish the right of all to participate in the tragic; vain was every attempt to open this heavenly kingdom to the poor in spirit.'[5]

With his insight into the connection of tragedy to legend, and the independence of the tragic from the ethos, Nietzsche's work lays the foundation for theses such as this. It is not necessary to refer to the prejudice of the next generation of scholars in order to explain the delay, not to say the laboriousness, with which these insights exerted their influence. It was rather that the Schopenhauerian and Wagnerian metaphysics necessarily vitiated the best aspects of Nietzsche's work. They are already influential in the definition of myth. 'The myth leads the world of manifestation to its limits where it denies itself and seeks to flee back again into the womb of the true and only reality . . . Thus we use the experiences of the truly aesthetic listener to bring to mind the tragic artist himself as he creates his figures like a fecund divinity of individuation (so his work can hardly be understood as an "imitation of nature") and as his vast Dionysian impulse then devours his entire world of manifestations, in order to let us sense beyond it, and through its destruction, the highest artistic primal joy, in the bosom of the primordially One.'[6] For Nietzsche, as is sufficiently clear from this passage, the tragic myth is a purely aesthetic creation, and the interplay of Apollonian and Dionysian energy remains equally confined to the aesthetic sphere, as appearance and the dissolution of appearance. Nietzsche's renunciation of any understanding of the tragic myth in historical–philosophical terms is a high price to pay for his emancipation from the stereotype of a morality in which the tragic occurrence was usually clothed. The classic formulation of this renunciation is as follows: 'For to our humiliation *and* exaltation, one thing above all must be clear to us. The entire comedy of art is neither performed for our betterment or education nor are we the true authors of this art world. On the contrary, we may assume that we are merely images and artistic projections for the true author, and that we have our highest dignity in our significance as works of art – for it is only as an *aesthetic phenomenon* that the existence and the world are eternally *justified* – while of course our consciousness of our own significance hardly differs from that which the soldiers painted on canvas have of the battle represented on it.'[7] The abyss of aestheticism opens up, and this brilliant intuition was finally to see all its concepts disappear into it, so that gods and heroes, defiance and suffering, the pillars of the tragic edifice, fall away into nothing. Where art so firmly occupies the centre of existence as to make man one of its manifestations instead of recognizing him above all as its basis, to see man's existence as the eternal subject of its own creations instead of recognizing him as its own creator, then all sane reflection is at an end. And whether, with the removal of man from the centre of art, it is Nirvana, the slumbering will to life, which takes his place, as in Schopenhauer, or whether it is the 'dissonance become man'[8] which, as in Nietzsche, has created both the manifestations of the human world and man himself, it makes no difference; it is the same pragmatism. For what does it matter whether it is the will to life or the will to destroy life which is supposed to inspire every work of art, since the latter, as a product of the absolute will, devalues itself along with the world? The nihilism lodged in the depths of the artistic philosophy of Bayreuth nullified – it could do no other – the concept of the hard, historical actuality of Greek tragedy. 'Image sparks, lyrical poems, which in their highest development are called tragedies and dramatic dithyrambs'[9] – tragedy is dissolved into visions of the chorus and the spectators. Nietzsche argues that one must 'always keep in mind that the public at an Attic tragedy found itself in the chorus of the orchestra, and there was at bottom no opposition between public and chorus; everything is merely a great sublime chorus of dancing and singing satyrs or of those who permit themselves to be represented by such satyrs ... The satyr chorus is, first of all, a vision of the Dionysian mass of spectators, just as the world of the stage, in turn, is a vision of this satyr chorus.'[10] It is not permissible to lay such extreme emphasis on the

Apollonian illusion, a pre-condition of the aesthetic dissolution of tragedy. As far as the philologist is concerned 'there is no basis in the cult for the tragic chorus'[11]; while the ecstatic, whether in the form of the mass or the individual, is – so long as he is not transfixed – only to be conceived in the state of most violent action. It is not possible to make the chorus, which intervenes in the tragedy in a considered and reflective way, at the same time into the subject which experiences the visions; especially not a chorus which would be both itself the vision of a mass of people and the bearer of further visions. Above all, there is no kind of unity between the choruses and the public. This needs to be said, insofar as the gulf between them, the orchestra, does not demonstrate it by its very presence.

Nietzsche turned his back on the tragic theories of the epigones without refuting them. For he saw no reason to take issue with their central doctrine of tragic guilt and tragic atonement, because he was only too willing to leave the field of moral debates to them. His neglect of such criticism barred the way to those concepts from the philosophy of history or the philosophy of religion in which the definition of tragedy is ultimately expressed. Wherever the discussion begins there is one, apparently unchallengeable, prejudice which it cannot tolerate. This is the assumption that the actions and attitudes encountered in fictional characters may be used in the discussion of moral problems in a similar way to an anatomical model. Although, in general, one hardly dare treat it so unquestioningly as a faithful imitation of nature, the work of art is unhesitatingly accepted as the exemplary copy of moral phenomena without any consideration of how susceptible such phenomena are to representation. The object in question here is not the significance of moral content for the criticism of a work of art; the question is a different one, indeed a double one. Do the actions and attitudes depicted in a work of art have moral significance as images of reality? And: can the content of a work of art, in the last analysis, be adequately understood in terms of moral insights? Their assent to – or rather their failure to consider – these two questions is what, more than anything else, determines the character of the customary interpretation and theory of the tragic. And yet a negative answer is precisely what is required to show the necessity of understanding the moral content of tragic poetry, not as its last word, but as one aspect of its integral truth: that is to say in terms of the history of philosophy. Certainly, the denial of the first proposition can, in different contexts, be more readily justified than that of the second, which is primarily the concern of a philosophy of art. But this much is true even of the former: fictional characters exist only in literature. They are woven as tightly into the totality of the literary work as are the subjects of Gobelins into their canvas, so that they cannot be removed from it as individuals. In this respect the human figure in literature, indeed in art as such, differs from the human figure in reality, where physical isolation, which in so many ways is only apparent isolation, has its true meaning as a perceptible expression of moral seclusion with God. 'Thou shalt not make unto thee any graven image' – this is not only a warning against idolatry. With incomparable emphasis the prohibition of the representation of the human body obviates any suggestion that the sphere in which the moral essence of man is perceptible can be reproduced. Everything moral is bound to life in its extreme sense, that is to say where it fulfils itself in death, the abode of danger as such. And from the point of view of any kind of artistic practice this life, which concerns us morally, that is in our unique individuality, appears as something negative, or at least should appear so. For art cannot, for its part, allow itself, in its works, to be appointed a councillor of the conscience and it cannot permit what is represented, rather than the actual representation, to be the object of attention. The truth content of this totality, which is never encountered in the abstracted lesson, least of all the moral lesson, but only in the critical elaboration of the work itself,[12] includes moral warnings only in the most indirect form.[13] Where they obtrude as the main purpose of the investigation, which is the case in the criticism of tragedy as practised by the German idealists – how typical is Solger's essay on Sophocles![14] – then this means that the very much more worthwhile struggle to ascertain the place of a work or a form in terms of the history of philosophy has been abandoned in favour of a cheap reflection which is figurative, and therefore less relevant than any moral doctrine, however philistine. As far as tragedy is concerned, this struggle will find reliable guidance in the consideration of its relationship to legend.

Wilamowitz gives the following definition: 'an Attic tragedy is a self-contained piece of heroic legend, poetically adapted in the sublime style for presentation by a chorus of Attic citizens and two or three actors, and intended for performance as part of the public worship at the shrine of Dionysus.'[15] Elsewhere he writes: 'thus any consideration ultimately leads back to the relationship of tragedy to legend. Tragedy has its essential roots in legend, from here it derives its special strengths and weaknesses, and herein lies the difference between Attic tragedy and every other kind of dramatic poetry.'[16] This is where the philosophical definition of tragedy has to begin, and it will do so with the perception that tragedy cannot be understood simply as legend in dramatic form. For legend is, by its very nature, free of tendentiousness. Here the streams of tradition, which surge down violently, often from opposite directions, have finally come to rest beneath the epic surface which conceals a divided, many-armed river-bed. Tragic poetry is opposed to epic poetry as a tendentious re-shaping of the tradition. The Oedipus-theme shows just how intensively and how significantly it was able to re-shape it.[17] Nevertheless, older theoreticians such as Wackernagel, are right when they declare that invention is incompatible with tragedy. For the re-shaping of the legend is not motivated by the search for tragic situations, but it is undertaken with a tendentious purpose which would lose all its significance if the tendency were not expressed in terms of the legend, the primordial history of the nation. The signature of tragedy does not therefore consist in a 'conflict of levels'[19] between the hero and the environment as such, which is what Scheler declares to be characteristic in his study *Zum Phänomen des Tragischen*, but the unique Greek form of such conflicts. Where is this to be sought? What tendency is hidden in the tragic? For what does the hero die? Tragic poetry is based on the idea of sacrifice. But in respect of its victim, the hero, the tragic sacrifice differs from any other kind, being at once a first and a final sacrifice. A final sacrifice in the sense of the atoning sacrifice to gods who are upholding an ancient right; a first sacrifice in the sense of the representative action, in which new aspects of the life of the nation become manifest. These are different from the old, fatal obligations in that they do not refer back to a command from above, but to the life of the hero himself; and they destroy him because they do not measure up to the demands of the individual will, but benefit only the life of the, as yet unborn, national community. The tragic death has a dual significance: it invalidates the ancient rights of the Olympians, and it offers up the hero to the unknown god as the first fruits of a new harvest of humanity. But this dual power can also reside in tragic suffering, as Aeschylus depicts it in the *Oresteia*, and Sophocles in *Oedipus*. If the expiatory character of the sacrifice stands out less prominently in this form, all the clearer is its transformation, in which the subjection of the hero to death is replaced by a paroxysm which just as surely does justice to the old conception of gods and sacrifice, as it is patently clad in the form of the new conception. Death thereby becomes salvation: the crisis of death. One of the oldest examples is the replacement of the execution of the victim at the altar with his escape from the knife of the sacrificial priest; the destined victim thus runs around the altar, finally seizing it, so that the altar becomes a place of refuge, the angry god a merciful god, the victim a prisoner and servant of god. This is the whole schema of the *Oresteia*. In its narrow concentration on the subject of death, its absolute dependence on the community, and above all in the absence of any guarantee of finality from the solution and salvation with which it concludes, this agonal prophecy is free of all epic-didactic elements. But what justification have we for speaking of an 'agonal' representation? For the hypothetical derivation of the tragic event from the sacrificial race around the *thymele* is scarcely enough to provide such a justification. This shows, in the first instance, that the Attic stage plays took the form of contests. Not only did the dramatists compete with each other, but also the protagonists, even the *choragi*. But the inner justification lies in the dumb anguish which every tragic performance both communicates to the spectators and displays in its characters. Here it comes about in the speechless contest of the *agon*. In his analysis of 'meta-ethical man', Franz Rosenzweig has demonstrated that the inarticulacy of the tragic hero, which distinguishes the main figure in Greek tragedy from all his successors, is one of the foundation stones of the theory of tragedy. 'For this is the mark of the self, the seal of its greatness and the token of its weakness alike: it is silent. The tragic hero has only one language that is completely proper to him: silence. It has been so from the very beginning. The tragic devised itself the artistic form of the drama precisely so as to be able to present silence . . . In his silence the hero burns the bridges connecting him to god and the world, elevates himself above the realm of personality, which in speech, defines itself against others and individualizes itself, and so enters the icy loneliness of the self. The self knows of nothing other than itself; its loneliness is absolute. How else can it activate this loneliness, this rigid and defiant self-sufficiency, except in silence. And so it is in the tragedies of Aeschylus, as even contemporaries noticed.'[20] Yet tragic silence, as presented in this important description, must not be thought of as being dominated by defiance alone. Rather, this defiance is every bit as much a consequence of the experience of speechlessness as a factor which intensifies the condition. The content of the hero's achievements belongs to the community, as does speech. Since the community of the nation denies these achievements, they remain unarticulated in the hero. And he must therefore all the more forcefully enclose within the confines of his physical self every action and every item of knowledge the greater and the more potentially effective it is. It is the achievement of his *physis* alone, not of language, if he is able to hold fast to his cause, and he must therefore do so in death. Lukács has the same thing in mind when, in his account of tragic decision, he observes: 'The essence of these great moments in life is the pure experience of selfhood.'[21] A passage in Nietzsche shows more clearly that the meaning of tragic silence had not escaped him. Although he had no suspicion of its significance as a manifestation of the agonal in the tragic sphere, he nevertheless puts his finger on it in his contrast of image and speech. Tragic 'heroes speak, as it were, more superficially than they act; the myth does not at all obtain adequate objectification in the spoken word. The structure of the scenes and the visual images reveal a deeper wisdom than the poet himself can put into words and concepts.'[22] This can, of course, hardly be a question of failure, as Nietzsche goes on to suggest. The greater the discrepancy between the tragic word and the situation – which can no longer be called tragic when there is no discrepancy – the more surely has the hero escaped the ancient statutes to which, when they finally overtake him, he throws only the dumb shadow of his being, the self, as a sacrifice, while his soul finds refuge in the word of a distant community. The tragic presentation of legend thereby acquired inexhaustible topicality. In the presence of the suffering hero the community learns reverence and gratitude for the word with which his death endowed it – a word which shone out in another place as a new gift whenever the poet extracted some new meaning from the legend. Tragic silence, far more than tragic pathos, became the storehouse of an experience of the sublimity of linguistic expression, which is generally so much more intensely alive in ancient than in later literature. The decisive confrontation with the demonic world-order which takes place in Greek literature also gives tragic poetry its signature in terms of the history of philosophy. The tragic is to the demonic what the paradox is to ambiguity. In all the paradoxes of tragedy – in the sacrifice, which, in complying with ancient statutes, creates new ones, in death, which is an act of atonement but which sweeps away only the self, in the tragic ending, which grants the victory to man, but also to god – ambiguity, the stigma of the daimons, is in decline. There are indications of this everywhere, however slight. For instance in the silence of the hero, which neither looks for nor finds any justification, and therefore throws suspicion back onto his persecutors. For its meaning is inverted: what appears before the public is not the guilt of the accused but the evidence of speechless suffering, and the tragedy which appeared to be devoted to the judgment of the hero is transformed into a hearing about the Olympians in which the latter appears as a witness and, against the will of the gods, displays the honour of the demi-god.'[23] The profound Aeschylean impulse to justice[24] inspires the anti-Olympian prophecy of all tragic poetry. 'It was not in law but in tragedy that the head of the genius first emerged above the cloud of guilt, for in tragedy the hold of demonic fate is broken. Not, however, in the replacement of the inscrutable pagan concatenation of guilt and atonement by the purity of man, absolved and reconciled with the pure god. It is rather that in tragedy pagan man realizes that he is better than his gods, but this realization strikes him dumb, and it remains unarticulated. Without declaring itself, it secretly endeavours to gather strength . . . There is here no question whatever of a restitution of the "moral order of the universe", but it is the attempt of moral man, still dumb, still inarticulate – as such he bears the name of hero – to raise himself up amid the agitation of that painful world. The paradox of the birth of the genius in moral speechlessness, moral infantility, constitutes the sublime element in tragedy.'[25]

It would be otiose to point out that the sublimity of the content is not explained by the rank and lineage of the characters, were it not for the fact that the royal status of so many heroes has been the source of certain curious speculations and obvious confusions. Both have arisen from a consideration of this royal status as such, in the modern sense. Yet it could not be more obvious that it is an incidental factor, arising from the material of the tradition on which tragic poetry is based. For in primeval times it is the ruler who occupies the central position here, so that royal descent is an indication of the dramatic character's origin in the heroic age. This is the sole significance attaching to this descent, but it is, of course, a decisive significance. For the forthrightness of the heroic self – which is not a character-trait, but the historical-philosophical signature of the hero – corresponds to his position of authority. By contrast to this simple state of affairs, Schopenhauer's interpretation of kingship in tragedy seems to be one of those levellings into the universally human which obscure the essential difference between ancient and modern drama. 'For the heroes of their tragedies the Greeks generally took royal persons and the moderns for the most part have done the same. This is certainly not because rank gives more dignity to the person who acts or suffers; and as it is merely a question of setting human passions in play, the relative worth of the objects by which this is done is a matter of indifference, and farms achieve as much as is achieved by kingdoms . . . Persons of great power and prestige are nevertheless best adapted for tragedy, because the misfortune in which we should recognize the fate of human life must have sufficient magnitude, in order to appear terrible to the spectator, be he who he may . . . But the circumstances that plunge a bourgeois family into want and despair are in the eyes of the great or wealthy often very insignificant, and can be removed by human aid, sometimes indeed by a trifle; therefore such spectators cannot be tragically shaken by them. On the other hand, the misfortunes of the great and powerful are unconditionally terrible, and are inaccessible even to help from outside; for kings must either help themselves through their own power, or be ruined. In addition to this is the fact that the fall is greatest from a height. Bourgeois characters lack the height from which to fall.'[26] What is here explained as the tragic character's dignity of rank – and explained in a thoroughly baroque way on the basis of the unhappy events of the 'tragedy' – has nothing whatever to do with the status of the timeless heroic figures; the princely estate does, however, have for the modern *Trauerspiel* the exemplary and far more precise significance which has been considered in the appropriate context. What distinguishes the *Trauerspiel* from Greek tragedy in respect of this deceptive affinity has not yet been perceived even by the most recent research. There is an extreme, involuntary irony about Borinski's commentary on Schiller's tragic experiments in *Die Braut von Messina*, which, because of the romantic attitude, could not but revert sharply to the *Trauerspiel*; following Schopenhauer, Borinski observes, with reference to the high rank of the characters, which is persistently emphasized by the chorus: 'How right were renaissance poetics – not in a spirit of "pedantry", but in a vital human way – to adhere rigidly to the "kings and heroes" of ancient tragedy.'[27]

Schopenhauer conceived of tragedy as *Trauerspiel*; of the great German metaphysicians after Fichte there is scarcely another so lacking in sympathy for Greek drama. In modern drama he saw a higher stage of development, and in this comparison, however inadequate it may be, he did at least locate the problem. 'What gives to everything tragic, whatever the form in which it appears, the characteristic tendency to the sublime, is the dawning of the knowledge that the world and life can afford us no true satisfaction, and are therefore not worth our attachment to them. In this the tragic spirit consists; accordingly, it leads to resignation. I admit that rarely in the tragedy of the ancients is this spirit of resignation seen and directly expressed . . . Stoic equanimity is fundamentally distinguished from Christian resignation by the fact that it teaches only calm endurance and unruffled expectation of unalterably necessary evils, but Christianity teaches renunciation, the giving up of willing. In just the same way the tragic heroes of the ancients show resolute and stoical subjection under the unavoidable blows of fate; the Christian tragedy, on the other hand, shows the giving up of the whole will to live, cheerful abandonment of the world in the consciousness of its worthlessness and vanity. But I am fully of the opinion that the tragedy of the moderns is at a higher level than that of the ancients.'[28] This diffuse appreciation, inhibited by anti-historical metaphysics, needs only to be contrasted with a few sentences by Rosenzweig for us to realize what progress has been made in the philosophical history of the drama with the discoveries of this thinker. 'This is one of the profoundest differences between the new tragedy and the old . . . its figures are all different from each other, different in the way every personality is different from another . . . In ancient tragedy this was not so; here only the actions were different; the hero, as tragic hero, always remained the same, always the same self, defiantly buried in itself. The demand that he be essentially conscious, that is to say conscious when he is alone with himself, is repugnant to the necessarily limited consciousness of the modern hero. Consciousness always demands clarity; limited consciousness is imperfect . . . The goal of modern tragedy is therefore quite unknown to ancient tragedy: it is the tragedy of the absolute man in his relationship to the absolute object . . . The barely recognized goal . . . is as follows: to replace the unlimited multiplicity of characters with one absolute character, a modern hero, who is every bit as much a single and unchanging hero as the ancient hero. This point of convergence, at which the lines of all tragic characters would meet, this absolute man . . . is none other than the saint. The tragedy of the saint is the secret longing of the tragedian . . . It makes no difference . . . whether this is an attainable goal for the tragic poet or not; even if it is beyond the reach of tragedy as a work of art, it is, nonetheless, for the modern consciousness, the exact counterpart to the hero of ancient tragedy.'[29] The 'modern tragedy', whose deduction from ancient tragedy is the object of these sentences, bears – it hardly needs saying – the far from insignificant name: *Trauerspiel*. With this the reflections which conclude the above passage transcend the theoretical nature of the problem. The *Trauerspiel* is confirmed as a form of the tragedy of the saint by means of the martyrdrama. And if one only learns to recognize its characteristics in many different styles of drama from Calderón to Strindberg it must become clear that this form, a form of the mystery play, still has a future.

Here it is a question of its past. This leads us far back to a turning-point in the history of the Greek spirit itself: the death of Socrates. The martyrdrama was born from the death of Socrates as a parody of tragedy. And here, as so often, the parody of a form proclaims its end. Wilamowitz testifies to the fact that it meant the end of tragedy for Plato: 'Plato burnt his tetralogy; not because he was renouncing the ambition to be a poet in the sense of Aeschylus, but because he recognized that the tragedian could no longer be the teacher and master of the nation. He did of course attempt – so great was the power of tragedy – to create a new art form of tragic character, and he created a new cycle of legend to replace the obsolete heroic legends, the legend of Socrates.'[30] This legend of Socrates is a comprehensive secularization of the heroic legend by the submission of its demonic paradoxes to reason. Superficially, of course, the death of the philosopher resembles tragic death. It is an act of atonement according to the letter of an ancient law, a sacrificial death in the spirit of a new justice which contributes to the establishment of a new community. But this very similarity reveals most clearly the real significance of the agonal character of the genuinely tragic: that silent struggle, that mute flight of the hero, which in the [Platonic] *Dialogues*, has given way to such a brilliant display of speech and consciousness. The agonal has disappeared from the drama of Socrates – even in his philosophical struggles it is only a question of going through the motions – and in one stroke the death of the hero has been transformed into that of a martyr. Like the Christian hero of the faith – which explains both the sympathy of many a father of the Church and the hatred of Nietzsche, who unerringly detected this – Socrates dies voluntarily, and voluntarily, with inexpressible superiority and without any defiance, he becomes mute as he becomes silent. 'But that he was sentenced to death, not exile, Socrates himself seems to have brought about with perfect awareness and without any natural awe of death . . . *The dying Socrates* became the new ideal, never seen before, of noble Greek youths.'[31] Plato could not have indicated more expressively the remoteness of this ideal from that of the tragic hero than he did by making immortality the subject of his master's final conversation. If, according to the *Apology*, the death of Socrates could still have appeared to be tragic – in much the same way as death in the *Antigone*, where it is already illuminated by an all too rational concept of duty – the Pythagorean tone of the *Phaedo*, on the other hand shows this death to be free of all tragic association. Socrates looks death in the face as a mortal – the best and most virtuous of mortals, one may insist – but he recognizes it as something alien, beyond which, in immortality, he expects to return to himself. Not so the tragic hero; he shrinks before death as before a power that is familiar, personal, and inherent in him. His life, indeed, unfolds from death, which is not its end but its form. For tragic existence acquires its task only because it is intrinsically subject to the limits of both linguistic and physical life which are set within it from its very beginning. This has been expressed in many different ways. Perhaps nowhere better than in a casual reference to tragic death as 'merely . . . the outward sign that the soul has died'.[32] The tragic hero may, indeed, be described as soulless. Out of his profound inner emptiness echo the distant, new divine commands, and from this echo future generations learn their language. Just as in the ordinary creature the activity of life is all-embracing, so, in the tragic hero, is the process of dying, and tragic irony always arises whenever the hero – with profound but unsuspected justification – begins to speak of the circumstances of his death as if they were the circumstances of life. 'The determination of the tragic character to die is also . . . only apparently heroic, only in a context of human psychology; the dying heroes of tragedy – thus, approximately, wrote a young tragedian – have already long been dead before they actually die.'[33] In his spiritual-cum-physical existence the hero is the framework of the tragic process. If the 'power of the framework', as it has appropriately been called, is really one of the essential features which distinguish the ancient attitude from the modern, in which the infinite and varied range of feelings or situations seems to be self-evident, then this power cannot be separated from that of tragedy itself. 'It is not the intensity but the duration of high feeling which makes the high man.' This monotonous duration of heroic feeling is vouchsafed solely in the pre-ordained framework of the hero's life. The oracle in tragedy is more than just a magical incantation of fate; it is a projection of the certainty that there is no tragic life which does not take place within its framework. The necessity which appears to be built into the framework, is neither a causal nor a magical necessity. It is the unarticulated necessity of defiance, in which the self brings forth its utterances. At the slightest breath of the word it would melt away like snow before the south wind. But the only word which could bring this about is an unknown one. Heroic defiance contains this word enclosed within it; that is what distinguishes it from the *hubris* of a man whose hidden significance is no longer acknowledged by the fully developed consciousness of the community.

Only antiquity could know tragic *hubris*, which pays for the right to be silent with the hero's life. The hero, who scorns to justify himself before the gods, reaches agreement with them in a, so to speak, contractual process of atonement which, in its dual significance, is designed not only to bring about the restoration but above all the undermining of an ancient body of laws in the linguistic constitution of the renewed community. Athletic contests, law, and tragedy constitute the great agonal trinity of Greek life – in his *Griechische Kulturgeschichte* Jacob Burckhardt refers to the *agon* as a scheme[34] – and they are bound together under the sign of this contract. 'Legislation and legal procedure were founded in Hellas in the struggle against self-help and the law of the jungle. Where the tendency to take the law into one's own hands declined, or the state succeeded in restraining it, the trial did not at once assume the character of a search for a judicial decision, but that of an attempt at conciliation ... In the framework of such a procedure the principal aim was not to establish the absolute right, but to prevail upon the injured party to renounce vengeance; and so sacral forms for proof and verdict could not but acquire a particularly high significance, because of the impact they had even on the losers.'[35] In antiquity the trial – especially the criminal trial – is a dialogue, because it is based on the twin roles of prosecutor and accused, without official procedure. It has its chorus: partly in the sworn witnesses (in ancient Cretan law, for instance, the parties proved their case with the help of compurgators, that is to say character-witnesses, who originally stood surety for the right of their party with weapons in the trial by ordeal), partly in the array of comrades of the accused begging the court for mercy, and finally in the adjudicating assembly of the populace. The important and characteristic feature of Athenian law is the Dionysian outburst, the fact that the intoxicated, ecstatic word was able to transcend the regular perimeter of the *agon*, that a higher justice was vouchsafed by the persuasive power of living speech than from the trial of the opposed factions, by combat with weapons or prescribed verbal forms. The practice of the trial by ordeal is disrupted by the freedom of the *logos*. This is the ultimate affinity between trial and tragedy in Athens. The hero's word, on those isolated occasions when it breaks through the rigid armour of the self, becomes a cry of protest. Tragedy is assimilated in this image of the trial; here too a process of conciliation takes place. So it is that in Sophocles and Euripides the heroes learn 'not to speak ... only to debate'; and this explains why 'the love-scene is quite alien to ancient drama'.[36] But if in the mind of the dramatist the myth constitutes the negotiation, his work is at one and the same time a depiction and a revision of the proceedings. And with the inclusion of the amphitheatre the dimensions of this whole trial have increased. The community is present at this re-opening of the proceedings as the controlling, indeed as the adjudicating authority. For its part it seeks to reach a decision about the settlement, in the interpretation of which the dramatist renews the memory of the achievements of the hero. But the conclusion of the tragedy is always qualified by a *non liquet*. The solution is always, it is true, a redemption; but only a temporary, problematic, and limited one. The satyric drama which precedes or follows the tragedy is an expression of the fact that the élan of comedy is the only proper preparation for, or reaction to, the *non liquet* of the represented trial. And even this is not free from the awe which surrounds the inscrutable conclusion: 'The hero, who awakens fear and pity in others, himself remains an unmoved, rigid self. And again in the spectator these emotions are at once turned inwards, and make him, too, a totally self-enclosed self. Each keeps to himself; each remains self. No community emerges. And yet there is an element common to them all. The selves do not come together, and yet the same note resounds in them all, the feeling of their own self.'[37] A disastrous and enduring effect of the forensic dramaturgy of tragedy has been the doctrine of the unities. This most concrete explanation of the unities is overlooked even in the profound interpretation which argues: 'Unity of place is the self-evident, immediately obvious symbol of this remaining-at-a-standstill amid the perpetual change of surrounding life; hence the technically necessary way to its expression. The tragic is but a single moment: that is what is meant by the unity of time.'[38] There is, of course, no doubt about this – the temporally limited emergence of the hero from the underworld lends the greatest emphasis to this interruption of the passage of time. Jean Paul's rhetorical question about tragedy is nothing less than a disavowal of the most astonishing divination: 'who will present gloomy worlds of shades at public festivals before a crowd?'[39] None of his contemporaries imagined anything of the kind. But here, as always, the most fruitful layer of metaphysical interpretation is to be found on the level of the pragmatic. Here unity of place is the court of judgment; unity of time, the duration of the court session, which has always been limited – either by the revolution of the sun or otherwise; and unity of action, that of the proceedings. These are the circumstances which make the conversations of Socrates the irrevocable epilogue of tragedy. In his own lifetime the hero not only discovers the word, but he acquires a band of disciples, his youthful spokesmen. His silence, not his speech, will now be informed with the utmost irony. Socratic irony, which is the opposite of tragic irony. What is tragic is the indiscretion by which, unconsciously, the truth of heroic life is touched upon: the self, whose reticence is so profound that it does not stir even when it calls out its own name in its dreams. The ironic silence of the philosopher, the coy, histrionic silence, is conscious. In place of the sacrificial death of the hero Socrates sets the example of the pedagogue. But, in Plato's work, the war which the rationalism of Socrates declared on tragic art is decided against tragedy with a superiority which ultimately affected the challenger more than the object challenged. For this does not happen in the rational spirit of Socrates, so much as in the spirit of the dialogue itself. At the end of the *Symposium*, when Socrates, Agathon, and Aristophanes are seated alone, facing one another – why should it not be the sober light of his dialogues which Plato allows to fall over the discussion of the nature of the true poet, who embodies both tragedy and comedy, as dawn breaks over the three? The dialogue contains pure dramatic language, unfragmented by its dialectic of tragic and comic. This purely dramatic quality restores the mystery which had gradually become secularized in the forms of Greek drama: its language, the language of the new drama, is, in particular, the language of the *Trauerspiel*.

Given the equation of the tragedy and the *Trauerspiel* it ought to have seemed very odd that the *Poetics* of Aristotle make no mention of mourning [*Trauer*] as the resonance of the tragic. But far from it, it has often been believed that modern aesthetics has, in the concept of the tragic, itself discovered a feeling, the emotional reaction to tragedy and *Trauerspiel*. Tragedy is a preliminary stage of prophecy. It is a content, which exists only in language: what is tragic is the word and the silence of the past, in which the prophetic voice is being tried out, or suffering and death, when they are redeemed by this voice; but a fate in the pragmatic substance of its entanglements is never tragic. The *Trauerspiel* is conceivable as pantomime; the tragedy is not. For the struggle against the demonic character of the law is dependent on the word of the genius. The evaporation of the tragic under the scrutiny of psychology goes hand in hand with the equation of tragedy and *Trauerspiel*. The very name of the latter already indicates that its content awakens mourning in the spectator. But it does not by any means follow that this content could be any better expressed in the categories of empirical psychology than could the content of tragedy – it might far rather mean that these plays could serve better to describe mourning than could the condition of grief. For these are not so much plays which cause mourning, as plays through which mournfulness finds satisfaction: plays for the mournful. A certain ostentation is characteristic of these people. Their images are displayed in order to be seen, arranged in the way they want them to be seen. Thus the Italian renaissance theatre, which is in many ways an influential factor in the German baroque, emerged from pure ostentation, from the *trionfi*,[40] the processions with explanatory recitation, which flourished in Florence under Lorenzo de Medici. And in the European *Trauerspiel* as a whole the stage is also not strictly fixable, not an actual place, but it too is dialectically split. Bound to the court, it yet remains a travelling theatre; metaphorically its boards represent the earth as the setting created for the enactment of history; it follows its court from town to town. In Greek eyes, however, the stage is a cosmic *topos*. 'The form of the Greek theatre recalls a lonely valley in the mountains: the architecture of the scene appears like a luminous cloud formation that the Bacchants swarming over the mountains behold from a height – like the splendid frame in which the image of Dionysus is revealed to them.'[41] Whether this beautiful description is correct or not, whether or not the courtroom analogy, the statement 'the scene becomes a tribunal', must hold good for every excited community, the Greek trilogy is, in any case, not a repeatable act of ostentation, but a once-and-for-all resumption of the tragic trial before a higher court. As is suggested by the open theatre and the fact that the performance is never repeated identically, what takes place is a decisive cosmic achievement. The community is assembled to witness and to judge this achievement. The spectator of tragedy is summoned, and is justified, by the tragedy itself; the *Trauerspiel*, in contrast, has to be understood from the point of view of the onlooker. He learns how, on the stage, a space which belongs to an inner world of feeling and bears no relationship to the cosmos, situations are compellingly presented to him. The linguistic indications of the connection between mourning and ostentation, as it finds expression in the theatre of the baroque, are terse. For instance:

'T[rauer] bühne' 'fig. the earth as a setting for mournful events . . .';
'das T[rauer] gepränge; das T[rauer] gerüst, a frame draped in cloth and
furnished with decorations, emblems, etc., on which the body of a prominent person is displayed in his coffin (catafalque, *castrum doloris, Trauer-
bühne)*.[42] The word *Trauer* is always to hand for these compounds, and
it extracts the marrow of its significance, so to speak, from its companion
word.[43] The following words of Hallmann are thoroughly characteristic
of the extreme sense in which the term is used in the baroque, a sense
which is not at all governed by aesthetic considerations: 'Solch Traur-
spiel kommt aus deinen Eitelkeiten! | Solch Todten-Tantz wird in der
Welt gehegt!'[44]*

The subsequent period owed to the baroque the assumption that the
historical subject was particularly suited to the *Trauerspiel*. And just as
the transformation of history into natural history in the baroque drama
was overlooked, so too, in the analysis of tragedy, was the discrimination
between legend and history. In this way the concept of historical tragedy
emerged. Here too the equation of *Trauerspiel* and tragedy was the consequence, and it acquired the theoretical function of concealing the problematic character of the historical drama as devised by German classicism.
The uncertainty in the relationship to the historical material is one of the
clearest aspects of this problematic character. Any freedom in the interpretation of history will always fall short of the precision of the tendentious renewal of myth in tragedy; on the other hand, whereas the
chronicler's strict adherence to sources, which was required of the
baroque *Trauerspiel*, is perfectly compatible with poetic culture, it is only
with great risk that this kind of drama can allow itself to be bound to the
'essence' of history. In contrast, complete freedom of plot is fundamentally
suited to the *Trauerspiel*. The highly significant development of this form
in the *Sturm und Drang* can, if one so wishes, be seen as a realization of its

---

* Such a *Trauerspiel* springs from thy vanities! Such a dance of death is cherished in the
world!

latent potentialities, and an emancipation from the arbitrary restriction of the chronicle. In a different way this influence of the formal world of the baroque is confirmed by the figure of the *Kraftgenie* [Man of power and genius], a bourgeois hybrid of tyrant and martyr. Minor observed such a synthesis in the *Attila* of Zacharias Werner.[45] There is even a survival of the true martyr and the dramatic presentation of his suffering in the starvation of [Gerstenberg's] Ugolino or in the castration-motif in [Lenz's] *Der Hofmeister*. The drama of the creature thus definitely continues, except that death is now replaced by love. But even here transience has the last word. 'Alas that man passes over the earth without leaving a trace, like a smile over the face or the song of a bird through the forest!'[46] It was as such laments that the *Sturm und Drang* read the choruses of tragedy, thereby retaining an element of the baroque interpretation of tragedy. In his criticism of [Lessing's] *Laocoön* in the first part of the *Kritische Wälder* Herder writes, as a spokesman of the Ossianic age, of the loudly lamenting Greeks with their 'susceptibility . . . to gentle tears'.[47] Really the chorus of tragedy does not lament. It remains detached in the presence of profound suffering; this refutes the idea of surrender to lamentation. It is a superficial view of such detachment to seek to explain it in terms of indifference or even pity. Choric diction, rather, has the effect of restoring the ruins of the tragic dialogue to a linguistic edifice firmly established – in ethical society and in religious community – both before and after the conflict. Far from dissolving the tragic action into lamentations, the constant presence of the members of the chorus, as Lessing already observed,[48] actually sets a limit on the emotional outburst even in the dialogue. The conception of the chorus as a *Trauerklage* [lamentation], in which 'the original pain of creation resounds',[49] is a genuinely baroque reinterpretation of its essence. For the chorus of the German *Trauerspiel* does, at least partially, have this function. Its second function is less obvious. The choruses of the baroque drama are not so much interludes, like those of ancient drama, as frames enclosing the act, which bear the same relationship to it as the ornamental borders in Renaissance printing to the type area. They serve to emphasize the nature of the act as part of a mere spectacle. The chorus of the *Trauerspiel* is therefore usually more elaborate and less directly connected to the action than the chorus of tragedy. In the classicistic versions of the historical drama the later, apocryphal life of the *Trauerspiel* assumes a quite different form from that which it assumed in the *Sturm und Drang*. No writer of modern times has struggled more intensely than Schiller to re-create the pathos of antiquity in subjects which have no connection with tragic myth. He believed that in the form of history he could renew the irrepeatable prerequisite which tragedy possessed in the myth. But neither a tragic element in the ancient sense, nor a fatal element in the romantic sense is fundamentally proper to history, unless they were to cancel each other out in the concept of causal necessity. The historical drama of classicism comes dangerously close to this vague modernist view, and neither a morality which is released from the tragic nor a reasoning which has escaped the dialectic of fate is capable of supporting its structure. Where Goethe's inclination was for mediating compromises which were both important and quite justified by the subject treated – it is not without reason that the experimental fragment, which follows Calderón in taking a subject from Carolingian history, goes by the curiously apocryphal title, a '*Trauerspiel* from Christendom' – Schiller sought to base the drama on the spirit of history as understood by German idealism. And although in other respects his dramas may be deemed the works of a great artist, it cannot be denied that with them he introduced the form of the epigones into the world. In doing so he wrested from classicism the possibility of giving a reflection of fate as the antipode of individual freedom. But in pursuing this experiment, and adapting the romantic tragedy of fate in *Die Braut von Messina*, he inevitably came closer and closer to the form of the *Trauerspiel*. It is a mark of his superior artistic understanding that, the idealist theorems notwithstanding, he had recourse to the astrological in *Wallenstein*, the miraculous effects of Calderón in *Die Jungfrau von Orléans*, and Calderónesque opening motifs in *Wilhelm Tell*. Of course, the romantic form of the *Trauerspiel*, whether in the drama of fate or anywhere else, could scarcely be more than a revival of Calderón. Hence Goethe's statement that Calderón could have become dangerous to Schiller. He could justifiably believe himself safe from this danger when, in the concluding scenes of *Faust*, he consciously and coolly, and with a force surpassing even Calderón's, did precisely the thing towards which Schiller might have felt himself half unwillingly pushed, half irresistibly drawn.

The aesthetic limitations of the historical drama necessarily emerged most clearly in its most radical and therefore most clumsy form, the *Haupt- und Staatsaktion*. This is the popular, southern counterpart to the erudite *Trauerspiel* of the north. It is significant that the only evidence, not of this particular insight, but of any insight into it at all stems from romanticism. In his history of the *Poesie und Beredsamkeit der Deutschen* the *littérateur* Franz Horn, gives a surprisingly perceptive account of the *Haupt- und Staatsaktionen*, without however dwelling unduly on the subject. He writes: 'When Velthem was alive the so-called *Haupt- und Staatsaktionen* were especially popular, although almost all subsequent literary historians have poured scorn upon them, without actually explaining why. These *Aktionen* are truly German in origin and entirely suited to the German character. Love of so-called pure tragedy was never common, but the inherent romantic impulse demanded rich sustenance, as did the delight in farce, which is usually most alive in the most thoughtful dispositions. However there is one other characteristically German inclination, which was not completely satisfied by all these genres: that is the inclination to seriousness in general, to solemnity, sometimes to expansiveness, sometimes to sententious concision and – ellipsis. The response to this was the invention of those so-called *Haupt- und Staatsaktionen*, which took their subject-matter from the historical parts of the Old Testament (?), Greece and Rome, Turkey, etc., but seldom from Germany... The kings and princes appear with their crowns of gilt paper, very melancholy and mournful, and they assure the sympathetic public that nothing is more difficult than to rule, and that a wood-cutter sleeps much more soundly at night; the generals and officers hold fine speeches, and recount their great deeds; the princesses are, as is fitting, exceedingly virtuous and, as is equally fitting, are sublimely in love, usually with one of the generals ... The ministers are correspondingly less popular with these authors, and are usually portrayed as evil-intentioned and with a black, or at least a grey, character . . . The clown and fool is often a nuisance to the *dramatis personae*; but they simply cannot get rid of this incarnation of parody who, as such, is of course immortal.'[50] It is no coincidence that this evocative description calls to mind the puppet-play. Stranitzky, the outstanding Viennese exponent of the genre, also owned a puppet-theatre. Even if those texts by him which have survived were not performed there, it is inconceivable that the actual repertoire of this puppet theatre did not have numerous points of contact with the *Aktionen*, whose parodistic epigones could probably still have found a place in it. The miniature, into which the *Haupt- und Staatsaktionen* thus tend to be transformed, shows how very closely they resemble the *Trauerspiel*. Whether the latter chooses the subtle reflection of the Spanish style or the bombastic gesture of the German, it still possesses the playful eccentricity which has a descendant in the hero of the puppet-play. 'Were not the bodies of Papinian and his son . . . perhaps represented by dummies? At any rate this must have been the case when the corpse of Leo was dragged on, and in the representation of the bodies of Cromwell, Irreton, and Bradshaw on the gallows . . . The horrible relic, the burned head of the steadfast Princess of Georgia, also belongs here . . . In Eternity's prologue to *Catharina* a whole collection of stage properties are lying scattered about the floor, similar perhaps to what is shown in the engraving on the title-page of the 1657 edition. As well as sceptre and crozier there are "Schmuck, Bild, Metal und ein gelehrt Papier".* According to what she says, eternity tramples . . . on father and son. If they were in fact represented, they, like the Prince who is also mentioned, could only have been dummies.'[51] Political philosophy, which must have held such points of view as sacrilegious, provides the counter-test. Salmasius writes: 'Ce sont eux qui traittent les testes des Roys comme des ballons, qui se ioüent des Couronnes comme les enfans font d'vn cercle, qui considerent les Sceptres des Princes comme des marottes, et qui n'ont pas plus de veneration pour les liurées de la souueraine Magistrature, que pour des quintaines.'[52]† In their physical appearance the actors them-

---

*Jewellery, a picture, metal and a learned manuscript.

† It is they who treat the heads of kings like balls, who play with crowns as children play with hoops, who regard the sceptres of princes as jesters' staffs, and who have no more respect for the insignia of sovereign magistracy than for quintains.

selves, especially the king, who was clad in ceremonial robes, could have had a stiff, puppet-like effect. 'Die Fürsten / denen ist der Purpur angebohrn / I Sind ohne Scepter kranck.'[53]* These lines of Lohenstein justify the comparison between the rulers of the baroque stage and the kings of playing cards. In the same play Micipsa speaks of the fall of Masinissa, 'der schwer von Kronen war'.[54]† Our final example is provided by Haugwitz: 'Reicht uns den rothen Sammt / und dies geblümte Kleid I Und schwartzen Atlass / dass man / was den Sinn erfreut / I Und was den Leib betrübt / kan auff den Kleidern lesen / I Und sehet wer wir sind in diesem Spiel gewesen / I Indem der blasse Tod den letzten Auffzug macht.'[55]‡

Among the several features of the *Staatsaktionen* listed by Horn, the most significant for the study of the *Trauerspiel* is ministerial intrigue. This does of course play a role in the high poetic drama too; alongside the 'Pralereyen / Klag'Reden / endlich auch Begräbnise(n) und Grabschriften', Birken includes 'Meineid und Verrätherey . . . Betrüge und Practiken'[56]§ in the subject-matter of the *Trauerspiel*. But the figure of the scheming adviser does not operate with total freedom in the scholarly drama; this happens in the more popular plays. And here he is in his element as the comic figure. So it is with 'Doctor Babra, ein verwihrter Jurist und Favorit des Königs'. His 'Politischen Staats- Streiche und verstelte Einfalth . . . gibt denen Staats-Scenen eine Modeste Unterhaltung'.[57] ¶ With the intriguer comedy is introduced into the *Trauerspiel*. But not as an episode. Comedy – or more precisely: the pure joke – is the essential inner side of mourning which from time to time, like the

---

* Princes, who are born to the purple, are sick without their sceptre.

† who was heavy with crowns

‡ Give us red velvet and this floral dress and black satin, so that what rejoices our senses and what distresses our body can be seen from our clothes; and so see our role in this play, in which pale death provides the final costume.

§ boasts, lamentations, and finally burials and funeral inscriptions . . . perjury and treachery . . . deception and trickery

¶ Doctor Babra a confused lawyer and favourite of the king. His political coups and his feigned simplicity . . . provide the stages with a modest degree of entertainment.

lining of a dress at the hem or lapel, makes its presence felt. Its representative is linked to the representative of mourning. 'Kein Zorn, wir sind gutte Freundt, werden ia die Herrn Collegen einander nichts thun',[58]* says Hanswurst to the 'Person dess Messinischen Wüttrichs Pelifonte'.† Or as in the epigram above an engraving depicting a stage on which there stand, to the left, a buffoon and, to the right, a prince: 'Wann die Bühne nu wird leer / I Gilt kein Narr und König mehr.'[59]‡ Rarely, if ever, has speculative aesthetics considered the affinity between the strict joke and the cruel. Who has not seen children laugh where adults are shocked? The alternation of the sadist between such childlike laughter and such adult shock can be seen in the intriguer. This is evident in Mone's excellent description of the rogue in a fourteenth-century play about the childhood of Christ. 'It is clear that this figure is an embryonic form of the court-jester . . . What is the fundamental trait in the character of this person? Scorn for human pride. That is what distinguishes this rogue from the aimless merry maker of later times. There is a certain harmlessness about the Hanswurst, but this older rogue has a bitingly provocative scorn, which leads directly to the horrible child-murder. There is something devilish at work here; and it is only because this rogue is, so to speak, a part of the devil, that he necessarily belongs in this tragedy: in order to circumvent salvation, if that were possible, by the murder of the child Jesus.'[60] It is quite appropriate to the secularization of the passion-plays in the baroque drama that the official should take the place of the devil. Inspired perhaps by this account of Mone's, a description of the Viennese *Haupt- und Staatsaktionen* refers back to the rogue in order to characterize the intriguer. The 'Hanswurst' of the *Staatsaktionen* appeared 'armed with the weapons and irony and scorn, usually got the better of his fellows – such as Scapin and Riepl – and did not even have any inhibitions about taking over the task of directing the intrigue of the play . . . As in the contemporary secular drama, the rogue had already, in the religious dramas of the fifteenth century, taken over the role of the comic figure, and, as now, this role was already perfectly adapted to the struc-

---

* Do not be angry, we are good friends; colleagues will do one another no harm.
† Pelifonte, the tyrant of Messina.
‡ When the stage is empty, fool and king will no longer count for anything.

ture of the play and exerted a fundamental influence on the development of the action.'[61] But this role is not, as is implied here, an amalgamation of heterogeneous elements. The cruel joke is just as original as harmless mirth; originally the two are close to each other; and it is precisely through the figure of the intriguer that the – so frequently high-flown – *Trauerspiel* derives its contact with the solid ground of wonderfully profound experiences. If the mourning of a prince and the mirth of his adviser are so close to each other this is, in the last analysis, only because the two provinces of the satanic realm were represented in them. And mourning, the specious sanctity of which makes the absorption of the ethical man into such a threat, appears in all its desperation unexpectedly not devoid of hope, compared with mirth which does not conceal the snarling grimace of the devil. Nothing shows more clearly the limitations of the art of the German baroque drama than the fact that the expression of this significant relationship was left to the popular spectacle. In England, on the other hand, Shakespeare had based such figures as Iago and Polonius on the old model of the demonic fool. With them the *Lustspiel* [comedy] enters into the *Trauerspiel*. Through their modulations these two forms are not only empirically connected but in terms of the law of their structure they are as closely bound to each other as classical tragedy and comedy are opposed; their affinity is such that the *Lustspiel* enters into the *Trauerspiel*: the *Trauerspiel* could never develop in the form of the *Lustspiel*. There is a certain good sense to the following image: the *Lustspiel* shrinks and is, so to speak, absorbed into the *Trauerspiel*. Lohenstein writes: 'Ich irrdisches Geschöpff und Schertz der Sterblichkeit'.[62]* Again we should recall the diminution of the reflected characters. The comic figure is a *raisonneur*; in reflection he appears to himself as a marionette. The finest exemplifications of the *Trauerspiel* are not those which adhere strictly to the rules, but those in which there are playful modulations of the *Lustspiel*. For this reason Calderón and Shakespeare created more important *Trauerspiele* than the German writers of the seventeenth century, who never progressed beyond the rigidly orthodox type. Novalis wrote: '*Lustspiel* and *Trauerspiel* profit

---

* I, earthly creature, and joke of mortality.

considerably and only become genuinely poetic through their subtle, symbolic combination';[63] and this is certainly true, at least as far as the *Trauerspiel* is concerned. He sees this demand fulfilled by the genius of Shakespeare. 'In Shakespeare there is indeed an alternation between the poetic and the anti-poetic, harmony and disharmony, the common, the base, the ugly and the romantic, the lofty, the beautiful, the real and the imagined: in Greek tragedy the opposite is true.'[64] In fact the gravity of the German baroque drama may well be one of the few features which can be explained by reference to Greek drama, even though it is in no way derived from the latter. Under the influence of Shakespeare the *Sturm und Drang* endeavoured to restore to view the comic interior of the *Trauerspiel*, and at once the figure of the comic schemer re-emerges.

German literary history has responded to the offspring of the baroque *Trauerspiel*: the *Haupt- und Staatsaktionen*, the drama of the *Sturm und Drang*, the fate-tragedy, with a reserve which is accounted for not so much by incomprehension as by a hostility, whose real object first becomes apparent when the form is subject to metaphysical ferment. In respect of the forms mentioned, this reserve, indeed scorn, seems to be most justified where the fate-drama is concerned. It *is* justified if one considers the quality of certain of the later manifestations of this genre. The traditional argument, however, rests on the schema of these dramas and not on an incomplete inventory of details. And so an examination of them is indispensable because this schema, as has already been indicated, is so closely related to that of the baroque *Trauerspiel*, that it must be seen as one of its varieties. In the work of Calderón especially, it emerges very clearly and significantly as such. It is impossible to pass over this flourishing territory of the drama with deprecatory remarks about the supposed limitation of its master, as Volkelt attempts to do in his theory of the tragic, which contains a fundamental denial of all the genuine problems associated with its theme. He writes: 'it must never be forgotten that this writer [was subject] to the pressure of an uncompromising Catholic faith and an absurdly intense conception of honour'.[65] Goethe has already replied to such divagations: 'Think of Shakespeare and Calderón! They stand immaculate before the highest seat of aesthetic judgment, and if someone versed in the art of discrimination should stubbornly criticize them for certain passages, they would smilingly show a picture of the nation and the age for which they worked, and not thereby merely secure indulgence, but actually win new laurels because they were able to adapt so successfully.'[66] Goethe therefore calls for the study of the Spanish dramatist, not so as to forgive him his limitations, but in order to learn to understand the nature of his freedom. This deference is absolutely decisive if we are to acquire insight into the drama of fate. For fate is not a purely natural occurrence – any more than it is purely historical. Fate, whatever guise it may wear in a pagan or mythological context, is meaningful only as a category of natural history in the spirit of the restoration-theology of the Counter-Reformation. It is the elemental force of nature in historical events, which are not themselves entirely nature, because the light of grace is still reflected from the state of creation. But it is mirrored in the swamp of Adam's guilt. For the ineluctable chain of causality is not in itself fateful. However often it is repeated, it will never be true that the task of the dramatist is to exhibit the causal necessity of a sequence of events on the stage. Why should art reinforce a thesis which it is the business of deterministic philosophy to advance? The only philosophical laws which have any place in the work of art are those which refer to the meaning of existence; theories concerning the operation of natural laws in the world-process, even if they do apply to it in its totality, are irrelevant. The deterministic outlook cannot influence any art-form. But the genuine notion of fate is different; its essential motive should be sought in an eternal sense of such determination. There is no need for events to follow a pattern which conforms to the laws of nature; a miracle can just as easily evoke this sense. It is not rooted in factual inevitability. The core of the notion of fate is, rather the conviction that guilt (which in this context always means creaturely guilt – in Christian terms, original sin – not moral transgression on the part of the agent), however fleeting its appearance, unleashes causality as the instrument of the irresistibly unfolding fatalities. Fate is the entelechy of events within the field of guilt. The isolation of the field within which the latter exerts its power is what distinguishes fate; for here everything intentional or accidental is so intensified that the complexities – of honour for instance – betray, by their paradoxical vehemence, that the action of this play has been inspired by fate. It would be absolutely wrong to argue: 'If we encounter improbable accidents, contrived situations, unduly complicated intrigues . . . then the impression of fatality is destroyed'.[67] For it is precisely the far-fetched combinations, those which are anything other than natural, which correspond to the various fates in the various fields of the action. In the German tragedy of fate there is of course no field of such ideas as is required for the representation of fate. The theological intention of a writer such as Werner could not compensate for the absence of a pagan-cum-Catholic convention, which, in the work of Calderón, endows brief episodes of life with the effectiveness of a cosmic or magical fate. In the drama of the Spanish dramatist fate emerges as the elemental spirit of history, and it is logical that the king alone, the great restorer of the disturbed order of creation, is able to conciliate it. Cosmic fate – sovereign majesty; these are the two poles of Calderón's world. The German baroque *Trauerspiel*, on the other hand, is characterized by an extreme paucity of non-Christian notions. For this reason – and one is almost tempted to say for this reason alone – it was not able to develop the drama of fate. Particularly striking is the extent to which the astrological was suppressed by respectable Christianity. It is true that Lohenstein's Masnissa observes: 'Des Himmels Reitzungen kan niemand überwinden',[68]* and that the 'Vereinbarung der Sterne und der Gemüther'† brings with it a reference to Egyptian theories of the dependence of nature on the movement of the constellations,[69] but these are isolated cases and are ideological in character. The middle ages on the other hand – and this is a counterpart to the error of modern criticism in regarding the drama of fate from the point of view of the tragic – looked for astrological destiny in Greek tragedy. In the eleventh century, in the work of Hildebert of Tours, it is 'already judged entirely in terms of the grotesque features, which the modern view attributed to it in the "tragedy of fate". That is to say it is

---

* No one can overcome the promptings of the heavens.

† correspondence between the stars and the dispositions of men

judged in terms of the crudely mechanical, or, as it was then understood in accordance with the average image of the pagan world-view of antiquity, the astrological intelligence. Hildebert calls his (regrettably unfinished) wholly independent, free adaptation of the Oedipus-problem a "*liber mathematicus*".'[70]

Fate leads to death. Death is not punishment but atonement, an expression of the subjection of guilty life to the law of natural life. That guilt which has often been the focal point of the theory of the tragic has its home in fate and the drama of fate. This guilt, which according to the ancient statutes falls upon men from without through misfortune, is taken over by a hero in the course of the tragic action and absorbed into himself. By reflecting it in his consciousness of himself, he escapes its demonic jurisdiction. If 'consciousness of the dialectic of their fate' was looked for in tragic heroes, and 'mystic rationalism' was found in the tragic reflections,[71] then what is meant here is perhaps the new, the tragic guilt of the hero – although the context leaves it open to doubt, and makes the words extremely problematical. A paradox, like every manifestation of the tragic order, this guilt consists only in the proud consciousness of guilt, in which the heroic character escapes from his enslavement, as an 'innocent', by demonic guilt. What Lukács says is true in respect of the tragic hero, and of him alone: 'From an external point of view there is no guilt and there can be none; each sees the guilt of the other as a chance ensnarement, as something which the slightest difference, even in a puff of wind, might have made turn out differently. But in the assumption of guilt, man assents to everything that has befallen him . . . Exalted men . . . let go of nothing, once it has been a part of their lives; tragedy is therefore their prerogative.'[72] This is a variation on Hegel's famous statement: 'It is a point of honour with such great characters that they are guilty.' This is always the guilt of those who are guilty by their actions, not their will; whereas in the field of demonic fate it is the act and the act alone which, by malicious accident, throws the guiltless into the abyss of general guilt.[73] In tragic poetry the ancient curse which has been passed down from generation to generation, becomes the inner, self-discovered possession of the tragic character. And it is thus extinguished. In the drama of fate, on the other hand, it is worked out; and so a distinction between the tragedy and the *Trauerspiel* illuminates the remark that the tragic usually moves 'to and fro, like some restless spirit, between the persons of the bloody "tragedies"'.[74] 'The subject of fate cannot be determined.'[75] The *Trauerspiel* therefore has no individual hero, only constellations of heroes. The majority of the main characters found in so many baroque dramas – Leo and Balbus in *Leo Armenius*, Catharina and Chach Abas in *Catharina von Georgien*, Cardenio and Celinde in the drama of that name, Nero and Agrippina, Masinissa and Sophonisbe in Lohenstein's drama – are not tragic characters, but are suited to the mournful play.

Destiny is not only divided among the characters, it is equally present among the objects. 'It is characteristic of the tragedy of fate not only that a curse or guilt is inherited within whole families, but also that this is associated with . . . a fatal stage property.'[76] For once human life has sunk into the merely creaturely, even the life of apparently dead objects secures power over it. The effectiveness of the object where guilt has been incurred is a sign of the approach of death. The passionate stirrings of creaturely life in man – in a word, passion itself – bring the fatal property into the action. It is nothing other than the seismographic needle, which registers its vibrations. In the drama of fate the nature of man, which is expressed in blind passion, and the nature of things, which is expressed in blind fate, are both equally subject to the law of fate. The more adequate the instrument which registers it, the more clearly this law can be seen. It is not therefore a matter of no importance whether, as in so many German tragedies of fate, some trivial stage-property bears down on the victim in a series of unworthy twists of the plot, or whether, as in the work of Calderón, ancient motifs come to light on such occasions. The full truth of A. W. Schlegel's remark that he knew of 'no dramatist who was equally skilled in giving a poetic quality to theatrical effect',[77] becomes clear in this context. Calderón was a master of this art, because theatrical effect is an essential, inner constituent of his most characteristic form, the drama of fate. And the mysterious externality of this dramatist does not consist so much in the way the stage-property constantly comes to the fore in the twists of the dramas of fate, but in the precision with which the passions themselves take on the nature of stage-properties. In a drama of jealousy the dagger becomes identical with the passions which guide it because in the work of Calderón jealousy is as sharp and as functional as a dagger. His whole mastery lies in the extreme exactitude with which, in a play like the Herod-drama, the passion is distinguished from that psychological motive to action which the modern reader looks for in it. This has been observed, but only as an object of criticism. 'The natural thing would have been to motivate the death of Marianne by Herod's jealousy. Indeed this particular solution was quite compellingly obvious, and the purposefulness with which Calderón worked against it, in order to give the "tragedy of fate" its appropriate conclusion, is plain to see.'[78] For Herod does not kill his wife *out of* jealousy; rather is it *through* jealousy that she loses her life. Through jealousy Herod is subject to fate, and in its sphere fate makes the same use of jealousy, the dangerously inflamed nature of man, as it does of the dagger to bring about disaster and to serve as a sign of disaster. And chance, in the sense of the breaking down of the action into fragmented elements or things, corresponds entirely to the meaning of the stage-property. The stage-property is therefore the criterion by which the genuine romantic drama of fate is distinguished from ancient tragedy which fundamentally renounces any order of fate.

The tragedy of fate is implicit in the *Trauerspiel*. Only the introduction of the stage-property lies between it and the German baroque drama. Its exclusion is a sign of the genuine influence of antiquity, or a genuine Renaissance trait. For there is hardly any more pronounced distinction between modern and ancient drama than the absence from the latter of the profane world of things. And the same is true of the classical period of the baroque in Germany. But if tragedy is completely released from the world of things, this world towers oppressively over the horizon of the *Trauerspiel*. The function of the mass of scholarly annotations is to point to the nightmare burden of *realia* on the action. In the developed form of the tragedy of fate there is no getting away from the stage-property. But alongside it there are dreams, ghostly apparitions, the terrors of the end, and all of these are part of the stock-in-trade of its basic form, the *Trauerspiel*. All of these are more or less closely orientated around the theme of death, and in the baroque they are fully developed, being transcendental phenomena whose dimension is temporal, in contrast to the immanent, predominantly spatial phenomena of the world of things. Gryphius, in particular, set great store by everything associated with the world of spirits. The German language has him to thank for the mar-vellous translation of *deus ex machina* in the following sentence: 'Obs jemand seltsam vorkommen dörffte, dass wir nicht mit den alten einen gott aus dem gerüste, sondern einen geist aus dem grabe herfür bringen, der bedencke, was hin und wieder von den gespensten geschrieben.'[79]* He either devoted, or intended to devote *De Spectris*, to his ideas on this subject; nothing is known for certain about this. Like ghostly apparitions, prophetic dreams are an almost obligatory ingredient of the drama, which occasionally begins by relating them as a kind of prologue. They generally foretell the end of the tyrant. It may have been the belief of the drama-turgists of the age that this was a way of introducing the Greek oracle into the German theatre; here it is worth pointing out that these dreams belonged to the natural domain of fate and so could only be related to certain of the Greek oracles, most particularly the telluric ones. On the other hand, the assumption that the significance of these dreams lay in the fact that 'the spectator [would be] prompted to make a rational com-parison between the action and its metaphorical anticipation',[80] is a delusion of intellectualism. As can be deduced from dream visions and ghostly happenings, night plays a major role. From here it is but a step to the drama of fate, where the witching hour plays a dominant part. *Carolus Stuardus* by Gryphius, and *Agrippina* by Lohenstein begin at

---

* If anyone should find it odd that we do not bring forth a god from the machine, like the ancients, but rather a spirit from the grave, then let him consider what has occasionally been written about ghosts.

midnight; others do not only take place at night, as the unity of time frequently required, but, like *Leo Armenius, Cardenio und Celinde*, and *Epicharis*, contain great scenes which derive their poetic quality from the night. There is a good reason for associating the dramatic action with night, especially midnight. It lies in the widespread notion that at this hour time stands still like the tongue of a scale. Now since fate, itself the true order of eternal recurrence, can only be described as temporal in an indirect, that is parasitical sense,[81] its manifestations seek out the temporal dimension. They stand in the narrow frame of midnight, an opening in the passage of time, in which the same ghostly image constantly reappears. One way of illuminating to its very depths the gulf which separates tragedy from *Trauerspiel* is to read in the strictest literal sense the excellent comment of the Abbé Bossu, author of a *Traité sur la poésie épique*, which is quoted by Jean Paul. It says that 'no tragedy should be set at night-time'. The midnight hour of the *Trauerspiel* stands in contrast to the daytime setting required by every tragic action. ''Tis now the very witching time of night, | When churchyards yawn, and hell itself breathes out | Contagion to this world.'[82] The spirit world is ahistorical. To it the *Trauerspiel* consigns its dead. 'O wehe, ich sterbe, ia, ia, Verfluchter, ich sterbe, aber du hast die Rache von mir annoch zu befürchten: auch unter der Erden werd ich dein grimmiger Feindt und rachgieriger Wüttrich dess Messinischen Reichs verbleiben. Ich werde deinen Thron erschittern, das Ehebeth, deine Liebe und Zufriedenheit beunruhigen und mit meinem Grimme dem König und dem Reich möglichsten Schaden zufügen.'[83]* It has been rightly said of the English *Trauerspiel* before Shakespeare that it has 'no proper end, the stream continues on its course'.[84] This is true of the *Trauerspiel* in general; its conclusion does not mark the end of an epoch, as the death of the tragic hero so emphatically does, in both an historical and an individual sense. This individual sense – which also has the historical meaning of the end of the myth – is explained in the words that tragic life is 'the most exclusively immanent

---

* Alas I die, yes, yes, accursed one, I die, but thou hast still to fear my vengeance: even beneath the earth shall I remain thy bitter enemy and the vengeance-seeking tyrant of the kingdom of Messina. I shall shake thy throne, disturb thy marriage bed, thy love, and thy contentment, and in my wrath do the utmost harm to king and kingdom

of all kinds of life. For this reason its limits always merge into death . . . For tragedy death – the ultimate limit – is an ever immanent reality, which is inextricably bound up with each of its occurrences.'[85] Death, as the form of tragic life, is an individual destiny; in the *Trauerspiel* it frequently takes the form of a communal fate, as if summoning all the participants before the highest court. 'In dreien Tagen solln zu Recht sie stehen: | Sie sind geladen hin vor Gottes Throne; | Nun lasst sie denken, wie sie da bestehen.'[86]* Whereas the tragic hero, in his 'immortality', does not save his life, but only his name, in death the characters of the *Trauerspiel* lose only the name-bearing individuality, and not the vitality of their role. This survives undiminished in the spirit-world. 'After a *Hamlet* it might occur to another dramatist to write a *Fortinbras*; no one can stop me from allowing all the characters to meet again in hell or in heaven, and settling their accounts anew.'[87] The author of this remark has failed to perceive that this is determined by the law of the *Trauerspiel*, and not at all by the work referred to, let alone its subject-matter. In the face of such great *Trauerspiele* as *Hamlet*, which have constantly been the subject of renewed critical attention, the irrelevance of the absurd concept of tragedy which has been used to judge these works ought to have been clear long ago. For, with reference to the death of Hamlet, what is the point of attributing to Shakespeare a final 'residue of naturalism and the imitation of nature, which causes the tragic poet to forget that it is not his job to provide a physiological reason for death'? What is the point of arguing that in *Hamlet* death has 'absolutely no connection with the conflict. Hamlet, who is inwardly destroyed because he could find no other solution to the problem of existence than the negation of life, is killed by a poisoned rapier! That is, by a completely external accident . . . Strictly speaking this naive death-scene completely destroys the tragedy of the drama.'[88] This is what is produced by a criticism which, in the arrogance of its philosophical knowledgeability, spares itself any profound study of the works of a genius. The death of Hamlet, which has no more in common with tragic death than the Prince himself has with Ajax, is in its

---

* In three days they must be judged: they are summoned before God's throne; let them now consider how they will justify themselves

drastic externality characteristic of the *Trauerspiel*; and for this reason alone it is worthy of its creator: Hamlet, as is clear from his conversation with Osric, wants to breathe in the suffocating air of fate in one deep breath. He wants to die by some accident, and as the fateful stage-properties gather around him, as around their lord and master, the drama of fate flares up in the conclusion of this *Trauerspiel*, as something that is contained, but of course overcome, in it. Whereas tragedy ends with a decision – however uncertain this may be – there resides in the essence of the *Trauerspiel*, and especially in the death-scene, an appeal of the kind which martyrs utter. The language of the pre-Shakespearian *Trauerspiel* has been aptly described as a 'bloody legal dialogue' ['blutiger Akten-dialog'].[89] The legal analogy may reasonably be taken further and, in the sense of the mediaeval literature of litigation, one may speak of the trial of the creature whose charge against death – or whoever else was indicted in it – is only partially dealt with and is adjourned at the end of the *Trauerspiel*. Its resumption is implicit in the *Trauerspiel*, and sometimes it actually emerges from its latent state. Though this, of course, is also something which only happens in the richer, Spanish variant. In *La vida es sueño* the repetition of the principal situation is placed right at the centre. Again and again the *Trauerspiele* of the seventeenth century treat the same subjects, and treat them in such a way as to permit, indeed necessitate, repetition. But the same old theoretical prejudices have meant that this has not been understood, and Lohenstein has been accused of 'curious errors' about the nature of the tragic, 'such as the error that the tragic effect of the action is intensified if the scope of this action is extended by the addition of similar occurrences. Instead of giving his action greater plasticity and bringing it to a head with new, important events, Lohenstein prefers to embellish its principal elements with arbitrary arabesques, as if a statue would be made more beautiful by the doubling of its most artistically sculpted limbs!'[90] These dramas should not have had an odd number of acts, as was the case in imitation of the drama of the Greeks; an even number is much more appropriate to the repeatable actions which they describe. In *Leo Armenius*, at least, the action is complete by the end of the fourth act. With its emancipation from the three-act and five-act scheme, modern drama has secured the triumph of one of the tendencies of the baroque.[91]

> Ich finde nirgends Ruh / muss selber mit mir zancken /
> Ich sitz / ich lieg / ich steh / ist alles in Gedancken.
>   Andreas Tscherning: *Melancholey Redet selber**

The great German dramatists of the baroque were Lutherans. Whereas in the decades of the Counter-Reformation Catholicism had penetrated secular life with all the power of its discipline, the relationship of Lutheranism to the everyday had always been antinomic. The rigorous morality of its teaching in respect of civic conduct stood in sharp contrast to its renunciation of 'good works'. By denying the latter any special miraculous spiritual effect, making the soul dependent on grace through faith, and making the secular-political sphere a testing ground for a life which was only indirectly religious, being intended for the demonstration of civic virtues, it did, it is true, instil into the people a strict sense of obedience to duty, but in its great men it produced melancholy. Even in Luther himself, the last two decades of whose life are filled with an increasing heaviness of soul, there are signs of a reaction against the assault on good works. 'Faith', of course, carried him through, but it did not prevent life from becoming stale. 'What is a man, I If his chief good and market of his time I Be but to sleep and feed? a beast, no more. I Sure, he that hath made us with such large discourse, I Looking before and after, gave us not I That capability and god-like reason I To fust in us unused.'[1] – these words of Hamlet contain both the philosophy of Wittenberg and a protest against it. In that excessive reaction which ultimately denied good works as such, and not just their meritorious and penitential character, there was an element of German paganism and the grim belief in the subjection of man to fate. Human actions were deprived of all value.

---

* Nowhere do I find rest, I must even quarrel with myself. I sit, I lie, I stand, but am always in thought.

Andreas Tscherning: *Melancholy speaks herself*

Something new arose: an empty world. In Calvinism – for all its gloominess – the impossibility of this was comprehended and in some measure corrected. The Lutheran faith viewed this concession with suspicion and opposed it. What was the point of human life if, as in Calvinism, not even faith had to be proved. If, on the one hand, faith was naked, absolute, effective, but on the other, there was no distinction between human actions? There was no answer to this except perhaps in the morality of ordinary people – 'honesty in small things', 'upright living' – which developed at this time, forming a contrast to the *taedium vitae* of richer natures. For those who looked deeper saw the scene of their existence as a rubbish heap of partial, inauthentic actions. Life itself protested against this. It feels deeply that it is not there merely to be devalued by faith. It is overcome by deep horror at the idea that the whole of existence might proceed in such a way. The idea of death fills it with profound terror. Mourning is the state of mind in which feeling revives the empty world in the form of a mask, and derives an enigmatic satisfaction in contemplating it. Every feeling is bound to an *a priori* object, and the representation of this object is its phenomenology. Accordingly the theory of mourning, which emerged unmistakably as a *pendant* to the theory of tragedy, can only be developed in the description of that world which is revealed under the gaze of the melancholy man. For feelings, however vague they may seem when perceived by the self, respond like a motorial reaction to a concretely structured world. If the laws which govern the *Trauerspiel* are to be found, partly explicit, partly implicit, at the heart of mourning, the representation of these laws does not concern itself with the emotional condition of the poet or his public, but with a feeling which is released from any empirical subject and is intimately bound to the fullness of an object. This is a motorial attitude which has its appointed place in the hierarchy of intentions and is only called a feeling because it does not occupy the highest place. It is determined by an astounding tenacity of intention, which, among the feelings is matched perhaps only by love – and that not playfully. For whereas in the realm of the emotions it is not unusual for the relation between an intention and its object to alternate between attraction and repulsion, mourning is capable of a special intensification, a progressive deepening of its intention. Pensiveness is characteristic above all of the mournful. On the road to the object – no: within the object itself – this intention progresses as slowly and solemnly as the processions of the rulers advance. The passionate interest in the pomp of the *Haupt- und Staatsaktionen*, in part an escape from the restrictions of pious domesticity, was also a response to the natural affinity of pensiveness for gravity. In the latter it recognizes its own rhythm. The relationship between mourning and ostentation, which is so brilliantly displayed in the language of the baroque, has one of its sources here; so too does the self-absorption, to which these great constellations of the worldly chronicle seem but a game, which may, it is true, be worthy of attention for the meaning which can reliably be deciphered from it, but whose never-ending repetition secures the bleak rule of a melancholic distaste for life. Even from the heritage of the renaissance did this age derive material which could only deepen the contemplative paralysis. It is only one step from stoic ἀπάθεια to mourning, but of course a step which only becomes possible in Christianity. Like all the other antique qualities of the baroque, its stoicism too is pseudo-antique. The influence of rational pessimism is less important than the desolation with which the practice of stoicism confronts man. The deadening of the emotions, and the ebbing away of the waves of life which are the source of these emotions in the body, can increase the distance between the self and the surrounding world to the point of alienation from the body. As soon as this symptom of depersonalization was seen as an intense degree of mournfulness, the concept of the pathological state, in which the most simple object appears to be a symbol of some enigmatic wisdom because it lacks any natural, creative relationship to us, was set in an incomparably productive context. It accords with this that in the proximity of Albrecht Dürer's figure, *Melencolia*, the utensils of active life are lying around unused on the floor, as objects of contemplation. This engraving anticipates the baroque in many respects. In it the knowledge of the introvert and the investigations of the scholar have merged as intimately as in the men of the baroque. The Renaissance explores the universe; the baroque explores libraries. Its meditations are devoted to books. 'Kein grösseres Buch weiss die Welt als sich selbst; dessen fürnehmstes Theil aber ist der Mensch, welchem Gott anstatt eines schönen Titulbildes sein unvergleichliches,

Ebenbild hat vorgedruckt, überdas ihn zu einem Auszuge, Kern und Edelgesteine der übrigen Theile solches grossen Weltbuches gemacht.'2* The 'Book of nature' and the 'Book of the times' are objects of baroque meditation. In them it possesses something housed and roofed. But they also contain evidence of the social prejudice of the imperially crowned poet, who had long since forfeited the dignity of a Petrarch, and here looks down in superiority on the divertissements of his 'leisure hours'. Not least the book served as a permanent monument in a natural scene rich in literature. In a preface to the works of Ayrer, which is remarkable for the emphasis that is placed on melancholy as the mood of the times, the publisher seeks to recommend the book as an *arcanum*, immune to the assaults of melancholy. 'In bedenckung dessen, das die Pyramides, Seulen und Büldnussen allerhand materien mit der zeit schadhafft oder durch gewalt zerbrochen werden oder wol gar verfallen ... das wol gantze Städt versuncken, vntergangen vnd mit wasser bedeckt seien, da hergegen die Schrifften vnd Bücher dergleichen vntergang befreyet, dann was jrgendt in einem Landt oder Ort ab vnd vntergehet, das findet man in vielen andern vnd vngohlichen orten vnschwer wider, also das, Menschlicher weiss davon zu reden, nichts Tauerhaffters vnd vnsterblichers ist, als eben die Bücher.'3† It is a consequence of this same mixture of complacency and contemplativeness that 'baroque nationalism' 'never took the form of political action ... any more than baroque hostility to convention ever became concentrated into something similar to the revolutionary will of the *Sturm und Drang* or the romantic onslaught on the philistinism of state and public life'.4 The vain activity of the intriguer was regarded as the undignified antithesis of passionate contemplation, to which alone was attributed the power to release those in high places from the satanic

---

* The world knows no greater book than itself; but the greatest part of this book is man, before whom, in place of a fine frontispiece, God has printed his own likeness, and, besides, God has made him into an abstract, kernel, and jewel of the other parts of this great book of the world.

† Considering that pyramids, pillars, and statues of all kinds of material become damaged by time, or destroyed by violence, or simply decay ... that whole cities have sunk, disappeared, and are covered with water, whereas writings and books are immune from such destruction, for any that disappear or are destroyed in one country or place are easily found again in countless other places, so that in human experience there is nothing more enduring and immortal than books.

ensnarement of history, in which the baroque recognized only the political aspect. And yet: introversion also led only too easily into the abyss. This is illustrated by the theory of the melancholy disposition.

In this imposing heritage which the baroque received from the renaissance, and which was the result of almost two thousand years of work, posterity possesses a more direct commentary on the *Trauerspiel* than the poetics could provide. There is a harmonious relationship between this and the philosophical ideas and political convictions which underlie the representation of history as a, *Trauerspiel*. The prince is the paradigm of the melancholy man. Nothing demonstrates the frailty of the creature so drastically as the fact that even he is subject to it. In one of the most powerful passages of the *Pensées* Pascal gives voice to the feeling of his age with this very reflection. 'L'Ame ne trouve rien en elle qui la contente. Elle n'y voit rien qui ne l'afflige quand elle y pense. C'est ce qui la contraint de se répandre au dehors, et de chercher dans l'application aux choses extérieures, à perdre le souvenir de son état véritable. Sa joie consiste dans cet oubli; et il suffit, pour la rendre misérable, de l'obliger de se voir et d'être avec soi.'[5]* 'La dignité royale n'est-elle pas assez grande d'elle-même pour rendre celui qui la possède heureux par la seule vue de ce qu'il est? Faudra-t-il encore le divertir de cette pensée comme les gens du commun? Je vois bien que c'est rendre un homme heureux que de le détourner de la vue de ses misères domestiques, pour remplir toute sa pensée du soin de bien danser. Mais en sera-t-il de même d'un Roi? Et sera-t-il plus heureux en s'attachant à ces vains amusements qu'à la vue de sa grandeur? Quel objet plus satisfaisant pourrait-on donner à son esprit? Ne serait-ce pas faire tort à sa joie d'occuper son âme à penser à ajuster ses pas à la cadence d'un air, ou à placer adroitement une

---

* The soul finds nothing in itself that it can like; it sees nothing in itself but what makes it sad when it thinks of it: This is it which makes her look abroad, and to strive by the using of exteriour things, to lose the remembrance of her true State; her Joy consists in this forgetfulness, and 'tis enough to make her miserable, to oblige her to look upon her self, and to be with her self.

balle, au lieu de le laisser jouir en repos de la contemplation de la gloire majestueuse qui l'environne? Qu'on en fasse l'épreuve; qu'on laisse un Roi tout seul, sans aucune satisfaction des sens, sans aucun soin dans l'esprit, sans compagnie, penser à soi tout à loisir, et l'on verra qu'un Roi qui se voit est un homme plein de misères, et qu'il les ressent comme un autre. Aussi on évite cela soigneusement et il ne manque jamais d'y avoir auprès des personnes des Rois un grand nombre de gens qui veillent à faire succéder le divertissement aux affaires, et qui observent tout le temps de leur loisir pour leur fournir des plaisirs et des jeux, en sorte qu'il n'y ait point de vide. C'est-à-dire qu'ils sont environnés de personnes qui ont un soin merveilleux de prendre garde que le Roi ne soit seul et en état de penser à soi, sachant qu'il sera malheureux, tout Roi qu'il est, s'il y pense.'[6]* This is echoed on numerous occasions in the German *Trauerspiel*. No sooner is it uttered, than it is re-echoed. Leo Armenius speaks of the prince as follows: 'Er zagt vor seinem schwerdt. Wenn er zu tische geht, | Wird der gemischte wein, der in crystalle steht, | In gall und gifft verkehrt. Alsbald der tag erblichen, | Kommt die beochwärste schaar, das heer der angst geschlichen, | Und wacht in seinem bett. Er kan in helffenbein, | In purpur und scharlat niemahl so ruhig seyn | Als die, so ihren leib vertraun der harten erden. | Mag ja der kurtze schlaff ihm noch zu theile werden, | So fällt ihm Morpheus an und

---

* The Royal Dignity, is it not sufficiently great of itself to render him happy that enjoys it, by the sole considering what he is? What, must he yet be diverted from this Thought, as the commoner sort of Men? I see it is to make a Man Happy, to divert him from the sight of his domestick Troubles, by filling his Mind with the Thoughts of dancing well. But would it be the same to a King? And would he be happier in following these vain amusements, than in considering his Greatness? What more pleasing Object can one offer to his Mind? Would it not interrupt his Joy, to trouble his Thoughts about ordering his Steps, to keep time with the Musick or in compleatly ordering a Ball, instead of letting him in rest and quiet, enjoy the Pleasure of Contemplating the Majestical Glory wherewith he is invested? Let this be put to the Tryal; let a King be left all alone, without any satisfaction of the Senses, without any care of the Mind, without company, to think of himself at all leisure, and it will be found, that a King that sees himself, is a Man full of Miseries, and one that feels them as well as any other common Person. Also this is very carefully avoided, and there never fails to have near the Persons of Kings, a great many that continually watch to make Divertisements succeed after Business, and observe all their leisure time; to supply them with Pleasures and Pastimes, that there might be none of their time vacant. That is to say, that they are compass'd round with Persons that are wonderfully careful that the King should not be alone, and in a Condition to think of himself, knowing very well, that he would be Miserable, all King as he is, if he should.

mahlt ihm in der nacht I Durch graue bilder vor, was er bey lichte dacht, I Und schreckt ihn bald mit blut, bald mit gestürztem throne, I Mit brandt, mit ach un tod und hingeraubter crone.'[7]* Or in an epigram: 'Wo scepter, da ist furcht!'[8]† Or else: 'Die traurige Melankoley wohnt mehrenteiles in Pallästen.'[9]‡ These statements apply as much to the internal disposition of the sovereign as to his external situation, and can justifiably be associated with Pascal. For the melancholic is 'initially . . . like someone who has been bitten by a mad dog: he experiences terrifying dreams and is afraid for no good reason'.[10] Thus writes Aegidius Albertinus, the Munich didacticist, in *Lucifers Königreich und Seelengejäidt*, a work which contains much that is characteristic of the popular conception, precisely because it was uninfluenced by later speculations. The same book also says: 'An den Herrnhöfen ist es gemeinklich Kalt / vnnd allzeit Winter / dann die Sonn der Gerechtigkeit ist weit von jhnen . . . derowegen Zittern die Hofleut auss lauter Kälte / Forcht vnd Trawrigkeit.'[11] § These courtiers resemble the stigmatized courtier, as described by Guevara, whom Albertinus translated, and if one thinks here of the intriguer and visualizes the tyrant, then the image of the court is not so different from the image of hell, which is, after all, known as the place of eternal mournfulness. Moreover the 'Trauergeist'[12] ¶ which figures in Harsdörffer, is presumably none other than the devil. The same melancholy, whose domination over man is marked by shudders of fear, is regarded by scholars as the source of those manifestations which form the obligatory accompaniment when despots meet their end. It is taken for granted that serious cases culminate in violent insanity. Even in his down-

---

* He quails before his own sword. When he dines, the mingled wine that is served in crystal turns to gall and poison. As soon as the day is over the sabled throng, the army of dread creeps up and lies awake in his bed. In ivory, purple, and scarlet he can never be so peaceful as those who entrust their bodies to the hard earth. And if he should still be granted a short sleep, then Morpheus assails him and paints before him, at night-time, in gloomy pictures, what he thought by day, terrifying him with blood, with disenthronement, with conflagration, with woe and death and the loss of his crown.

† Where there is a sceptre, there is fear.

‡ Mournful melancholy mostly dwells in palaces.

§ In royal courts it is usually cold and the season is always winter, for the sun of righteousness is far away . . . and so courtiers shiver from sheer cold, fear, and mournfulness.

¶ spirit of mourning

fall the tyrant remains a model. 'He loses his senses while his body remains alive, for he no longer sees and hears the world which lives and moves about him, but only the lies which the devil paints in his brain and blows into his ears, until in the end he begins to rave and sinks into despair.' This is how Aegidius Albertinus describes the end of the melancholic. It is characteristic, though odd, that there is an attempt in *Sophonisbe* to refute the allegorical figure of 'Jealousy' by modelling its behaviour on that of the insane melancholic. If the allegorical refutation of jealousy seems strange here,[13] for Syphax's jealousy of Masruissa is more than justified, then it is most remarkable that at first the foolishness of Jealousy is characterized as a deception of the senses – in that beetles, grasshoppers, fleas, shadows, etc. are seen as rivals – but that then Jealousy, despite enlightenment by Reason, and recalling certain myths, suspects these creatures of being divine rivals in disguise. The whole is not therefore the characterization of a passion, but of a severe mental disorder. Albertinus explicitly recommends that melancholics be put in chains, 'damit auss solchen Fanatasten keine Wütrich / Tyrannen vnd der Jugendt oder Weibermörder gebrütet werden'.[14]* And Hunold's Nebuchadnezzar does indeed appear in chains.[15]

The codification of this syndrome dates from the high middle ages, and the form given to the theory of the temperaments by the leader of the medical school of Salerno, Constantinus Africanus, remained in force until the renaissance. According to this theory the melancholic is 'envious, mournful, greedy, avaricious, disloyal, timorous, and sallow',[16] and the *humor melancholicus* is the 'least noble complexion'.[17] The pathology of the humours saw the cause of these manifestations in an excess of the dry and cold element in man. This element was believed to be the black bile – *bilis innaturalis* or *atra* in contrast to *bilis naturalis* or *candida* – in the same way as the wet and warm (sanguinary) temperament was thought to be based in the blood, the wet and cold (phlegmatic) tem-

---

* lest such eccentrics turn into oppressors, tyrants, and murders of women and children

perament in water, and the dry and warm (choleric) temperament in the yellow bile. Further, according to this theory the spleen was a decisive factor in the formation of the noxious black bile. The thick and dry blood which flows into it and gets the upper hand, inhibits a man's gaiety and evokes hypochondria. The physiological explanation of melancholy – 'Oder ists nur phantasey, die den müden geist betrübet, | Welcher, weil er in dem cörper, seinen eignen kummer liebet?'[18]* asks Gryphius – could not but make an impression on the baroque, which had such a clear vision of the misery of mankind in its creaturely estate. If melancholy emerges from the depths of the creaturely realm to which the speculative thought of the age felt itself bound by the bonds of the church itself, then this explained its omnipotence. In fact it is the most genuinely creaturely of the contemplative impulses, and it has always been noticed that its power need be no less in the gaze of a dog than in the attitude of a pensive genius. 'Sir, sorrow was not ordained for beasts but men, yet if men do exceed in it they become beasts',[19] says Sancho Panza to Don Quixote. With a theological twist – and hardly as a result of his own deductions – the same idea occurs in Paracelsus. 'Die Fröligkeit vnn die Traurigkeit / ist auch geboren von Adam vnn Eua. Die Fröligkeit ist in Eua gelegen / vnn die Traurigkeit in Adam . . . So ein frölichs Mensch / als Eua gewesen ist / wirdt nimmermehr geboren: Dessgleichen als traurig als Adam gewesen ist / wirdt weiter kein Mensch geboren. Dann die zwo Materien Adae vnd Euae haben sich vermischt / dass die Traurigkeit temperiert ist worden vonn der Fröligkeit / vnnd die Fröligkeit dessgleichen von der Traurigkeit . . . Der Zorn / Tyranney, vnnd die Wuetend Eigenschafft / dessgleichen die Mildte / Tugentreiche / vnnd Bescheidenheit / ist auch von ihn beyden hie: dass Erste von Eua, das Ander von Adamo, und durch vermischung eingetheilt inn alle Proles.'[20]† Adam, as

---

* Or is it only imagination that oppresses the tired spirit, which, because it is in the body, loves its own affliction?

† Joyfulness and mournfulness were also born of Adam and Eve. Joyfulness was imparted to Eve and mournfulness to Adam . . . As joyful a person as Eve will never be born again: and similarly, as sorrowful a man as Adam will never be born again. For the two elements of Adam and Eve have been mingled so that mournfulness has been tempered with joyfulness, and joyfulness with mournfulness . . . Anger, tyranny, and the quality of violence, mildness, virtue, and modesty also derive from these two: the former from Eve, the latter from Adam, and by being mingled they have been divided among all their descendants.

the first born, a pure creation, possesses the creaturely mournfulness; Eve, created to cheer him, possesses joyfulness. The conventional association of melancholy and madness is not observed; Eve had to be designated as the instigator of the Fall. This gloomy conception of melancholy is not of course the original way of seeing it. In antiquity it was, rather, seen in a dialectical way. In a canonic passage in Aristotle genius is linked with madness within the concept of melancholy. The theory of the melancholy syndrome, as expounded in the thirtieth chapter of the *Problemata*, was effective for more than two thousand years. Hercules Aegyptiacus is the prototype of the genius who soars to the most lofty deeds before collapsing into madness. When they are so closely juxtaposed 'the antithesis of the most intense spiritual activity and its profoundest decline'[21] will always affect the beholder with the same deep horror. Apart from this, melancholy genius tends particularly to be revealed in the activity of divination. The view that prophetic ability is furthered by melancholy is an ancient one, and is derived from Aristotle's essay *De divinatione somnium*. And this survival from the propositions of antiquity emerges in the mediaeval tradition of the prophetic dreams granted precisely to melancholics. In the seventeenth century too such characteristics are encountered, though, of course, here they are always given a sombre twist: 'Allgemeine Traurigkeit ist eine Wahrsagerin alles zukünftigen Unheils.'* There is a most emphatic statement of the same idea in Tscherning's beautiful poem 'Melancholey Redet selber': 'Ich Mutter schweren bluts / ich faule Last der Erden I Wil sagen / was ich bin / und was durch mich kan werden. I Ich bin die schwartze Gall / 'nechst im Latein gehört / I Im Deutschen aber nun / und keines doch gelehrt. I Ich kan durch wahnwitz fast so gute Verse schreiben / I Als einer der sich läst den weisen Föbus treiben / I Den Vater aller Kunst. Ich fürchte nur allein I Es möchte bey der Welt der Argwohn von mir seyn / I Als ob vom Höllengeist ich etwas wolt' ergründen / I Sonst könt' ich vor der Zeit / was noch nicht ist / verkünden / I Indessen bleib ich doch stets eine Poetinn / I Besinge meinen fall / und was ich selber bin. I Und diesen Ruhm hat mir mein edles Blut geleget I Und Himmelischer

---

* General mournfulness is a prophet of all future woe

Geist / wann der sich in mir reget / I Entzünd ich als ein Gott die Hertzen
schleunig an / I Da gehn sie ausser sich / und suchen eine Bahn I Die mehr
als Weltlich ist. Hat jemand was gesehen / I Von der Sibyllen Hand so ists
durch mich geschehen.'[22]* The persistence of the deeper anthropological
analyses of this by no means contemptible scheme is astonishing. Even
Kant still painted the picture of the melancholic in the colours in which it
appeared in the work of the older theoreticians. In the *Beobachtungen über
das Gefühl des Schönen und Erhabenen* 'vengefulness . . . inspirations,
visions, temptations, . . . significant dreams, presentiments, and miraculous portents'[23] are ascribed to the melancholic.

Just as the ancient pathology of the humours was revived in the school of
Salerno, under the mediating influence of Arabian science, so too did
Arabia preserve the other Hellenistic science which nourished the doctrine of the melancholic: astrology. The principal source of the mediaeval
wisdom of the stars has been shown to be the astronomy of Abû Ma Sar,
which itself is dependent on the astronomy of late antiquity. The theory
of melancholy has a very close connection with the doctrine of stellar
influences. And of such influences only the most baleful, that of Saturn,
could rule over the melancholy disposition. However obvious the distinction between the astrological and the medical systems in the theory of the
melancholy temperament – Paracelsus, for instance, wanted to exclude
melancholy entirely from the latter and place it in the former[24] – however
obvious it must seem that the harmonious speculations, which were con-
cocted out of both, had only a coincidental relationship to empirical

---

* I, thick-blooded mother, rotten burden of the earth, wish to declare what I am, and what
can be accomplished through me. I am the black bile, first found in Latin, but now in German, but without being taught. Through madness I can write verses almost as good as one
who allows himself to be inspired by wise Phoebus, the father of all art. I fear only that the
world might be distrustful of me, lest I should want in some way to penetrate the spirit of
hell. Otherwise I could, before the day, foretell what has not yet come to pass. Meanwhile I
remain ever a poetess, singing of my own condition and what I am. This glory I owe to my
noble blood, and when the heavenly spirit moves me I swiftly enflame hearts like a god; they
are then beside themselves, and seek a path which transcends the earthly. If anyone has seen
anything from the hands of the Sibyls, then this was brought about by me.

reality, all the more astonishing, all the more difficult to explain, is the wealth of anthropological insight to which the theory gives rise. Out-of-the-way details, such as the melancholic's inclination for long journeys, crop up: hence the horizon of the sea in the background of Dürer's *Melencolia*; but also the fanatical exoticism of Lohenstein's dramas, and the delight of the age in descriptions of journeys. The astronomic explanation of this is obscure. But not if the distance of the planet from the earth and the consequently long duration of its orbit are no longer conceived in the negative sense of the Salerno doctors, but rather in a beneficent sense, with reference to the divine reason which assigns the menacing star to the remotest place, and if, on the other hand, the introspection of the melancholy man is understood with reference to Saturn which 'as the highest planet and the one farthest from everyday life, the originator of all deep contemplation, calls the soul from externalities to the inner world, causes it to rise ever higher, finally endowing it with the utmost knowledge and with the gift of prophecy.'[25] Re-interpretations of this kind, which give the transformation of these doctrines its fascination, reveal a dialectical trait in the idea of Saturn, which corresponds astonishingly to the dialectic of the Greek conception of melancholy. In their discovery of this most vital function of the Saturn-image Panofsky and Saxl have, in their fine study, *Dürers 'Melencolia I'*, completed and perfected the discoveries made by their predecessor, Giehlow, in his remarkable studies, *Dürers Stich 'Melencolia I' und der maximilianische Humanistenkreis*. The more recent work states: 'Now this *extremitas* which, for all subsequent centuries, made melancholy, in contrast to the other three "temperaments", so significant and problematic, so enviable and uncanny . . . – this also explains the deepest and most decisive correspondence between melancholy and Saturn . . . Like melancholy, Saturn too, this spirit of contradictions, endows the soul, on the one hand, with sloth and dullness, on the other, with the power of intelligence and contemplation; like melancholy, Saturn also constantly threatens those who are subject to him, however illustrious they may be in and for themselves, with the dangers of depression or manic ecstasy – he who . . . in the words of Ficino, "seldom imprints his mark on ordinary characters and ordinary destinies, but on men who are different from others, who are divine or bestial, happy or bowed down under the profoundest misery".[26] As far as this dialectic of Saturn is concerned, it requires an explanation 'which can only be sought in the inner structure of the mythological idea of Cronos as such . . . The idea of Cronos is not only dualistic where the god's outward activity is concerned, but also in relation to his own, as it were personal, destiny; and it is, moreover, dualistic to such an extent and to such a degree that Cronos could be described quite simply as a god of extremes. On the one hand he is the ruler of the golden age . . . – on the other he is the mournful, dethroned and dishonoured god . . .; on the one hand he creates (and devours) countless children – on the other he is condemned to eternal sterility; on the one hand he is . . . a monster to be outwitted by low cunning – on the other he is the old wise god who . . . is respected as the supreme intelligence, as a προμήθευς and προμάντιος . . . This immanent polarity of the Cronos-concept . . . is the ultimate explanation of the particular character of the astrological idea of Saturn – that character which is ultimately determined by an especially prominent and funda-mental dualism.'[27] 'In his commentary on Dante, Jacopo della Lana, for instance, was giving yet another clear elaboration and penetrating expla-nation of this immanent set of antitheses, when he argued that Saturn, by virtue of its quality as an earthly, cold, and dry planet, gives birth to totally material men, suited only to hard agricultural labour – but, in absolute contrast, by virtue of its position as the highest of the planets it gives birth to the most extremely spiritual *religiosi contemplativi*, who turn their backs on all earthly life.'[28] The history of the problem of melancholy unfolds within the perimeter of this dialectic. Its climax is reached with the magic of the Renaissance. Whereas the Aristotelian in-sights into the psychical duality of the melancholy disposition and the antithetical nature of the influence of Saturn had given way, in the middle ages, to a purely demonic representation of both, such as conformed with Christian speculation; with the Renaissance the whole wealth of ancient meditations re-emerged from the sources. The great achievement of Giehlow and the superior beauty of his work consist in the discovery of this turning point and the way it is presented with all the force of a drama-tic *peripeteia*. According to Warburg, in the Renaissance, when the re-interpretation of saturnine melancholy as a theory of genius was carried out with a radicalism unequalled even in the thought of antiquity, 'dread of Saturn . . . [occupied] the central position in astrological belief'.[29] In the middle ages the saturnine outlook had been taken over in many variants. The ruler of the months, 'the Greek god of time and the Roman spirit of the crops' have become Death the reaper, with his scythe, which is not destined for the corn but for the human race, just as it is no longer the annual cycle with its recurrence of seedtime, harvest and fallow winter, which rules the passage of time, but the implacable progression of every life towards death. But for this age, which was bent at all costs on gaining access to the sources of occult insight into nature, the melancholic posed the question of how it might be possible to discover for onself the spiritual powers of Saturn and yet escape madness. The problem was to separate sublime melancholy, the *melencolia 'illa heroica'* of Marsilius Ficinus, and of Melanchthon,[31] from the ordinary and pernicious kind. A precise regimen of body and soul is combined with astrological magic: the ennoblement of melancholy is the principal theme of the work by Marsilius Ficinus, *De vita triplici*. The magic square, which is inscribed on the tablet at the head of Dürer's *Melencolia*, is the planetary sign of Jupiter, whose influence counteracts the dismal forces of Saturn. Beside this tablet there hangs a balance as a reference to the constellation of Jupiter. 'Multo generosior est melancholia, si coniunctione Saturni et Iouis in libra temperetur, qualis uidetur Augusti melancholia fuisse.'[32]* Under the influence of Jupiter the harmful inspirations are transformed into beneficial ones, Saturn becomes the protector of the most sublime investigations; astrology itself is under his sway. Thus it was that Dürer could arrive at the intention 'of expressing the spiritual concentration of the prophet in the facial features of Saturn'.[33]

The theory of melancholy became crystallized around a number of ancient emblems, into which it was, of course, the unparalleled interpretative

---

* Melancholy is much more generous if it is tempered by the conjunction of Saturn and Jupiter in Libra, as the melancholy of Augustus seems to have been.

genius of the Renaissance which first read the imposing dialectic of these dogmas. One of the properties assembled around Dürer's figure of Melancholy is the dog. The similarity between the condition of the melancholic, as described by Aegidius Albertinus, and the state of rabies, is not accidental. According to ancient tradition 'the spleen is dominant in the organism of the dog'.[34] This he has in common with the melancholic. If the spleen, an organ believed to be particularly delicate, should deteriorate, then the dog is said to lose its vitality and become rabid. In this respect it symbolizes the darker aspect of the melancholy complexion. On the other hand the shrewdness and tenacity of the animal were borne in mind, so as to permit its use as the image of the tireless investigator and thinker. 'In his commentary on this hieroglyph Pierio Valeriano says explicitly that the dog which "faciem melancholicam prae se ferat"* would be the best at tracking and running.'[35] In Dürer's engraving, especially, the ambivalence of this is enriched by the fact that the animal is depicted asleep: bad dreams come from the spleen, but prophetic dreams are also the prerogative of the melancholic. As the common lot of princes and martyrs they are a familiar element in the *Trauerspiel*. But even these prophetic dreams are to be seen as arising from geomantic slumber in the temple of creation, and not as sublime or even sacred inspiration. For all the wisdom of the melancholic is subject to the nether world; it is secured by immersion in the life of creaturely things, and it hears nothing of the voice of revelation. Everything saturnine points down into the depths of the earth; and so the nature of the ancient god of agriculture is preserved. According to Agrippa of Nettesheim 'the seed of the depths and . . . the treasures of the earth'[36] are the gifts of Saturn. Here the downward gaze is characteristic of the saturnine man, who bores into the ground with his eyes. Tscherning shares this view: 'Wem ich noch unbekandt / der kennt mich von Geberden | Ich wende fort und für mein' Augen hin zur Erden / | Weil von der Erden ich zuvor entsprossen bin / | So seh ich nirgends mehr als auff die Mutter hin.'[37]† For the melancholic the inspirations of mother earth dawn from the night of

---

* Bears a melancholy face.

† Whosoever knows me not will recognise me from my attitude. I turn my eyes ever to the ground, because I once sprung from the earth, and so I now look only on my mother.

contemplation like treasures from the interior of the earth; the lightning-flash of intuition is unknown to him. The earth, previously important only as the cold, dry element acquires the full wealth of its esoteric meaning in a scientific reflection of Ficinus. Through the new analogy between the force of gravity and mental concentration, the old symbol is brought into the great interpretative process of the Renaissance philosophers. 'Naturalis autem causa esse videtur, quod ad scientias, praesertim difficiles consequendas, necesse est animum ab externis ad interna, tamquam a circumferentia quadam ad centrum sese recipere atque, dum speculatur, in ipso (ut ita dixerim) hominis centro stabilissime permanere. Ad centrum vero a circumferentia se colligere figique in centro, maxime terrae ipsius est proprium, cui quidem atra bilis persimilis est. Igitur atra bilis animum, ut se et colligat in unum et sistat in uno comtempleturque, assidue provocat. Atque ipsa mundi centro similis ad centrum rerum singularum cogit investigandum, evehitque ad altissima quaeque comprehendenda.'[38] Panofsky and Saxl are right to point out here, in contradiction of Giehlow, that there is no question of Ficinus 'recommending' concentration to the melancholic.[39] But their assertion is of little significance in comparison to the sequence of analogies which embraces thought – concentration – earth – gall, and this not simply in order to proceed from the first to the last link in the chain, but also, surely, in an unmistakable allusion to a new interpretation of the earth within the framework of the ancient wisdom of the theory of the temperaments. According to ancient opinion the earth owes its spherical form and so, as was already argued by Ptolemy, its perfection and its position at the centre of the universe, to the centripetal force of concentration. And so Giehlow's supposition that the sphere in Dürer's engraving is a symbol of the con-

---

*But it seems to be a natural principle that in the pursuit of especially abstruse patterns of intellectual enquiry the mind must be directed from outward matters to inward matters, from the circumference to the centre, as it were, and, while in pursuit of its speculations, should remain firmly established at the centre of the individual, so to speak. But the mental activity of being drawn away from the periphery and becoming fixed at the centre is the special characteristic of that area of the mind to which melancholy is akin. Melancholy therefore continually challenges the mind to concentrate itself and come to rest in one place and to practise contemplation. And since melancholy is in itself like the centre of the world, even so, it compels an investigation which reaches out to the centre of every individual object of enquiry, and leads to an understanding of the very deepest truths.

templative man must not simply be set aside.[40] And this, the 'ripest and most mysterious fruit of the cosmological culture of Maximilian's circle',[41] as Warburg has called it, may well be considered as a seed in which the allegorical flower of the baroque, still held in check by the power of a genius, lies ready to burst into bloom. There is, however, one symbol which seems to have been passed over in the re-discovery of the older symbols of melancholy embodied in this engraving and in contemporary speculation, and it seems equally to have escaped the attention of Giehlow and other scholars. This is the stone. Its place in the inventory of emblems is assured. Aegidius Albertinus writes of the melancholic: 'Die Trübsal, als welche sonsten das Herz in Demut erweicht, machet ihn nur immer störrischer in seinem verkehrten Gedanken, denn seine Tränen fallen ihm nicht ins Herz hinein, dass sie die Härtigkeit erweichten, sondern es ist mit ihm wie mit dem Stein, der nur von aussen schwitzt, wenn das Wetter feucht ist';[42]* and in reading these words one can barely restrain oneself from seeing, and following up, a special meaning. But the image is changed in Hallmann's funeral oration for Herr Samuel von Butschky: 'Er war von Natur tieffsinnig und Melancholischer Complexion, welche Gemüther einer Sache beständiger nachdencken / und in allen Actionibus behuttsam verfahren. Das Schlangenvolle Medusen Haupt / wie auch das Africanische Monstrum, nebst dem weinenden Crocodille dieser Welt konten seine Augen nicht verführen / viel weniger seine Glieder in einen unarthigen Stein verwandeln.'[43]† And the stone appears for a third time in Filidor's beautiful dialogue between melancholy and joy: 'Melankoley. Freude. Jene ist ein altes Weib / in verächtlichen Lumpen gekleidet / mit verhülleten [sic] Haupt / sitzet auff einem Stein / unter einem dürren Baum / den Kopff in den Schooss legend / Neben ihr stehet eine Nacht-Eule . . . Melankoley: Der harte Stein / der dürre Baum / | Der abgestorbenen Zypressen / | Giebt meiner Schwermuth sichern Raum | und

---

* The grief, which otherwise moves the heart to meekness, only makes him more and more obstinate in his perverse thoughts, for his tears do not fall into his heart and soften its hardness, but he resembles a stone which, when the weather is damp, only sweats outwardly;

† He was by nature pensive and of a melancholy complexion, which dispositions ponder a matter more constantly and proceed cautiously in all their actions. Neither the serpent-headed Medusa, nor the African monster, nor the weeping crocodile of this world could mislead his gaze, still less transform his limbs into an unfeeling stone.

macht der Scheelsucht mich vergessen . . . Freude: Wer ist diss Murmel-
thier I hier an den dürren Ast gekrümmet? I Der tieffen Augen röthe I
straalt / wie ein Blut Comete / I der zum Verderb und Schrecken glimmet
. . . I Jetzt kenn ich dich / du Feindin meiner Freuden / I Melanckoley /
erzeugt im Tartarschlund I vom drey geköpfften Hund'. O! sollt' ich dich
in meiner Gegend leiden? I Nein / warlich / nein! I der kalte Stein / I der
Blätterlose Strauch / I muss aussgerottet seyn I und du / Unholdin /
auch.'44*

It may be that all that is to be seen in the emblem of the stone are the most
obvious features of the cold, dry earth. But it is quite conceivable and, in
view of the passage from Albertinus, by no means improbable, that in the
inert mass there is a reference to the genuinely theological conception of
the melancholic, which is to be found in one of the seven deadly sins. This
is *acedia*, dullness of the heart, or sloth. The feeble light and the slowness
of Saturn in its orbit establish a connection between this condition and
the melancholic, for which there is evidence – on an astrological or some
other basis – in a manuscript of the thirteenth century. 'Von der tracheit.
Du vierde houbet sunde ist. tracheit. an gottes dienste. Du ist so ich mich
kere. von eime erbeitsamen. unt sweren guoten werke. zuo einer itelen
ruowe. So ich mih kere. von deme guoten werke. wande ez mir svere ist.
da von kumet bitterkeit des hercen.'45† In Dante *acedia* is the fifth link
in the order of the principal sins. In its circle of hell icy cold rules, and this
refers back to the data of the pathology of the humours, the cold, dry

* Melancholy. Joy. The former is an old woman, dressed in contemptible rags with her
head shrouded, scated on a stone beneath a dead tree, supporting her head in her hand;
beside her stands a night-owl . . . Melancholy: The hard stone, the dead cypress tree provide
a secure place for my heaviness of heart, and allow me to forget jealousy . . . Joy: What is
this marmot, crouching here by the withered branch? Its red eyes gleam like a bloody comet
threatening destruction and horror . . . Now I recognise you, enemy of my joys, Melancholy,
begotten in the jaws of Tartarus by the three-headed dog. Oh! must I suffer you in my
presence? No, truly no! The cold stone, the leafless bush, must be uprooted, and you,
monster, too.
† On Sloth. The fourth principal sin is sloth in the service of God. That is if I should turn
from a laborious and demanding good work to idle rest. If I turn from the good work when it
becomes heavy, this gives rise to bitterness of the heart.

constitution of the earth. The melancholy of the tyrant appears in a new, clearer light when seen as *acedia*. Albertinus expressly includes *acedia* in the melancholy syndrome: 'Artlich wirdt die Accidia oder Trägheit dem Biss eines wütigen Hundts verglichen / dann wer von demselbigen gebissen wird / der vberkompt alsbaldt erschröckliche Träum / er förchtet sich im Schlaf / wird Wütig / Vnsinnig / verwirfft alles Getranck / förchtet das Wasser / bellet wie ein Hund / vnd wirdt dermassen forchtsamb / dass er auss forcht niderfellt. Dergleichen Leut sterben auch bald / wann jhnen nicht geholfen wirdt.'[46]* The indecisiveness of the prince, in particular, is nothing other than saturnine *acedia*. Saturn causes people to be 'apathetic, indecisive, slow'.[47] The fall of the tyrant is caused by indolence of the heart. Just as this characterizes the figure of the tyrant so does unfaithfulness – another feature of saturnine man – characterize the figure of the courtier. It is not possible to conceive of anything more inconstant than the mind of the courtier, as depicted in the *Trauerspiel*: treachery is his element. It is not a sign of superficiality or clumsy characterization on the part of the authors that, at critical moments, the parasites abandon the ruler, without any pause for reflection, and go over to the other side. It is rather that their action reveals an unscrupulousness, which is in part a consciously Machiavellian gesture, but is also a dismal and melancholy submission to a supposedly unfathomable order of baleful constellations, which assumes an almost material character. Crown, royal purple, sceptre are indeed ultimately properties, in the sense of the drama of fate, and they are endowed with a fate, to which the courtier, as the augur of this fate, is the first to submit. His unfaithfulness to man is matched by a loyalty to these things to the point of being absorbed in contemplative devotion to them. Only in this hopeless loyalty to the creaturely, and to the law of its life, does the concept behind this behaviour attain its adequate fulfilment. In other words, all essential decisions in relation to men can offend against loyalty; they are subject to higher laws. Loyalty is completely appropriate only to the relationship of man to the

---

* *Acedia* or sloth is comparable in kind to the bite of a mad dog, for whoever is bitten by the same is immediately assailed by horrible dreams, he is terrified in his sleep, becomes enraged and senseless, rejects all drink, is afraid of water, barks like a dog, and becomes so fearful that he falls down in terror. Such men die very soon if they receive no help.

world of things. The latter knows no higher law, and loyalty knows no object to which it might belong more exclusively than the world of things. And indeed this world is constantly calling upon it; and every loyal vow or memory surrounds itself with the fragments of the world of things as its very own, not-too-demanding objects. Clumsily, indeed unjustifiably, loyalty expresses, in its own way, a truth for the sake of which it does, of course, betray the world. Melancholy betrays the world for the sake of knowledge. But in its tenacious self-absorption it embraces dead objects in its contemplation, in order to redeem them. The poet, of whom the following has been said, speaks from the spirit of melancholy. 'Péguy used to speak of that irredeemability of things, that recalcitrance, that heaviness of things, indeed of beings, which in the end allows a little ash to survive from the efforts of heroes and saints.'[48] The persistence which is expressed in the intention of mourning, is born of its loyalty to the world of things. This is how we should understand that unfaithfulness which almanacs attribute to saturnine man, and this is how we should interpret that completely isolated dialectic contrast, the 'faithfulness in love' which Abû Ma sar ascribes to saturnine man.[49] Faithfulness is the rhythm of the emanatively descending levels of intention which reflect the appropriately transformed ascending ones of neo-Platonic theosophy.

In the German *Trauerspiel* the characteristic attitude is that of the reaction of the Counter-Reformation, and so the determining factor in the creation of dramatic types is the mediaeval scholastic image of melancholy. But in its formal totality this drama diverges fundamentally from such a typology; its style and language are inconceivable without that audacious twist thanks to which the speculations of the Renaissance were able to recognize in the features of the sorrowful Contemplator[50] the reflection of a distant light, shining back from the depths of self-absorption. This age succeeded (at least once) in conjuring up the human figure who corresponded to this dichotomy between the neo-antique and the mediaeval light in which the baroque saw the melancholic. But Germany was not the country which was able to do this. The figure is Hamlet. The secret of his person is contained within the playful, but for that very reason firmly circumscribed, passage through all the stages in this complex of intentions, just as the secret of his fate is contained in an action which, according to this, his way of looking at things, is perfectly homogeneous. For the *Trauerspiel* Hamlet alone is a spectator by the grace of God; but he cannot find satisfaction in what he sees enacted, only in his own fate. His life, the exemplary object of his mourning, points, before its extinction, to the Christian providence in whose bosom his mournful images are transformed into a blessed existence. Only in a princely life such as this is melancholy redeemed, by being confronted with itself. The rest is silence. For everything that has not been lived sinks beyond recall in this space where the word of wisdom leads but a deceptive, ghostly existence. Only Shakespeare was capable of striking Christian sparks from the baroque rigidity of the melancholic, un-stoic as it is un-Christian, pseudo-antique as it is pseudo-pietistic. If the profound insight with which Rochus von Liliencron recognized the ascendancy of Saturn and marks of *acedia* in Hamlet,[51] is not to be deprived of its finest object, then this drama will also be recognized as the unique spectacle in which these things are overcome in the spirit of Christianity. It is only in this prince that melancholy self-absorption attains to Christianity. The German *Trauerspiel* was never able to inspire itself to new life; it was never able to awaken within itself the clear light of self-awareness. It remained astonishingly obscure to itself, and was able to portray the melancholic only in the crude and washed-out colours of the mediaeval complexion-books. What then is the purpose of this excursus? The images and figures presented in the German *Trauerspiel* are dedicated to Dürer's genius of winged melancholy. The intense life of its crude theatre begins in the presence of this genius.

Allegory and Trauerspiel

Wer diese gebrechliche Hüten / wo das Elend alle
Ecken zieret / mit einem vernünftigen Wortschlusse
wolte begläntzen / der würde keinen unförmlichen
Ausspruch machen / noch das Zielmass der gegründe-
ten Wahrheit überschreiten / wann er die Welt nennte
einen allgemeinen Kauffladen / eine Zollbude des
Todes / wo der Mensch die gangbahre Wahre / der Tod
der wunderbahre Handels-Mann / Gott der gewisseste
Buchhalter / das Grab aber das versiegelte Gewand und
Kauff-Hauss ist.
Christoph Männling: *Schaubühne des Todes | oder
Leich-Reden**

For over a hundred years the philosophy of art has been subject to the
tyranny of a usurper who came to power in the chaos which followed in
the wake of romanticism. The striving on the part of the romantic
aestheticians after a resplendent but ultimately non-committal knowledge
of an absolute has secured a place in the most elementary theoretical
debates about art for a notion of the symbol which has nothing more than
the name in common with the genuine notion. This latter, which is the

---

* Whosoever would grace this frail cottage, in which poverty adorns every corner, with a
rational epitome, would be making no inapt statement nor overstepping the mark of well-
founded truth if he called the world a general store, a customs-house of death, in which man
is the merchandise, death the wondrous merchant, God the most conscientious book-
keeper, but the grave the bonded drapers' hall and ware house.

Christoph Männling: *Theatre of death, or funeral orations*

one used in the field of theology, could never have shed that sentimental twilight over the philosophy of beauty which has become more and more impenetrable since the end of early romanticism. But it is precisely this illegitimate talk of the symbolic which permits the examination of every artistic form 'in depth', and has an immeasurably comforting effect on the practice of investigation into the arts. The most remarkable thing about the popular use of the term is that a concept which, as it were categorically, insists on the indivisible unity of form and content, should nevertheless serve the philosophical extenuation of that impotence which, because of the absence of dialectical rigour, fails to do justice to content in formal analysis and to form in the aesthetics of content. For this abuse occurs wherever in the work of art the 'manifestation' of an 'idea' is declared a symbol. The unity of the material and the transcendental object, which constitutes the paradox of the theological symbol, is distorted into a relationship between appearance and essence. The introduction of this distorted conception of the symbol into aesthetics was a romantic and destructive extravagance which preceded the desolation of modern art criticism. As a symbolic construct, the beautiful is supposed to merge with the divine in an unbroken whole. The idea of the unlimited imma-nence of the moral world in the world of beauty is derived from the theosophical aesthetics of the romantics. But the foundations of this idea were laid long before. In classicism the tendency to the apotheosis of existence in the individual who is perfect, in more than an ethical sense, is clear enough. What is typically romantic is the placing of this perfect individual within a progression of events which is, it is true, infinite but is nevertheless redemptive, even sacred.[1] But once the ethical subject has become absorbed in the individual, then no rigorism – not even Kantian rigorism – can save it and preserve its masculine profile. Its heart is lost in the beautiful soul. And the radius of action – no, only the radius of the culture – of the thus perfected beautiful individual is what describes the circle of the 'symbolic'. In contrast the baroque apotheosis is a dialectical one. It is accomplished in the movement between extremes. In this eccentric and dialectic process the harmonious inwardness of classicism plays no role, for the reason that the immediate problems of the baroque, being politico-religious problems, did not so much affect the individual and his ethics as his religious community. Simultaneously with its profane concept of the symbol, classicism develops its speculative counterpart, that of the allegorical. A genuine theory of the allegory did not, it is true, arise at that time, nor had there been one previously. It is nevertheless legitimate to describe the new concept of the allegorical as speculative because it was in fact adapted so as to provide the dark background against which the bright world of the symbol might stand out. Allegory, like many other old forms of expression, has not simply lost its meaning by 'becoming antiquated'. What takes place here, as so often, is a conflict between the earlier and the later form which was all the more inclined to a silent settlement in that it was non-conceptual, profound, and bitter. The symbolizing mode of thought of around 1800 was so foreign to allegorical expression in its original form that the extremely isolated attempts at a theoretical discussion are of no value as far as the investigation of allegory is concerned – although they are all the more symptomatic of the depth of the antagonism. Taken out of its context, the following statement by Goethe may be described as a negative, *a posteriori* construction of allegory: 'There is a great difference between a poet's seeking the particular from the general and his seeing the general in the particular. The former gives rise to allegory, where the particular serves only as an instance or example of the general; the latter, however, is the true nature of poetry: the expression of the particular without any thought of, or reference to, the general. Whoever grasps the particular in all its vitality also grasps the general, without being aware of it, or only becoming aware of it at a late stage.'[2] Thus did Goethe, in response to Schiller, declare his position with regard to allegory. He cannot have regarded it as an object worthy of great attention. More expansive is a later remark by Schopenhauer on the same lines. 'Now, if the purpose of all art is the communication of the apprehended Idea . . .; further, if starting from the concept is objectionable in art, then we shall not be able to approve, when a work of art is intentionally and avowedly chosen to express a concept; this is the case in *allegory* . . . When, therefore, an allegorical picture has also artistic value, this is quite separate from and independent of what it achieves as allegory. Such a work of art serves two purposes simultaneously, namely the expression of a concept and the expression of an Idea. Only the latter can be an aim of art; the other is a foreign aim, namely the trifling amusement of carving a picture to serve at the same time as an inscription, as a hieroglyphic ... It is true that an allegorical picture can in just this quality produce a vivid impression on the mind and feelings; but under the same circumstances even an inscription would have the same effect. For instance, if the desire for fame is firmly and permanently rooted in a man's mind ... and if he now stands before the *Genius of Fame* [by Annibale Carracci] with its laurel crowns, then his whole mind is thus excited, and his powers are called into activity. But the same thing would also happen if he suddenly saw the word "fame" in large clear letters on the wall.'[3] For all that this last comment comes close to touching on the essence of allegory, these observations are nevertheless prevented from standing out in any way from among the perfunctory dismissals of the allegorical form by their excessively logical character, which, in accepting the distinction between 'the expression of a concept and the expression of an idea', accepts precisely that untenable modern view of allegory and symbol – despite the fact that Schopenhauer uses the concept of the symbol differently. Such arguments have continued to be the standard ones until very recently. Even great artists and exceptional theoreticians, such as Yeats,[4] still assume that allegory is a conventional relationship between an illustrative image and its abstract meaning. Generally authors have only a vague knowledge of the authentic documents of the modern allegorical way of looking at things, the literary and visual emblem-books of the baroque. The spirit of these works speaks so feebly in the late and more well-known epigones of the late eighteenth century that only the reader of the more original works experiences the allegorical intention in all its strength. These works were, however, excluded from consideration by neo-classical prejudice. That is, to put it briefly, the denunciation of a form of expression, such as allegory, as a mere mode of designation. Allegory – as the following pages will serve to show – is not a playful illustrative technique, but a form of expression, just as speech is expression, and, indeed, just as writing is. This was the *experimentum crucis*. Writing seemed to be a conventional system of signs, *par excellence*. Schopenhauer is not alone in dismissing allegory with the statement that it is not essentially different from writing. This objection is of fundamental importance for our attitude to every major object of baroque philology. And however difficult, however remote it may seem, the establishment of the philosophical basis of the latter is absolutely indispensable. And the discussion of allegory demands a central place in it; the beginnings are unmistakably evident in *Deutsche Barockdichtung* by Herbert Cysarz. But either because the declaration of the primacy of classicism as the entelechy of baroque literature frustrates any insight into the essence of this literature – and most especially the understanding of allegory – or because the persistent anti-baroque prejudice pushes classicism into the foreground as its own forefather, the new discovery that allegory 'is the dominant stylistic law, particularly in the high baroque',[5] comes to nothing because of the attempt to exploit the formulation of this new insight, quite incidentally, as a slogan. It is 'not so much the art of the symbol as the technique of allegory' which is characteristic of the baroque in contrast to classicism. The character of the sign is thus attributed to allegory even with this new development. The old prejudice, which Creuzer gave its own linguistic coinage in the term *Zeichenallegorie*[7] [sign-allegory], remains in force.

Otherwise, however, the great theoretical discussions of symbolism in the first volume of Creuzer's *Mythologie* are, indirectly, of immense value for the understanding of the allegorical. Alongside the banal older doctrine which survives in them, they contain observations whose epistemological elaboration could have led Creuzer far beyond the point he actually reached. Thus he defines the essence of symbols, whose status, that is to say whose distance from the allegorical, he is anxious to preserve, in terms of the following four factors: 'The momentary, the total, the inscrutability of its origin, the necessary';[8] and elsewhere he makes the following excellent observation about the first of these factors: 'That stirring and occasionally startling quality is connected to another, that of brevity. It is like the sudden appearance of a ghost, or a flash of lightning which suddenly illuminates the dark night. It is a force which seizes hold of our entire being . . . Because of its fruitful brevity they [the ancients] compare it in particular with laconism . . . In important situations in life, when every moment conceals a future rich in consequences, which holds the soul in suspense, in fateful moments, the ancients also were prepared for the divine signals which they . . . called *symbola*.'[9] On the other hand 'the requirements of the symbol' are 'clarity . . . brevity . . . grace and beauty';[10] The first and the last two of these reveal distinctly an outlook which Creuzer has in common with the classicistic theories of the symbol. This is the doctrine of the artistic symbol, which, in its supremacy, is to be distinguished from the restricted religious or even mystical symbol. There can be no question but that Winckelmann's veneration of Greek sculpture, whose divine images serve as examples in this context, exerted a decisive influence on Creuzer here. The artistic symbol is plastic. The spirit of Winckelmann speaks in Creuzer's antithesis of the plastic and the mystic symbol. 'What is dominant here is the inexpressible which, in seeking expression, will ultimately burst the too fragile vessel of earthly form by the infinite power of its being. But herewith the clarity of vision is itself immediately destroyed, and all that remains is speechless wonder.' In the plastic symbol 'the essence does not strive for the extravagant but, obedient to nature, adapts itself to natural forms, penetrates and animates them. That conflict between the infinite and the finite is therefore resolved by the former becoming limited and so human. Out of this purification of the pictorial on the one hand, and the voluntary renunciation of the infinite on the other, grows the finest fruit of all that is symbolic. This is the symbol of the gods, which miraculously unites the beauty of form with the highest fullness of being and which, because it receives its most perfect execution in Greek sculpture, may be called the plastic symbol.'[11] Classicism looked to 'the human' as the highest 'fullness of being', and, since it could not but scorn allegory, it grasped in this yearning only an appearance of the symbolic. Accordingly there is also to be found in Creuzer a comparison of the symbol 'with the allegory, which in everyday speech is so often confused with the symbol',[12] which is quite close to the theories then prevalent. The 'difference between symbolic and allegorical representation' is explained as follows: 'The latter signifies merely a general concept, or an idea which is different from itself; the former is the very incarnation and embodiment of the idea. In the former a process of substitution takes place . . . In the latter the concept itself has descended into our physical world, and we see it itself directly in the image.' But here Creuzer reverts to his original idea. 'The distinction between the two modes is therefore to be sought in the momentariness which allegory lacks . . . There [in the symbol] we have momentary totality; here we have progression in a series of moments. And for this reason it is allegory, and not the symbol, which embraces myth . . ., the essence of which is most adequately expressed in the progression of the epic poem.'[13] But far from this insight leading to a new evaluation of the allegorical mode, there is another passage in which, on the basis of these propositions, the following is said about the Ionian philosophers: 'They restore the symbol, supplanted by the more effusive legend, to its old rights: the symbol, which was originally a child of sculpture and is still incorporated in discourse, and which, because of its significant concision, because of the totality and the contained exuberance of its essence, is far better able than legend to point to the one and inexpressible truth of religion.'[14] Görres makes the following acute observation on these and similar arguments in a letter: 'I have no use for the view that the symbol is being, and allegory is sign . . . We can be perfectly satisfied with the explanation that takes the one as a sign for ideas, which is self-contained, concentrated, and which steadfastly remains itself, while recognizing the other as a successively progressing, dramatically mobile, dynamic representation of ideas which has acquired the very fluidity of time. They stand in relation to each other as does the silent, great and mighty natural world of mountains and plants to the living progression of human history.'[15] This puts many things right. For the conflict between a theory of the symbol, which emphasizes the organic, mountain and plant-like quality in the make-up of the symbol on the one hand, and Creuzer's emphasis of its momentary quality, points very clearly to the real state of affairs. The measure of time for the experience of the symbol is the mystical instant in which the symbol assumes the meaning into its hidden and, if one might say so, wooded interior. On the other hand, allegory is not free from a corresponding dialectic, and the contemplative calm with which it immerses itself into the depths which separate visual being from meaning, has none of the disinterested self-sufficiency which is present in the apparently related intention of the sign. The violence of the dialectic movement within these allegorical depths must become clearer in the study of the form of the *Trauerspiel* than anywhere else. That worldly, historical breadth which Görres and Creuzer ascribe to allegorical intention is, as natural history, as the earliest history of signifying or intention, dialectical in character. Within the decisive category of time, the introduction of which into this field of semiotics was the great romantic achievement of these thinkers, permits the incisive, formal definition of the relationship between symbol and allegory. Whereas in the symbol destruction is idealized and the transfigured face of nature is fleetingly revealed in the light of redemption, in allegory the observer is confronted with the *facies hippocratica* of history as a petrified, primordial landscape. Everything about history that, from the very beginning, has been untimely, sorrowful, unsuccessful, is expressed in a face – or rather in a death's head. And although such a thing lacks all 'symbolic' freedom of expression, all classical proportion, all humanity – nevertheless, this is the form in which man's subjection to nature is most obvious and it significantly gives rise not only to the enigmatic question of the nature of human existence as such, but also of the biographical historicity of the individual. This is the heart of the allegorical way of seeing, of the baroque, secular explanation of history as the Passion of the world; its importance resides solely in the stations of its decline. The greater the significance, the greater the subjection to death, because death digs most deeply the jagged line of demarcation between physical nature and significance. But if nature has always been subject to the power of death, it is also true that it has always been allegorical. Significance and death both come to fruition in historical development, just as they are closely linked as seeds in the creature's graceless state of sin. The perspective of allegory as a development of myth, which plays a role in Creuzer's work, ultimately appears, from the same baroque standpoint, as a moderate and more modern perspective. Significantly Voss opposes it: 'Like all sensible people Aristarchus took Homer's legends of universe and divinity as the naive beliefs of the Nestorian heroic age. Krates, however, regarded them as primordial symbols of mysterious orphic doctrines, principally from Egypt, and in this he was followed by the geographer, Strabo and the later grammarians. Such use of symbols, which arbitrarily transposed the experiences and articles of belief of the post-Homeric age back into the distant past, remained dominant throughout the monkish centuries and was generally called allegory.'[16] The writer disapproves of this association of myth and allegory; but he allows that it is conceivable, and it rests on a theory of legend such as was developed by Creuzer. The epic poem is in fact a history of signifying nature in its classical form, just as allegory is its baroque form. Given its relationship to both of these intellectual currents, romanticism was bound to bring epic and allegory closer together. And thus Schelling formulated the programme for the allegorical exegesis of epic poetry in the famous dictum: *The Odyssey* is the history of the human spirit, *The Iliad* is the history of nature.

It is by virtue of a strange combination of nature and history that the allegorical mode of expression is born. Karl Giehlow devoted his life to shedding light on this origin. Only since his monumental study, *Die Hieroglyphenkunde des Humanismus in der Allegorie der Renaissance, besonders der Ehrenpforte Kaisers Maximilian I*, has it been possible to establish historically both the fact and the nature of the difference between the modern allegory which arose in the sixteenth century and that of the middle ages. It is true – and the great significance of this will emerge in the course of this study – the two are precisely and essentially connected. Yet only where this connection stands out as a constant against the historical variable can it be recognized in its substance; and this distinction has only become possible since the discoveries of Giehlow. Among earlier investigators Creuzer, Görres, and – especially – Herder seem to have been the only ones to have had an eye for the riddles of this form of expression. With reference to the very epochs in question, this last-named concedes: 'The history of this age and its taste is still very obscure. [17] His own supposition is wrong on historical grounds: 'Painters imitated the old works of monks; but with great understanding and close observation of objects, so that I might almost call this age the emblematic age';[18] but he speaks from an intuitive understanding of the substance of this literature which sets him above the romantic mythologists. Creuzer refers to him in discussions of the modern emblem. 'Later, too, this love of the allegorical persisted, indeed it seemed to gain a new lease of life at the beginning of the sixteenth century . . . In the same period allegory among the Germans, because of the seriousness of their national character, took a more ethical direction. With the advances of the Reformation the symbolic inevitably lost its importance as an expression of religious mysteries . . . The ancient love of the visual expressed itself . . . in symbolic representations of a moral and political kind. Indeed allegory now had even to make manifest the newly discovered truth. One of our nation's great writers who, in keeping with his intellectual breadth, does not find this expression of German strength either childish or immature but dignified and worthy of consideration, finds cause in the prevalence of this mode of representation at that time, to call the age of the Reformation the emblematic age, and makes observations about it which are well worth taking to heart.'[19] Given the uncertainties that were then prevalent, even Creuzer could correct only the evaluation, not the understanding of allegory. Not until the appearance of Giehlow's work, a work of historical character, does it become possible to achieve an analysis of this form in historical-philosophical terms. He discovered the impulse for its development in the efforts of the humanist scholars to decipher hieroglyphs. In their attempts they adopted the method of a pseudo-epigraphical *corpus* written at the end of the second, or possibly even the fourth century A.D., the *Hieroglyphica* of Horapollon. Their subject – and this both establishes their character and was the basic determining factor in their influence on the humanists – consists entirely of the so-called symbolic or enigmatic hieroglyphs, mere pictorial signs, such as were presented to the hierogrammatist, aside from the ordinary phonetic signs, in the context of religious instruction, as the ultimate stage in a mystical philosophy of nature. The obelisks were approached with memories of this reading in mind, and a misunderstanding thus became the basis of the rich and infinitely widespread form of expression. For the scholars proceeded from the allegorical exegesis of Egyptian hieroglyphs, in which historical and cultic data were replaced by natural-philosophical, moral, and mystical commonplaces, to the extension of this new kind of writing. The books of iconology were produced, which not only developed the phrases of this writing, and translated whole sentences 'word for word by special pictorial signs',[20] but frequently took the form of lexica.[21] 'Under the leadership of the artist-scholar, Albertus, the humanists thus began to write with concrete images *(rebus)* instead of letters; the word "rebus" thus originated on the basis of the enigmatic hieroglyphs, and medallions, columns, triumphal arches, and all the conceivable artistic objects produced by the Renaissance, were covered with such enigmatic devices.'[22] Along with the Greek doctrine of the freedom of artistic vision, the Renaissance also took over from antiquity the Egyptian dogma of artistic constraint. These two views could not but stand in conflict; and if, at first, this conflict was suppressed by artists of genius, as soon as the world became dominated by a hieratic spirit, the latter inevitably triumphed.'[23] In the works of the mature baroque the distance from the beginnings of emblematics in the previous century becomes progressively more apparent, the similarity to the symbol becomes more fleeting, and the hieratic ostentation more assertive. Something approaching a natural theology of writing already plays a role in the *Libri de re aedificatoria decem* by Leon Battista Alberti. 'In the context of an investigation into the titles, signs and sculptures which are suitable for sepulchral monuments he takes the opportunity to draw a parallel between alphabetic script and the Egyptian signs. He sees it as a failing of the former that it is only known to its own age and therefore must inevitably fall into oblivion . . . and in contrast he extols the Egyptian system because it represents god, for instance, by an eye, nature by a vulture, time by a circle, peace by an ox.'[24] But at the same time speculation became applied to a less rational apologia for emblematics, which much more clearly acknowledges the hieratic quality of the form. In his commentary on *The Enneads* of Plotinus, Marsilius Ficinus observes that in hieroglyphics the Egyptian priests 'must have wanted to create something corresponding to divine thought, since divinity surely possesses knowledge of all things, not as a changing idea, but as the simple and fixed form of the thing itself, so to speak. Hieroglyphs, then, are an image of divine ideas! As an example he takes the hieroglyph of the winged snake biting its own tail, used to signify the concept of time. For the diversity and mobility of the human idea of time, how in its swift circle it links beginning and end, how it teaches wisdom, brings things and removes them, this entire sequence of thoughts is contained in the specific and fixed image of the circle formed by the snake.'[25] Nothing less than the theological conviction that the hieroglyphs of the Egyptians contain a hereditary wisdom, which illuminates every obscurity of nature, is expressed in the following sentence of Pierio Valeriano: 'Quippe cum hieroglyphice loqui nihil aliud sit, quam diuinarum humanarumque rerum naturam aperire.'[26]* The 'Epistola nuncupatoria' to these same *Hieroglyphica* contain the following remarks: 'Nec deerit occasio recte sentientibus, qui accommodate ad religionem nostram haec retulerint et exposuerint. Nec etiam arborum et herbarum consideratio nobis ociosa est, cum B. Paulus et ante eum Dauid ex rerum creatarum cognitione, Dei magnitudinem et dignitatem intellegi tradant. Quae cum ita sint, quis nostrum tam torpescenti, ac terrenis faecibusque immerso erit animo, qui se non innumeris obstrictum a Deo beneficiis fateatur, cum se hominem creatum uideat, et omnia quae coelo, aëre, aqua, terraque continent, hominis causa generata esse.'[27]† 'Hominis causa' should not be considered in terms of the teleology of the Enlightenment, for which human happiness was the supreme purpose of nature, but in terms of a quite different, baroque, teleology. Devoted neither to the earthly nor to the moral happiness of creatures, its exclusive aim is their mysterious instruction. From the point of view of the baroque, nature serves the purpose of expressing its meaning, it is the emblematic representation of its sense, and as an allegorical representation it remains irremediably different from its historical realization. In moral examples and in catastrophes history served only as an aspect of the subject matter

---

*Since speaking in hieroglyphic mode means unveiling the nature of things human and divine.

† Nor shall there be lacking any opportunity for men of proper sensibility to expound and explore these matters in a way which fits our religion. Not even a consideration of trees or of vegetation is gratuitous in our purposes, since Blessed Paul and David before him record that the majesty and awesomeness of God is understood by means of a knowledge of the created universe. Since this is how matters stand, who among us is possessed of a mind so slothful, a mind so immersed in things which perish and decay, that he is unable to confess that God surrounds him with benefits without number, when he recognizes, moreover, as a man, his own creatureliness, and that everything contained in heaven, the air, in water and on the earth has been produced for the sake of man.

of emblematics. The transfixed face of signifying nature is victorious, and history must, once and for all, remain contained in the subordinate role of stage-property. Mediaeval allegory is Christian and didactic – in the mystic and natural-historical respect the baroque is descended from antiquity: Egyptian antiquity, but subsequently Greek antiquity as well. The discovery of its secret storehouse of invention is attributed to Ludovico da Feltre, 'called "il Morto" because of his "grotesque" underground activities as a discoverer. And thanks to the mediation of an anchorite of the same name (in E. T. A. Hoffmann's *Die Serapionsbrüder*), the antique painter who was picked out from Pliny's much discussed passage on decorative painting as the classic of the grotesque, the "balcony-painter" Serapion, has also been used in literature as the personification of the subterranean-fantastic, the occult-spectral. For even at that time the enigmatically mysterious character of the effect of the grotesque seems to have been associated with its subterraneanly mysterious origin in buried ruins and catacombs. The word is not derived from *grotta* in the literal sense, but from the "burial" – in the sense of concealment – which the cave or grotto expresses... For this the eighteenth century still had the expression *das Verkrochene* [that which has crept away]. The enigmatic was therefore part of its effect from the very beginning.'[28] Winckelmann's position is not so very far removed from this. However severely he criticizes the stylistic principles of baroque allegory, his theory is still closely related to those of earlier authors in a number of ways. Borinski sees this very clearly in the *Versuch einer Allegorie*. 'Here, above all, Winckelmann still adheres to the general renaissance belief in *sapientia veterum* [the wisdom of the ancients], the spiritual bond between primordial truth and art, between intellectual science and archaeology ... In the authentic "allegory of the ancients", "breathed in" from the fullness of Homeric inspiration, he seeks the "psychic" panacea for the "sterility" of the endless repetition of scenes of martyrdom and mythology in the art of the moderns ... This kind of allegory alone teaches the artist "invention": and it is this which raises him to the same level as the poet.'[29] Thus allegory loses its simple didactic aspect even more radically than in the baroque.

As, in the course of their development, emblematics acquired further ramifications, so this form of expression became more obscure. Egyptian, Greek, Christian pictorial languages became intertwined. A typical example of the ready response of theology to this is provided by a work such as the *Polyhistor symbolicus*,[30] written by that very same jesuit, Caussinus, whose Latin *Felicitas* had been translated by Gryphius. Nor could any kind of writing seem better designed to safeguard the high political maxims of true worldly wisdom than an esoteric script such as this, which was comprehensible only to scholars. In his essay on Johann Valentin Andreä, Herder even speculated that it provided a refuge for many ideas which people were reluctant to voice openly before princes. The view of Opitz sounds more paradoxical. For while on the one hand he sees in the theological esotericism of this form of expression a sub-stantiation of the noble origins of poetry, he does, on the other hand, nevertheless believe that it was introduced in the interest of general comprehensibility. The proposition from the *Art poétique* of Delbène: 'La poésie n'était au premier âge qu'une théologie allégorique',* served as a model for a well-known formulation in the second chapter of Opitz's *Deutsche Poeterey*. 'Die Poeterey ist anfangs nichts anderes gewesen als eine verborgene Theologie.'† But on the other hand, he also writes: 'Weil die erste und rawe welt gröber und ungeschlachter war / als das sie hetten die lehren von weissheit und himmlischen dingen recht fassen und verstehen können / so haben weise Männer / was sie zu erbawung der gottesfurcht / guter sitten und wandels erfunden / in Reime und Fabeln / welche sonderlich der gemeine Pöfel zu hören geneiget ist / verstecken und verbergen müssen.'[31]‡ This remained the standard view, and for Harsdörffer, perhaps the most consistent allegorist, it provided the basis for the theory of this form of expression. Just as it established itself in

---

* Originally poetry was simply allegorical theology.

† Poetry was initially nothing other than concealed theology

‡ Because the earliest rude world was too crude and uncivilised and people could not therefore correctly grasp and understand the teachings of wisdom and heavenly things, wise men had to conceal and bury what they had discovered for the cultivation of the fear of God, morality, and good conduct, in rhymes and fables, to which the common people are disposed to listen.

every field of spiritual activity, from the broadest to the narrowest, from
theology, the study of nature, and morality, down to heraldry, occasional
poetry, and the language of love, so is the stock of its visual requisites
unlimited. With every idea the moment of expression coincides with a
veritable eruption of images, which gives rise to a chaotic mass of metaphors. This is how the sublime is presented in this style. 'Universa rerum
natura materiam praebet huic philosophiae (sc. imaginum) nec qvicqvam
ista protulit, qvod non in emblema abire possit, ex cujus contemplatione
utilem virtutum doctrinam in vita civili capere liceat: adeo ut qvemadmo-
dum Historiae ex Numismatibus, ita Morali philosophiae ex Emblematis
lux inferatur.'[32]* This is a particularly telling comparison. For where
nature bears the imprint of history, that is to say where it is a setting, does
it not have a numismatic quality? The same author – a reviewer in the
Acta eruditorum – writes elsewhere: 'Quamvis rem symbolis et emblemati-
bus praebere materiam, nec quic quam in hoc universo existere, quod non
idoneum iis argumentum suppeditet, supra in Actis . . . fuit monitum;
cum primum philosophiae imaginum tomum superiori anno editum
enarraremus. Cujus assertionis alter hic tomus,[33] qui hoc anno prodiit,
egregia praebet documenta; a naturalibus et artificialibus rebus, elemen-
tis, igne, montibus ignivomis, tormentis pulverariis et aliis machinis
bellicis, chymicis item instrumentis, subterraneis cuniculis, fumo
luminaribus, igne sacro, aere et variis avium generibus depromta
symbola et apposita lemmata exhibens.'[34]† A single illustration will suffice

---

*The universal nature of things adds weight to this line of philosophical enquiry (sc. into
the question of images), nor has anything disclosed this information which could not be
transmitted upon a piece of engraved work [*emblema*], in the beholding of which the individual might be enabled to derive useful information about virtue in civil life: so that, as in
the case of history, illumination can come from coins, so, in the case of moral philosophy, it
may come from engraved work.

† It was pointed out above, however, in the *Acta* that a thing shows its natural character
through symbols and ornamentation, and that no single thing exists in this entire universe
which cannot supply just such an appropriate representation as we explain in the first volume
of the philosophy of images, which came out in the previous year. In support of this assertion
the second volume of this book, which appeared this year, contributes excellent proofs, producing symbols and aptly related themes drawn from both natural and artificial material,
from the elements, from fire, from mountains which belch fire, from dusty siege engines and
other machines of war, from alchemical instruments too, from underground tunnels, from
smoke, from lamps, from sacred fire, from bronze coinage, and from the many species of
birds.

to show how far people went in this direction. The following passages occur in Böckler's *Ars heraldica*: 'Von Blättern. Man findet selten Blätter in den Wappen / wo sie aber gefunden werden / so führen sie die Deutung der Warheit / weilen sie etlicher Massen der Zungen und dem Hertzen gleichen.'[35] 'Von Wolcken. Gleichwie die Wolcken sich übersich (!) in die Höhe schwingen / hernach fruchtbaren Regen herab giessen / davon das Feld / Frücht und Menschen erfrischet und erquicket werden / also soll auch ein Adeliches Gemüth / in Tugend-Sachen gleichsam in die Höhe aufsteigen / alsdenn mit seinen Gaben / dem Vatterland zu dienen / beflissen seyn.'[36] 'Die weise (!) Pferde bedeuten den obsiegenden Frieden / nach geendigtem Krieg / und zugleich auch die Geschwindigkeit.'[37]* The most astonishing thing is a complete system of chromatic hieroglyphs, in the form of combinations of two different colours, towards which this book points. 'Roth zu Silber / verlangen sich zu rächen',[38] 'Blau . . . zu Roth / Unhöflichkeit',[39] 'Schwartz . . . zu Purpur / beständige Andacht',[40]† to mention but a few. 'The many obscurities in the connection between meaning and sign . . . did not deter, they rather encouraged the exploitation of ever remoter characteristics of the representative object as symbols, so as to surpass even the Egyptians with new subtleties. In addition to this there was the dogmatic power of the meanings handed down from the ancients, so that one and the same object can just as easily signify a virtue as a vice, and therefore more or less anything.'[41]

This brings us to the antinomies of the allegorical, the dialectical discussion of which is essential if the image of the *Trauerspiel* is to be evoked.

---

* On leaves. Leaves are rarely found in coats of arms, but where they are found, they signify truth because in many respects they resemble the tongue and the heart. . . . On clouds. Just as clouds pile up on each other into the heights, and thereafter fruitful rain falls from them, so that field, fruit, and men are refreshed and invigorated, so should a noble disposition rise to the heights, as it were, in matters of virtue, and then apply itself to serving the fatherland with its gifts. . . . White horses signify victorious peace after the conclusion of war, and also speed.

† Red and silver, the lust for vengeance, . . . blue . . . and red, discourtesy, . . . black . . . and purple, constant piety.

Any person, any object, any relationship can mean absolutely anything else. With this possibility a destructive, but just verdict is passed on the profane world: it is characterized as a world in which the detail is of no great importance. But it will be unmistakably apparent, especially to anyone who is familiar with allegorical textual exegesis, that all of the things which are used to signify derive, from the very fact of their pointing to something else, a power which makes them appear no longer commensurable with profane things, which raises them onto a higher plane, and which can, indeed, sanctify them. Considered in allegorical terms, then, the profane world is both elevated and devalued. This religious dialectic of content has its formal correlative in the dialectic of convention and expression. For allegory is both: convention *and* expression; and both are inherently contradictory. However, just as baroque teaching conceives of history as created events, allegory in particular, although a convention like every kind of writing, is regarded as created, like holy scripture. The allegory of the seventeenth century is not convention of expression, but expression of convention. At the same time expression of authority, which is secret in accordance with the dignity of its origin, but public in accordance with the extent of its validity. And the very same antinomies take plastic form in the conflict between the cold, facile technique and the eruptive expression of allegorical interpretation. Here too the solution is a dialectical one. It lies in the essence of writing itself. It is possible, without contradiction, to conceive of a more vital, freer use of the revealed spoken language, in which it would lose none of its dignity. This is not true of its written form, which allegory laid claim to being. The sanctity of what is written is inextricably bound up with the idea of its strict codification. For sacred script always takes the form of certain complexes of words which ultimately constitute, or aspire to become, one single and inalterable complex. So it is that alphabetical script, as a combination of atoms of writing, is the farthest removed from the script of sacred complexes. These latter take the form of hieroglyphics. The desire to guarantee the sacred character of any script – there will always be a conflict between sacred standing and profane comprehensibility – leads to complexes, to hieroglyphics. This is what happens in the baroque. Both externally and stylistically – in the extreme character of the typographical arrangement and in the use of highly charged metaphors – the written word tends towards the visual. It is not possible to conceive of a starker opposite to the artistic symbol, the plastic symbol, the image of organic totality, than this amorphous fragment which is seen in the form of allegorical script. In it the baroque reveals itself to be the sovereign opposite of classicism, as which hitherto, only romanticism has been acknowledged. And we should not resist the temptation of finding out those features which are common to both of them. Both, romanticism as much as baroque, are concerned not so much with providing a corrective to classicism, as to art itself. And it cannot be denied that the baroque, that contrasting prelude to classicism, offers a more concrete, more authoritative, and more permanent version of this correction. Whereas romanticism inspired by its belief in the infinite, intensified the perfected creation of form and idea in critical terms,[42] at one stroke the profound vision of allegory transforms things and works into stirring writing. Winckelmann still has this penetration of vision in the *Beschreibung des Torso des Hercules in Belvedere zu Rom*:[43] it is evident in the un-classical way he goes over it, part by part and limb by limb. It is no accident that the subject is a torso. In the field of allegorical intuition the image is a fragment, a rune. Its beauty as a symbol evaporates when the light of divine learning falls upon it. The false appearance of totality is extinguished. For the *eidos* disappears, the simile ceases to exist, and the cosmos it contained shrivels up. The dry rebuses which remain contain an insight, which is still available to the confused investigator. By its very essence classicism was not permitted to behold the lack of freedom, the imperfection, the collapse of the physical, beautiful, nature. But beneath its extravagant pomp, this is precisely what baroque allegory proclaims, with unprecedented emphasis. A deep-rooted intuition of the problematic character of art – it was by no means only the coyness of a particular social class, it was also a religious scruple which assigned artistic activity to the 'leisure hours' – emerges as a reaction to its self-confidence at the time of the Renaissance. Although the artists and thinkers of classicism did not concern themselves with what they regarded as grotesque, certain statements in neo-Kantian aesthetics give an idea of the ferocity of the controversy. The dialectic quality of this form of expression is misunderstood, and mistrusted as ambiguity. 'The basic characteristic of allegory, however, is ambiguity, multiplicity of meaning; allegory, and the baroque, glory in richness of meaning. But the richness of this ambiguity is the richness of extravagance; nature, however, according to the old rules of metaphysics, and indeed also of mechanics, is bound by the law of economy. Ambiguity is therefore always the opposite of clarity and unity of meaning.'[44] No less doctrinaire are the arguments of a pupil of Hermann Cohen, Carl Horst, who was restricted by his title, *Barock-probleme*, to a more concrete approach. Notwithstanding, allegory is said 'always to reveal a "crossing of the borders of a different mode", an advance of the plastic arts into the territory of the "rhetorical" arts. And,' the author continues, 'such violation of frontiers is nowhere more remorselessly punished than in the pure culture of sentiment, which is more the business of the pure "plastic arts" than the "rhetorical arts", and brings the former closer to music . . . In the unemotional permeation of the most varied human forms of expression with autocratic ideas . . . artistic feeling and understanding is diverted and violated. This is what allegory achieves in the field of the "plastic" arts. Its intrusion could therefore be described as a harsh disturbance of the peace and a disruption of law and order in the arts. And yet allegory has never been absent from this field, and the greatest artists have dedicated great works to it.'[45] This fact alone should have been enough to produce a different attitude to allegory. The undialectic neo-Kantian mode of thought is not able to grasp the synthesis which is reached in allegorical writing as a result of the conflict between theological and artistic intentions, a synthesis not so much in the sense of a peace as a *treuga dei* between the conflicting opinions.

When, as is the case in the *Trauerspiel*, history becomes part of the setting, it does so as script. The word 'history' stands written on the countenance of nature in the characters of transience. The allegorical physiognomy of the nature-history, which is put on stage in the *Trauer-spiel*, is present in reality in the form of the ruin. In the ruin history has physically merged into the setting. And in this guise history does not assume the form of the process of an eternal life so much as that of irresistible decay. Allegory thereby declares itself to be beyond beauty. Allegories are, in the realm of thoughts, what ruins are in the realm of things. This explains the baroque cult of the ruin. Borinski, less exhaustive in his argument than accurate in his account of the facts, is aware of this. 'The broken pediment, the crumbling columns are supposed to bear witness to the miracle that the sacred edifice has withstood even the most elemental forces of destruction, lightning and earthquake. In its artificiality, however, such a ruin appears as the last heritage of an antiquity which in the modern world is only to be seen in its material form, as a picturesque field of ruins.'[46] A footnote adds: 'The rise of this tendency can be traced by examining the ingenious practice of renaissance artists in setting the Birth of Christ and the Adoration in the ruins of an antique temple instead of the mediaeval stable. In Domenico Ghirlandaio (Florence, Accademia), for instance, these ruins still consisted simply of impeccably preserved showpieces; now they become an end in themselves, serving as a picturesque setting representing transitory splendour, in the plastic and colourful Nativity-scenes.'[47] What prevails here is the current stylistic feeling, far more than the reminiscences of antiquity. That which lies here in ruins, the highly significant fragment, the remnant, is, in fact, the finest material in baroque creation. For it is common practice in the literature of the baroque to pile up fragments ceaselessly, without any strict idea of a goal, and, in the unremitting expectation of a miracle, to take the repetition of stereotypes for a process of intensification. The baroque writers must have regarded the work of art as just such a miracle. And if, on the other hand, it seemed to be the calculable result of the process of accumulation, it is no more difficult to reconcile these two things than it was for the alchemist to reconcile the longed-for miraculous 'work' and the subtle theoretical recipes. The experimentation of the baroque writers resembles the practice of the adepts. The legacy of antiquity constitutes, item for item, the elements from which the new whole is mixed. Or rather: is constructed. For the perfect vision of this new phenomenon was the ruin. The exuberant subjection of antique elements in a structure which, without uniting them in a single whole, would, in destruction, still be superior to the harmonies of antiquity, is the purpose of the technique which applies itself separately, and ostentatiously, to realia, rhetorical figures and rules. Literature ought to be called *ars inveniendi*. The notion of the man of genius, the master of the *ars inveniendi*, is that of a man who could manipulate models with sovereign skill. 'Fantasy', the creative faculty as conceived by the moderns, was unknown as the criterion of a spiritual hierarchy. 'Dass bishero unsern Opitius niemand in der teutschen Poeterey nur gleichkommen, viel weniger überlegen sein können (welches auch ins künftige nicht geschehen wird), ist die vornehmste Ursache, dass neben der sonderbaren Geschicklichkeit der trefflichen Natur, so in ihm ist, er in der Latiner und Griechen Schriften sowohl [sic] belesen und selbe so artig auszudrücken und inventieren weiss.'[48]* The German language, moreover, as the grammarians of the time saw it, was in this context, only another nature, alongside that of the ancient models. Hankamer explains their view as follows: 'Linguistic nature, like material nature, is a repository of all secrets. [The writer] brings no power to it, creates no new truth from the spontaneous outpourings of the soul'.[49] The writer must not conceal the fact that his activity is one of arranging, since it was not so much the mere whole as its obviously constructed quality that was the principal impression which was aimed at. Hence the display of the craftsmanship, which, in Calderón especially, shows through like the masonry in a building whose rendering has broken away. Thus, one might say, nature remained the great teacher for the writers of this period. However, nature was not seen by them in bud and bloom, but in the over-ripeness and decay of her creations. In nature they saw eternal transience, and here alone did the saturnine vision of this generation recognize history. Its monuments, ruins, are, according to Agrippa von Nettesheim, the home of the saturnine beasts. In the process of decay, and in it alone, the events of history shrivel up and become absorbed in the setting. The quintessence of these decaying objects is the polar opposite to the idea of transfigured nature as conceived by the early renais-

---

* The principal reason why no one in German poetry has yet been able even to approach our Opitz, let alone surpass him (which will not occur in the future either), is that, apart from the remarkable agility of his excellent nature, he is so well read in Latin and Greek writings, and he himself possesses such powers of expression and invention.

sance. Burdach has demonstrated that this latter concept was 'quite different from our own'. 'For a long time it continues to remain dependent on the linguistic usage and the thinking of the middle ages, even if the evaluation of the word and the notion 'nature' does visibly rise. However, in artistic theory from the fourteenth to the sixteenth century, the imitation of nature means the imitation of nature as shaped by God.'[50] But it is fallen nature which bears the imprint of the progression of history. The penchant of the baroque for apotheosis is a counterpart to its own particular way of looking at things. The authorization of their allegorical designations bears the seal of the all-too-earthly. Never does their transcendence come from within. Hence their illumination by the artificial light of apotheosis. Hardly ever has there been a literature whose illusionistic virtuosity has more radically eliminated from its works that radiance which has a transcendent effect, and which was at one time, rightly, used in an attempt to define the essence of artistry. It is possible to describe the absence of this radiance as one of the most specific characteristics of baroque lyric. And the drama is no different. 'So muss man durch den Tod in jenes Leben dringen / I Das uns Aegyptens Nacht in Gosems Tag verkehrt / I Und den beperlten Rock der Ewigkeit gewehrt!'[51]* This is how Hallmann, from the point of view of the stage-manager, describes eternal life. Obdurate concentration on requisites frustrated the depiction of love. Unworldly voluptuousness, lost in its own fantasy, holds the floor. 'Ein schönes Weib ist ja, die tausend Zierden mahlen, I Ein unverzehrlich Tisch, der ihrer viel macht satt. I Ein unverseigend Quell, das allzeit Wasser hat, I Ja süsse Libes-Milch; Wenn gleich in hundert Röhre I Der linde Zukker rinnt. Es ist der Unhold Lehre, I Des schelen Neides Art, wenn andern man verwehrt I Die Speise, die sie labt, sich aber nicht verzehrt.'[52]† Any adequate masking of content is absent from the typical works of the baroque. The extent of their claims, even in the minor forms, is breathtaking. And they lack any feeling for the

---

* And so one must go through death to enter into that life which transforms Egypt's night into Gosen's day, and grants us the pearly robe of eternity!

† A beautiful woman, adorned with a thousand ornaments, is an inexhaustible table that satisfies many. An eternal spring from which water always flows, or rather love's sweet milk; as when sweet sugar runs in a hundred canes. It is the devil's doctrine, the way of squinting envy, to deny others the food which refreshes, but which is not consumed.

intimate, the mysterious. They attempt, extravagantly and vainly, to replace it with the enigmatic and the concealed. In the true work of art pleasure can be fleeting, it can live in the moment, it can vanish, and it can be renewed. The baroque work of art wants only to endure, and clings with all its senses to the eternal. This is the only way of explaining how, in the following century, readers were seduced by the liberating sweetness of the first *Tändeleyen*, and how, in the rococo, Chinoiserie became the counterpart to hieratic byzantinism. In speaking of the *Gesamtkunstwerk* as the summit of the aesthetic hierarchy of the age and the ideal of the *Trauerspiel* itself,[53] the baroque critic provides a new confirmation of this spirit of weightiness. As an experienced allegorist, Harsdörffer is, among many theoreticians, the one who spoke out most radically for the synthesis of all the arts. For this is precisely what is required by the allegorical way of looking at things. Winckelmann makes the connection abundantly clear when, with polemical overstatement, he remarks: 'Vain . . . is the hope of those who believe that allegory should be taken so far that one might even be able to paint an ode.'[54] More disconcerting is the question of how the literary works of the century are introduced: dedications, prefaces and epilogues, by the authors themselves or by others, testimonials, acknowledgements of the great masters – these are the rule. Without exception they provide an elaborate surrounding framework to the larger editions and the collected works. For it was only rarely that the eye was able to find satisfaction in the object itself. It was expected that works of art could be absorbed in the midst of ordinary every day affairs, and devotion to them was far less a private matter, for which account did not have to be given, than it was later to become. Reading was obligatory, and it was educational. The range of the products, their intentional bulkiness and lack of mystery should be understood as a correlative of such an attitude among the public. It was not felt that these products were intended to spread by growth over a period of time, so much as to fill up their allotted place here and now. And in many respects this was their reward. But for this very reason criticism is implied with rare clarity in the fact of their continued existence. From the very beginning they are set up for that erosion by criticism which befell them in the course of time. Beauty has nothing inalienable for the uninitiated. And for such people nothing is less approachable than the German *Trauerspiel*. Its outer form has died away because of its extreme crudity. What has survived is the extra-ordinary detail of the allegorical references: an object of knowledge which has settled in the consciously constructed ruins. Criticism means the mortification of the works. By their very essence these works confirm this more readily than any others. Mortification of the works: not then – as the romantics have it – awakening of the consciousness in living works,[55] but the settlement of knowledge in dead ones. Beauty, which endures, is an object of knowledge. And if it is questionable whether the beauty which endures does still deserve the name, it is nevertheless certain that there is nothing of beauty which does not contain something that is worthy of knowledge. Philosophy must not attempt to deny that it re-awakens the beauty of works. 'Science cannot lead to the naive enjoyment of art any more than geologists and botanists can awaken a feeling for the beauty of landscape';[56] this assertion is as incorrect as the analogy which is sup-posed to support it is false. The geologist and the botanist can indeed do just this. Without at least an intuitive grasp of the life of the detail in the structure, all love of beauty is no more than empty dreaming. In the last analysis structure and detail are always historically charged. The object of philosophical criticism is to show that the function of artistic form is as follows: to make historical content, such as provides the basis of every important work of art, into a philosophical truth. This transformation of material content into truth content makes the decrease in effectiveness, whereby the attraction of earlier charms diminishes decade by decade, into the basis for a rebirth, in which all ephemeral beauty is completely stripped off, and the work stands as a ruin. In the allegorical construction of the baroque *Trauerspiel* such ruins have always stood out clearly as formal elements of the preserved work of art.

Even the story of the life of Christ supported the movement from history to nature which is the basis of allegory. However great the retarding, secular tendency of its exegesis had always been – seldom did it reach such a degree of intensity as in the work of Sigmund von Birken. His poetics give, 'as examples of birth, marriage, and funeral poems, of eulogies and victory congratulations, songs on the birth and death of Christ, on his spiritual marriage with the soul, on his glory and his victory'.[57] The mystical instant [*Nu*] becomes the 'now' [*Jetzt*] of contemporary actuality; the symbolic becomes distorted into the allegorical. The eternal is separated from the events of the story of salvation, and what is left is a living image open to all kinds of revision by the interpretative artist. This corresponds profoundly to the endlessly preparatory, circumlocutious, self-indulgently hesitant manner of the baroque process of giving form. It has been quite correctly observed, by Hausenstein, that, in paintings of apotheoses, the foreground is generally treated with exaggerated realism so as to be able to show the remoter, visionary objects more reliably. The attempt to gather all worldly events into the graphic foreground is not undertaken only in order to heighten the tension between immanence and transcendence, but also in order to secure for the latter the greatest conceivable rigour, exclusiveness and inexorability. It is an unsurpassably spectacular gesture to place even Christ in the realm of the provisional, the everyday, the unreliable. The *Sturm und Drang* provides strong support; Merck writes that it 'cannot in any way detract from the great man if it is known that he was born in a stable and lay in swaddling clothes between an ox and an ass'.[58] Above all it is the offensive, the provocative quality of the gesture which is baroque. Where man is drawn towards the symbol, allegory emerges from the depths of being to intercept the intention, and to triumph over it. The same tendency is characteristic of baroque lyric. The poems have 'no forward movement, but they swell up from within'.[59] If it is to hold its own against the tendency to absorption, the allegorical must constantly unfold in new and surprising ways. The symbol, on the other hand, as the romantic mythologists have shown, remains persistently the same. How striking is the contrast between the uniform verses of the emblem-books, the 'vanitas vanitatum vanitas', and the fashionable bustle with which they appeared, on each others heels, from the middle of the century onwards! Allegories become dated, because it is part of their nature to shock. If the object becomes allegorical under the gaze of melancholy, if melancholy causes life to flow out of it and it remains behind dead, but eternally secure, then it is exposed to the allegorist, it is unconditionally in his power. That is to say it is now quite incapable of emanating any meaning or significance of its own; such significance as it has, it acquires from the allegorist. He places it within it, and stands behind it; not in a psychological but in an ontological sense. In his hands the object becomes something different; through it he speaks of something different and for him it becomes a key to the realm of hidden knowledge; and he reveres it as the emblem of this. This is what determines the character of allegory as a form of writing. It is a schema; and as a schema it is an object of knowledge, but it is not securely possessed until it becomes a fixed schema: at one and the same time a fixed image and a fixing sign. The baroque ideal of knowledge, the process of storing, to which the vast libraries are a monument, is realized in the external appearance of the script. Almost as much as in China it is, in its visual character, not merely a sign of what is to be known but it is itself an object worthy of knowledge. The romantics were the first to begin to become conscious of this aspect of allegory too. Particularly Baader. In his *Über den Einfluss der Zeichen der Gedanken auf deren Erzeugung und Gestaltung* he writes: 'It is well known that it is entirely up to us whether we use any particular object of nature as a conventional sign for an idea, as we see in symbolic and hieroglyphic writing, and this object only then takes on a new character when we wish to use it, not to convey its natural characteristics, but those which we have ourselves, so to speak, lent it.'[60] A note to this passage contains the following commentary: 'There is good reason for the fact that everything we see in external nature is, for us, already writing, a kind of sign-language, which nevertheless lacks the most essential feature: pronunciation; this must quite simply have come from somewhere else and been given to man.'[61] 'From somewhere else' the allegorist then takes it up, by no means avoiding that arbitrariness which is the most drastic manifestation of the power of knowledge. The wealth of ciphers, which the allegorist discovered in the world of the creature with its profound historical stamp, justifies Cohen's charge of 'extravagance'. It may not accord with the authority of nature; but the voluptuousness with which significance rules, like a stern sultan in the harem of objects, is without equal in giving expression to nature. It is indeed characteristic of the sadist that he humiliates his object and then – or thereby – satisfies it. And that is what the allegorist does in this age drunk with acts of cruelty both lived and imagined. This even applies to religious painting. The 'opening of the eyes', which baroque painting makes into 'a schema quite independent of the situation as conditioned by the subject in hand',[62] betrays and devalues things in an inexpressible manner. The function of baroque iconography is not so much to unveil material objects as to strip them naked. The emblematist does not present the essence implicitly, 'behind the image'.[63] He drags the essence of what is depicted out before the image, in writing, as a caption, such as, in the emblem-books, forms an intimate part of what is depicted. Basically, then, the *Trauerspiel*, too, which grew up in the sphere of the allegorical, is, in its form, a drama for the reader. Although this says nothing about the value or the possibility of its stage-performance. But it does make it clear that the chosen spectator of such examples of the *Trauerspiel* concentrated on them with at least the same thought and attentiveness as the reader; that the situations did not change very frequently, but that when they did, they did so in a flash, like the appearance of the print when a page is turned; and it explains how it is that, in a hostile and grudging intuition of the inner law of these dramas, the older school of research persisted in the view that they were never performed.

This view was certainly incorrect. For the only pleasure the melancholic permits himself, and it is a powerful one, is allegory. It is true that the overbearing ostentation, with which the banal object seems to arise from the depths of allegory is soon replaced by its disconsolate everyday countenance; it is true that the profound fascination of the sick man for the isolated and insignificant is succeeded by that disappointed abandonment of the exhausted emblem, the rhythm of which a speculatively inclined observer could find expressively repeated in the behaviour of apes. But the amorphous details which can only be understood allegorically keep coming up. For if the instructions are: 'everything [must be] considered in its own right, and then the intelligence [will] increase and taste be refined', [64] then the appropriate object of such intentions is ever present.

In his *Gesprächspiele* Harsdörffer sees the basis of a particular genre in the fact 'that, following the example of Judges, IX, 8, instead of the animals of Aesop's fables, lifeless objects, forests, trees, stones, may speak and act, while yet another genre emerges from the fact that words, syllables, and letters appear in personified form'.[65] As far as this latter trend is concerned, Christian Gryphius, the son of Andreas, distinguished himself with his didactic play *Der deutschen Sprache unterschiedene Alter*. It is perfectly clear that this fragmentation in the graphic aspects is a principle of the allegorical approach. In the baroque, especially, the allegorical personification can be seen to give way in favour of the emblems, which mostly offer themselves to view in desolate, sorrowful dispersal. A large part of Winckelmann's *Versuch einer Allegorie*, needs to be understood as a protest against this style. 'Simplicity consists in designing a picture which expresses the intended meaning in as few signs as possible, and this is the characteristic of allegories in the best periods of antiquity. In later times there arose the practice of bringing many concepts together, by means of just as many signs, in one single figure, like those divinities known as *panthei*, which are invested with the attributes of all the gods ... The best and most perfect allegory of one or of several concepts is comprised of one single figure, or should be thought of as such.'[66] This is the voice of the will to symbolic totality venerated by humanism in the human figure. But it is as something incomplete and imperfect that objects stare out from the allegorical structure. Even among the romantics the genuine theorists of this field had no use for them. They were weighed in the balance against the symbol and found wanting. 'The German emblem [*Sinnbild*] . . . is quite lacking in that dignity and substance. It ought therefore . . . to remain confined to the lower sphere, and be completely excluded from symbolic tests.'[67] Görres has the following to say about this statement of Creuzer: 'Since you explain the mystic symbol as the formal symbol in which the spirit aspires to transcend form and destroy the body, the plastic symbol, however, as the pure median between spirit and nature, you have omitted the opposite of the former, the real symbol, in which the bodily form absorbs the spiritual, and here the emblem, the German symbol [*Sinnbild*] in its restricted sense, fits in well.'[68] The romantic standpoint of both authors was still too precarious for them not to feel some hostility towards the rational didacticism, to which this form seemed suspiciously close; but on the other hand the straightforward, whimsical, popular quality of many of its products could not but have appealed to Görres. Yet he did not clarify his position. And even today it is by no means self-evident that the primacy of the thing over the personal, the fragment over the total, represents a confrontation between the allegory and the symbol, to which it is the polar opposite and, for that very reason, its equal in power. Allegorical personification has always concealed the fact that its function is not the personification of things, but rather to give the concrete a more imposing form by getting it up as a person. In this respect the insight of Cysarz is very penetrating. The baroque vulgarizes ancient mythology in order to see everything in terms of figures (not souls): this is the ultimate stage of externalization after the hieratic religious content had been aestheticized by Ovid and secularized by the neo-Latin writers. There is not the faintest glimmer of any spiritualization of the physical. The whole of nature is personalized, not so as to be made more inward, but, on the contrary – so as to be deprived of soul.'[69] That awkward heavy-handedness, which has been attributed either to lack of talent on the part of the artist or lack of insight on the part of the patron, is essential to allegory. It is therefore all the more remarkable that Novalis, who was incomparably more aware than the later romantics of what separated him from the ideals of classicism, shows a profound understanding of the essence of allegory in the few passages in which he touches on the subject. The attentive reader of the following note will immediately be able to see deep into the mind of the poet of the sixteenth century, a high official, experienced in privy affairs of state, and overwhelmed with duties: 'Business affairs can also be treated poetically . . . A certain archaism of style, a correct disposition and ordering of masses, a faint hint of allegory, a certain strangeness, respect, and bewilderment which shimmer through the writing – these are some of the essential features of this art.'[70] This is indeed the spirit in which the baroque approaches realia in practice. That there is an affinity between the romantic genius and baroque spiritual make-up in the field of the allegorical is equally clear from this further fragment: 'Poems, merely fine-sounding and full of beautiful words but without any meaning or coherence – no more than a few verses of which are comprehensible – like fragments of the most heterogeneous objects. True poetry can, at most, have an allegorical meaning as a whole, and its effect can, at most, be an indirect one, like that of music etc. Nature is therefore purely poetic, and so it is a magician's den, a physicist's laboratory, a children's nursery, an attic and a lumber-room.'[71] It must not be assumed that there is anything accidental about the fact that the allegorical is related in this way to the fragmentary, untidy, and disordered character of magicians' dens or alchemists' laboratories familiar above all to the baroque. Are not the works of Jean Paul, the greatest allegorist in German literature, just such children's nurseries and haunted rooms? Indeed a genuine history of the romantic style could do no better than show, with reference to his works, that even the fragment, and even irony are variants of the allegorical. In short: the technique of romanticism leads in a number of respects into the realm of emblematics and allegory. And the relationship between these two might be formulated as follows: in its fully developed, baroque, form allegory brings with it its own court; the profusion of emblems is grouped around the figural centre, which is never absent from genuine allegories, as opposed to periphrases of concepts. They seem to be arranged in an arbitrary way: *The confused 'court'* – the title of a Spanish *Trauerspiel* – could be adopted as the model of allegory. This court is subject to the law of 'dispersal' and 'collectedness'. Things are assembled according to their significance; indifference to their existence allowed them to be dispersed again. The disorder of the allegorical scenery stands in contrast to the galant boudoir. In the dialectic of this form of expression the fanaticism of the process of collection is balanced by the slackness with which the objects are arranged: the extravagant distribution of instruments of penance or violence is particularly paradoxical. Borinski has written brilliantly of baroque form that 'for its excessive structural demands this form compensates by being decorative or, to use its own term, "galant"' [72] and this confirms it as a contemporary of allegory. This remark is also relevant to stylistic criticism of baroque poetics. For in the theory of 'tragedy' the rules of ancient tragedy are taken separately, as lifeless components, and piled up around an allegorical figure representing the tragic muse. Thanks only to the classicistic misinterpretation of the *Trauerspiel*, such as the baroque practised in ignorance of its true self, could the 'rules' of ancient tragedy become the amorphous, binding, and emblematic rules according to which the new form developed. In such a context of allegorical decay and destruction the image of Greek tragedy seemed to be the only possible, the natural sign of 'tragic poetry'. Its rules become significant anticipations of the *Trauerspiel*; its texts are read as *Trauerspiel*-texts. The extent to which this was, and continued to be, possible can be seen from the Sophocles-translations of Hölderlin, which date from that late period which Hellingrath did not call the poet's 'baroque' period for nothing.

> Ihr kraft beraubte Wort', ihr seid zerstückte Stück',
> Und seichte schattenstreif, allein, entweicht zu rük;
> Vermehlet mit Gemähl ihr werdet zu gelassen,
> Wenn ein tief Sinnebild hilft das verborgne fassen.
> Franz Julius von dem Knesebeck:
> *Dreyständige Sinnbilder**

The philosophical understanding of allegory, and especially the dialectical understanding of its extreme form, is the only background against which the image of the *Trauerspiel* stands out in living and – if one may venture to say so – beautiful colours, the only background not darkened by the grey of retouching. In the chorus and the interlude the allegorical structure of the *Trauerspiel* is so conspicuous that it could never have entirely escaped the notice of the onlookers. But for that very reason these remained the critical points at which the edifice, which so boldly raised the claim to be a Greek temple, was stormed and eventually destroyed. Wackernagel writes: 'The chorus is the heritage and property of the Greek theatre: even there it is only the natural consequence of certain historical

---

* Ye words robbed of power, you are shattered fragments, and by itself a pale shadow vanishes away. Married to a painting, you will be admitted, when a profound emblem helps you to grasp that which is concealed.

premises. In Germany there was never any basis for the development of anything of this kind, and so the attempts of the German dramatists of the sixteenth and seventeenth centuries ... to transpose it to the German theatre could only come to grief.'[1] There can be no doubt about the dependence of the Greek chorus-drama on certain national conditions; but equally there can be no doubt that the same is true of the apparent imitations of the Greeks in the sixteenth and seventeenth centuries. The chorus of the baroque drama is not something external. It is as internal to it as is the carving of a Gothic altar behind the open wings on which stories from the lives of the saints are painted. In the chorus, or the inter-lude, allegory is no longer colourful, rich in historical associations, but pure and severe. At the end of the fourth act of Lohenstein's *Sophonisbe* Lechery and Virtue appear in conflict. Finally Lechery is unmasked, and allows itself to be addressed by Virtue as follows: 'Wol! wir wolln bald des Engels Schönheit sehn! I Ich muss dir den geborgten Rock ausziehen. I Kan sich ein Bettler in was ärgers nehn? I Wer wollte nicht für dieser Sclavin fliehen? I Wirff aber auch den Bettler-Mantel weg. I Schaut / ist ein Schwein besudelter zu schauen? I Diss ist ein Krebs- und diss ein Aussatz-Fleck. I Muss dir nicht selbst für Schwer- und Eyter grauen? I Der Wollust Kopff ist Schwan / der Leib ein Schwein. I Lasst uns die Schminck' im Antlitz auch vertilgen. I Hier fault das Fleisch / dort frisst die Lauss sich ein / I So wandeln sich in Koth der Wollust Liljen. I Noch nicht genug! zeuch auch die Lumpen aus; I Was zeigt sich nun? Ein Aass / ein todt Gerippe. I Besieh' itzt auch der Wollust innres Haus: I Dass man sie in die Schinder-Grube schippe!'[2]* This is the ancient allegorical motif of Dame World. From such striking passages an inkling of what is going on here occasionally penetrated even to the authors of the last century. Conrad Müller writes: 'In the baroque choruses Lohenstein's

---

* Good! Now let us see the angel's beauty. I must take off your borrowed dress. Can a beggar sew himself into anything worse? Who would not flee before this slave? But throw away the beggar's mantle too. Look, is a swine more foul to behold? This is a canker and this a leprous sore. Are you not yourself revolted by the swelling and pus? The head of Lechery is a swan; the body a swine's. Let us also remove the cosmetics from the face. Here the flesh is decaying, and here the louse is eating its way in. Thus do the lilies of Lechery change into filth. Not yet enough! Pull off the rags; and what is now revealed? A corpse, a skeleton. Now behold Lechery's innermost dwelling: may she be shovelled into the knacker's pit!

tendency to complexity weighs less heavily on his linguistic genius, because those verbal flourishes, which seem strange in the stylistic temple of tragedy, are quite in keeping with the fantastic decorations of allegory.'[3] And just as it is manifest in the word, so too is the allegorical manifest in the figural and the scenic. The high point is reached in the interludes, with their personified attributes, incarnations of the virtues and vices, without in any way being confined to them. For it is illuminating that a series of types such as is formed by king, courtier, and fool, has an allegorical significance. Here the divinations of Novalis are again correct: 'Scenes which are genuinely visual are the only ones which belong in the theatre. Allegorical characters, these are what people mostly see. Children are hopes, young girls are wishes and requests.'[4] With great insight this suggests connections between spectacle proper and allegory. In the baroque, of course, their figures were different and – in a Christian and courtly respect – more precisely defined than Novalis depicts them. The allegorical character of the figures is betrayed in the infrequency and the hesitancy with which the plot refers to their particular morality. In *Leo Armenius* it is left completely unclear whether he whom Balbus strikes is guilty or innocent. It is enough that he is the king. Nor is there any other way of explaining the fact that practically any character can find a place in the *tableau vivant* of an allegorical apotheosis. 'Virtue' extols Masinissa,[5] a pitiful rogue. Never did the German *Trauerspiel* succeed in distributing the person's characteristics so secretly in the thousand folds of allegorical drapery, after the manner of Calderón. Nor was it any more successful in the re-interpretation of the allegorical figure in unique new roles, after the manner of Shakespeare. 'Certain of Shakespeare's figures possess the physiognomic features of the morality-play allegory; but this is only recognizable to the practised eye; as far as these features are concerned, they move, as it were, in the allegorical cloak of invisibility. Such figures are Rosencrantz and Guildenstern.'[6] Because of its obsession with earnestness the German *Trauerspiel* never mastered the art of using allegory inconspicuously. Only comedy accorded the allegorical the rights of citizenship in the secular drama; but when comedy moves in seriously, then the consequences are unexpectedly fatal.

The growing significance of the interlude, which, in Gryphius' middle period, already occupies the place of the chorus before the dramatic catastrophe,[7] coincides with the increasing obtrusiveness of its display of allegorical pomp. It reaches its high point in the work of Hallmann. 'Just as the structural, logical meaning is obscured by the ornamental aspect of speech ... which becomes mannered to the point of catachresis, so ... too is the dramatic structure concealed by the ornamental tendency, which is borrowed from the style of the speech, and which takes the form, in the interludes, of staged *exemplum*, staged antithesis, and staged metaphor.'[8] These interludes are recognizably the consequences of that allegorical approach which has been discussed above. Whether, following the example of the Jesuit didactic drama, an allegorical, *spiritualiter* relevant *exemplum* is extracted from ancient history (in Hallmann: the Dido chorus from *Adonis und Rosibella*, the Callisto-chorus from *Catharina*[9]), whether, as Lohenstein prefers, the choruses expound an edifying psychology of the passions, or whether, as in Gryphius, religious reflection is dominant, it is more or less true that in all of these types the dramatic incident is not conceived as an isolated catastrophe, but rather as one that is necessary by nature and inherent in the way of the world. But even in its functional use allegory is not associated with the climax of the dramatic action, but it is an extended explanatory interlude. The acts do not follow rapidly from each other, but they are built up in the manner of terraces. The structure of the drama is such that there are several broad layers whose chronological perspective is identical, and the level represented by the interlude became the site for a display of expressive statuary. 'The mention of an *exemplum* in words is accompanied by a scenic representation of it as a *tableau vivant (Adonis)*; three, four, even as many as seven such *exempla* can be seen on stage together *(Adonis)*. The rhetorical apostrophe, "Look how ..." underwent the same transformation into scenic terms in the prophetic speeches of spirits. [10] With all the power at its disposal the will to allegory makes use of the 'dumb show' to bring back the fading word, in order to make it accessible to the unimaginative visual faculty. The tendency to achieve a balance, so to speak, between the atmosphere of the dramatic character's visionary perception and that of the spectator's profane perception – a theatrical gamble which even Shakespeare seldom risks – can be seen all the more clearly, the more unsuccessful these lesser masters were. The visionary description of the *tableau vivant* is one of the triumphs of baroque vigour and baroque antitheticism. 'Action and chorus are separate worlds, they are as different as dream and reality'.[11] 'The dramatic technique of Andreas Gryphius produces a clear distinction in action and chorus between the real world of objects and events and an ideal world of causes and meanings.'[12] If it is permissible to treat these two statements as premises, it is not far to the conclusion that the world which becomes perceptible in the chorus is the world of dreams, and of meaning. The melancholic possesses an intimate awareness of the unity of these two worlds. But the radical distinction between action and interlude also vanishes before the gaze of its chosen spectator. Here and there the connection is revealed in the dramatic action itself. When, for instance, in the chorus Agrippina finds herself rescued by mermaids. And, characteristically, nowhere more beautifully and more emphatically than in the person of a sleeper, the Emperor Bassian, in the intermezzo which follows the fourth act of *Papinian*. During his slumber a chorus enacts its significant play. 'Der Käyser erwachet und gehet traurig ab.'[13]* 'It would be idle to ask how the poet, for whom ghosts were a reality, conceived of the combination of them with allegories', observes Steinberg unjustly.[14] Ghosts, like the profoundly significant allegories, are manifestations from the realm of mourning; they have an affinity for mourners, for those who ponder over signs and over the future. The explanation for the strange appearance of the spirits of the living is not quite so clear. In the first chorus of Lohenstein's *Trauerspiel* 'die Seele der Sophonisbe'† confronts her passions,[15] while in Hallmann's scenario *Liberata*,[16] and in *Adonis und Rosibella*,[17] it is only a question of a ghostly disguise. If Gryphius has a spirit appear in the form of Olympia,[18] this is a new twist. This is not, of course, the utter 'nonsense'[19] which Kerckhoffs says it is; it is rather a remarkable testimony to the fanaticism with which even the absolutely singular, the individual character, is multiplied in the allegorical. There is

---

* The emperor awakes and makes a mournful exit.
† the soul of Sophonisbe

perhaps a case of much more bizarre allegorization in a stage direction which occurs in Hallmann's *Sophia*: when, as one must suppose, it is not two dead people but two incarnations of death, which as 'zwey Todte mit Pfeilen . . . ein höchst trauriges Ballet nebst untergemischten grausamen Geberden gegen die Sophie tantzen'.[20]* This sort of thing resembles certain emblematic illustrations. The *Emblemata selectiora*, for instance, contain a plate[21] which shows a rose simultaneously half in bloom and half faded, and the sun rising and setting in the same landscape. 'The essence of the baroque lies in the simultaneity of its actions',[22] writes Hausenstein rather crudely, but with some awareness. For where it is a question of a realization in terms of space – and what else is meant by its secularization other than its transformation into the strictly present – then the most radical procedure is to make events simultaneous. The duality of meaning and reality was reflected in the construction of the stage. The use of the drop-scene permitted the alternation between actions on the forestage and scenes which extended to the full depth of the stage. And 'the splendour that was uninhibitedly displayed could . . . only properly be displayed on the rear part of the stage'.[23] Since it was not feasible to bring about a resolution of the situation without the apotheosis of the finale, the complexities of plot could only be woven in the restricted area of the forestage; the solution took place in allegorical fullness. The same duality runs through the tectonic structure of the whole. It has already been suggested that the classicistic framework stands in contrast to the style of expression employed in these dramas. Hausenstein has observed something similar, and asserts that whereas the external structure of palace and house, and to some extent even church, are mathematically determined, the style of the interior is the province of uncontrolled imagination.[24] If indeed surprise, even complexity, has any meaning in the structure of these dramas, and should be emphasized by contrast to a classicistic transparency of plot, then exoticism in the choice of subject-matter is also not foreign to it. The *Trauerspiel* gives more emphatic encouragement to the invention of the literary plot than tragedy. And if reference should be made here to the *bürgerliches Trauerspiel*, then one might well

---

* two deaths with arrows . . . dance an extremely mournful ballet, mingled with cruel gestures at Sophia

wish to go so far as to recall the original title of Klinger's *Sturm und Drang*. *Der Wirrwarr* is the title the dramatist gave to his play. Complexity was what the baroque *Trauerspiel* sought with its vicissitudes and intrigues. And it is precisely here that it becomes palpably clear how allegory is related to it. The meaning of its action is expressed in a complicated configuration like letters in a monogram. Birken calls one kind of *Singspiel* (musical drama) a ballet, 'Thereby implying that the disposition of the figures and the external splendour are what is most essential. Such a ballet is nothing more than an allegorical picture executed with living figures, and with changes of scene. The spoken word makes no pretence to be dialogue; it is only a commentary on the images, spoken by the images themselves.'[25]

So long as they are not imposed too rigidly these explanations are relevant to the *Trauerspiel*. That this form is concerned with the display of allegorical types is clear from the custom of the double title alone. It would be well worth investigating why it is that only Lohenstein makes no use of it. One of the titles always refers to the subject matter, the other to its allegorical content. Following mediaeval linguistic practice the allegorical form is shown triumphant. The summary of the content of *Cardenio und Celinde* contains the following statement: 'Wie nun Catharine den sieg der heiligen liebe über den tod vorhin gewiesen, so zeigen diese den triumph oder das sieges-gepränge des todes über die irdische liebe'.[26]* Hallmann says of *Adonis und Rosibella*: 'Der Hauptzweck dieses Hirtenspieles Adonis und Rosibella, ist die Sinnreiche und über den Todt triumphierende Liebe.'[27]† 'Obsiegende Tugend' [Virtue triumphant] is the sub-title of Haugwitz's *Soliman*. The modern fashion for this form of expression came from Italy, where the *trionfi* were the dominant feature in the processions. The impressive translation of the

---

* Just as *Catharine* showed the victory of sacred love over death, so does this play show the triumph or victory parade of death over profane love.

† The main aim of this pastoral play is to show the significance of love and its triumph over death.

Trionfi which was published in Köthen in 1643 may have been influential in promoting the influence of this model. Italy, the home of emblematics, has always led the way in such matters. Or, as Hallmann puts it: 'Die Italiäner gleich wie sie in allen Erfindungen excelliren: also haben sie nichts weniger/ in Emblematischer Entschattung [der] Menschlichen Unglückseeligkeit . . . ihre Kunst erwiesen.'[29]* It is not uncommon for speech in the dialogues to be no more than a caption, conjured up from allegorical constellations in which the figures are related to one another. In short: as its caption, the maxim declares the stage-setting to be allegorical. The maxims can therefore quite properly be called 'schöne eingemengte Sprüche',[30]† as Klai calls them in the preface to his Herod-drama. Certain instructions for their disposition, derived from Scaliger, are still current. 'Die Lehr- und Dancksprüche (scil: Denksprüche) sind gleichsam des Trauerspiels Grundseulen; Solche aber müssen nicht von Dienern und geringen Leuten / sondern von den fürnemsten und ältsten Personen angeführet . . . werden.'[31]‡ Not only emblematic utterances,[32] but also entire speeches sound as if they properly belong beneath an allegorical engraving. For instance the hero's opening lines in *Papinian.* 'Wer über alle steigt und von der stoltzen höh | Der reichen ehre schaut, wie schlecht der pövel geh, | Wie unter ihm ein reich in lichten flammen krache, | Wie dort der wellen schaum sich in die felder mache | Und hier der himmel zorn, mit blitz und knall vermischt, | In thürm und tempel fahr, und was die nacht erfrischt, | Der heisse tag verbrenn, und seine sieges-zeichen | Sieht hier und dar verschränckt mit viel mahl tausend leichen, | Hat wol (ich geb es nach) viel über die gemein. | Ach! aber ach! wie leicht nimmt ihn der schwindel ein.'[33]§ The maxim has the

---

* Just as they excell in all inventions, so have the Italians equally demonstrated their skill . . . in the allegorical adumbration of human misfortune.

† beautiful, interspersed apophthegms

‡ The maxims and apophthegms are, so to speak, the basic pillars of the *Trauerspiel*; they must not, however, be spoken by servants and lesser persons, but by the most noble and senior characters.

§ Whoever rises above everyone and from the lofty heights of rich honour sees how ill the common people fare, how, below him, an empire bursts into bright flames, how here the foam of the waves bursts into the fields, and there the anger of the heavens, with both thunder and lightning, strikes tower and temple, and what is refreshed by the night is scorched by hot day, and sees how his trophies go hand in hand with many thousands of corpses, he may (I admit) have many advantages over ordinary men. But, alas, how easily he falls prey to giddiness.

same function here as lighting in baroque painting: it is a flash of light in the entangling darkness of allegory. Once again there is a connection with an older form of expression. In his *Uber die Kritische Behandlung der geistlichen Spiele* Wilken has compared the roles in such plays with the scrolls which 'in the old paintings are attached ... to the images of the persons from whose mouths they come',[34] and this applies to many passages in the texts of *Trauerspiele*. Only twenty-five years ago R. M. Meyer could write: 'We find it disturbing when in the paintings of old masters the figures have scrolls hanging out of their mouths ... and we find it almost horrifying that there was a time when every figure created by the hand of an artist had, so to speak, such a scroll in its mouth, which the observer was supposed to read like a letter, and then forget the bearer. However, we must not ... overlook the fact that this almost childish conception of the detail was based on a magnificent overall idea.'[35] Of course an *ad hoc* critical consideration of this idea will not stop at offering a half-hearted palliative, but will also necessarily depart as far from any understanding of it as this writer does with the explanation that the approach is derived from the 'primitive period', when 'everything was endowed with life'. The situation is rather – and this will be shown – that, in comparison to the symbol, the western conception of allegory is a late manifestation which has its basis in certain very fertile cultural conflicts. The allegorical maxim is comparable to the scrolls. Or again, it can be described as a conventional sector or frame, into which the action, in constant variations, intermittently penetrates, to reveal itself therein as an emblematic subject. The *Trauerspiel* is therefore in no way characterized by immobility, nor indeed by slowness of action (Wysocki has remarked: 'immobility is encountered in place of movement'[36]), but by the irregular rhythm of the constant pause, the sudden change of direction, and consolidation into new rigidity.

The greater the desire to emphasize the sententious quality of a line, the more lavishly the poet will decorate it with the names of objects which serve the emblematic description of what is meant. The stage-property, whose significance is implicit in the baroque *Trauerspiel* before it is made

explicit by courtesy of the drama of fate, is already stirring in the seventeenth century in the form of the emblematic metaphor. In a stylistic
history of this period – such as Erich Schmidt planned but did not complete [37] – a substantial chapter would have to be given over to illustrations of this mannerism. In all of these examples the exuberant use of
metaphor, the 'exclusively sensuous character'[38] of the figures of speech,
should be attributed to a penchant for an allegorical mode of expression,
and not to an oft-cited 'poetic sensuality', because, in its refined form, the
language of the time, including poetic language, avoids constant emphasis
of its basically metaphorical character. But, on the other hand, it is just as
wrong to see in this 'fashionable' linguistic mannerism 'the principle of . . .
divesting language of part of its sensuous character and making it more
abstract, [such] as is always evident in endeavours to make language
suitable for more cultivated social intercourse';[39] indeed it is a mis-
conceived application of a principle of the euphuistic language of the
Alamode period to the 'fashionable' language of the great poetry of the
earlier age. For the preciosity of the latter, as indeed of the baroque style
in general, consists to a great extent in an extreme recourse to concrete
words. And there is such a pronounced obsession with using these words
on the one hand and, on the other, displaying elegant antitheses, that
when an abstract word seems quite unavoidable, a concrete word is added
to it with quite uncommon frequency, so that new words are invented.
For instance: 'Verleumbdungs-Blitz',[40] 'Hoffahrts-Gifft',[41] 'Unschulds-
Zedern',[42]* 'Freundschaffts-Blut'.[43] Or else: 'So weil auch Mariamn'
als eine Natter beisst | Und mehr die Zwietrachts-Gall' als Friedens-
Zucker liebet.'[44]† The counterpart to such an approach is triumphantly
evident when the writer succeeds in significantly dividing a living entity
into the *disjecta membra* of allegory, as Hallmann does in an image of
court-life: 'Es hat Theodoric auch auff dem Meer geschifft / | Wo statt
der Wellen / Eiss; des Saltzes / heimlich Gifft / | Der Ruder / Schwerd und
Beil; der Seegel / Spinneweben; | Der Ancker / falsches Bley / des

---

* the lightning of calumny, the poison of Vainglory, the cedars of innocence, the blood of
friendship.
† Because Mariamne too bites like a viper and loves the gall of discord more than the sugar
of peace.

Nachens Glass umgeben.'⁴⁵* Cysarz observes pertinently: 'Every idea, however abstract, is compressed into an image, and this image, however concrete, is then stamped out in verbal form.' None of the dramatists was more prone to this mannerism than Hallmann. It destroys the unity of his dialogues. For hardly has an argument begun, than it is immediately transformed by one or other of the speakers into a metaphor which keeps on being extended as it is subjected to greater or lesser variation in numerous exchanges. With the remark: 'Der Tugenden Pallast kan Wollust nicht beziehn', Sohemus deeply insults Herod; but he, far from punishing him, sinks straight into allegory: 'Man siehet Eisenkraut bey edlen Rosen blühn.'⁴⁶† Thus it is that ideas evaporate in images.⁴⁷ Many a literary historian has given examples of the outlandish linguistic creations to which this writer was led in the search for conceits.⁴⁸ 'Mund und Gemüthe stehn in einem Meineids-Kasten I Dem hitz'ger Eifer nun die Riegel loss gemacht.'⁴⁹‡ 'Seht / wie dem Pheroras das traur'ge Sterbe-Kleid I Im Gifft-Glas wird gereicht.'⁵⁰§ 'Imfall die Warheit kan der Greuel-That erhell'n / I Dass Mariamnens Mund unreine Milch gesogen I Aus Tyridatens Brust / so werde stracks vollzogen / I Was Gott und Recht befihlt / und Rath und König schleusst.'⁵¹¶ There are certain words, in Hallmann the word 'comet' in particular, which acquire a grotesque allegorical usage. In order to describe the dire events taking place in the palace in Jerusalem, Antipater remarks that 'die Cometen sich in Salems Schloss begatten'.⁵²‖ Occasionally the imagery seems almost to get out of control, and the poetry to degenerate into flights of ideas. A prime example of this is provided by Hallmann: 'Die Frauen-List: Wenn meine Schlang' in edlen Rosen lieget / I Und Züngelnd saugt

---

* Theodoric too has embarked on that sea where his fragile boat is surrounded by ice instead of waves, secret poison instead of salt, sword and axe instead of oars, spider's webs instead of sails, perfidious lead instead of an anchor.

† Lechery cannot occupy the palace of virtue. . . . Ironwort blossoms beside noble roses.

‡ Mouth and mind are contained in one perjury-chest of which feverish zeal is now loosing the bolts.

§ Look how Pheroras is offered his mournful death-robe in the glass of poison.

¶ If truth can reveal the horrible deed of Mariamne in sucking impure milk from the breast of Tyridates, then what God and justice command, and council and king conclude will straightway be done.

‖ The comets are copulating in the castle of Salem.

den Weissheits-vollen Safft / I Wird Simson auch von Delilen besieget / I
Und schnell beraubt der überird'schen Krafft: I Hat Joseph gleich der
Juno Fahn getragen / I Herodes ihn geküsst auff seinem Wagen / I So
schaut doch / wie ein Molch [Dolch?] diss Karten-Blat zerritzt / I Weil
ihm sein Eh-Schatz selbst durch List die Bahre schnitzt.'[53]* In *Maria
Stuarda* by Haugwitz a lady-in-waiting to the queen says of God: 'Er
treibt die See von unsern Hertzen / I Dass derer Wellen stoltzer Guss I Uns
offt erziehlet heisse Schmertzen / I Doch ist es nur der Wunder-Fluss / I
Durch dessen unbegreifflichs regen / I Sich unsers Unglücks Kranckheit
legen.'[54]† This is every bit as obscure and allusive as the psalms of
Quirinus Kuhlmann. The rationalist criticism which has proscribed
these poems, begins with a polemic against their linguistic allegories.
'What a hieroglyphic and enigmatic obscurity casts its shadow over the
entire expression',[55] observes Breitinger, about a passage from Lohenstein's *Cleopatra*, in his *Critische Abhandlung von der Natur, den Absichten
und dem Gebrauche der Gleichnisse*; while Bodmer reproaches Hofmanns-
waldau in the same spirit: 'He wraps up the concepts in similes and figures
of speech as in a prison'.[57]

This poetry was in fact incapable of releasing in inspired song the profound meaning which was here confined to the verbal image. Its language
was heavy with material display. Never has poetry been less winged. The
re-interpretation of ancient tragedy is no less strange than the new
hymnic form which represented an attempt to equal the flights of Pindar –
however obscure and baroque these may have been. The baroque
Trauerspiel is not – as Baader says – endowed with the ability to make its

---

* Woman's cunning: When my serpent lies in noble roses and, hissing, sucks in the sap
of wisdom, Samson is vanquished by Delilah and quickly robbed of his supernatural
strength: if Joseph has carried the banner of Juno and Herod has kissed him in his chariot,
then look yet how a salamander [dagger?] tears up this card, because his marriage treasure
herself cunningly carves the bier.
† He stirs up the sea of our hearts so that the proud surge of its waves often causes us hot
pains, but this is only the miraculous tide through whose strange movement our sickness and
misfortune abate.

hieroglyphic element public. For its writing does not achieve transcendence by being voiced; rather does the world of written language remain self-sufficient and intent on the display of its own substance. Written language and sound confront each other in tense polarity. The relationship between them gives rise to a dialectic, in the light of which 'bombast' is justified as a consistently purposeful and constructive linguistic gesture. This view of the matter, one of the happiest and most fruitful, veritably falls into the lap of anyone who approaches the sources in a receptive frame of mind. Only when the power of reasoned enquiry was overcome by dizziness at the profundity of the abyss before it, could bombast become the bogey of epigonal stylistics. The division between signifying written language and intoxicating spoken language opens up a gulf in the solid massif of verbal meaning and forces the gaze into the depths of language. And although philosophical reflection on this subject was unknown to the baroque, the writings of Böhme provide a number of clear leads. Where he speaks of language Jacob Böhme, one of the greatest allegorists, upholds the value of sound over silent profundity. He developed the doctrine of the 'sensual' or natural language. This latter is not (and this is decisive) the emergence of the allegorical world into sound, for this remains confined to silence. 'Word-baroque' and 'image-baroque' – as Cysarz has only recently called these forms of expression – are rooted in each other as polar opposites. In the baroque the tension between the spoken and the written word is immeasurable. The spoken word, it might be said, is the ecstasy of the creature, it is exposure, rashness, powerlessness before God; the written word is the composure of the creature, dignity, superiority, omnipotence over the objects of the world. This, at least, is the case in the *Trauerspiel*, whereas in Böhme's more gentle outlook there is room for a more positive image of spoken language. 'Das ewige Wort oder Göttliche Hall oder Stimme / welche ein Geist ist / das hat sich in Formungen als in ein aussgesprochen Wort oder Hall mit der Gebährung des grossen Mysterii eingeführet / und wie das Freudenspiel im Geiste der ewigen Gebährung in sich selber ist / also ist auch der Werckzeug / als die aussgesprochene Form in sich selber / welches der lebendige Hall führet / und mit seinem eigenen ewigen Willen-geist schläget / dass es lautet und hallet / gleich wie eine Orgel von vielen

Stimmen mit einer einigen Lufft getrieben wird / dass eine jede Stimme / ja eine jede Pfeiffe ihren Thon gibt.'⁵⁷* 'Alles was von GOtt geredet / geschrieben oder gelehret wird / ohne die Erkäntnüss der Signatur, das ist stumm und ohne Verstand / dann es kommt nur aus einem historischen Wahn / von einem andern Mund / daran der Geist ohne Erkäntnüss stumm ist: So ihm aber der Geist die Signatur eröffnet / so verstehet er des andern Mund / und versteht ferner / wie sich der Geist . . . im Hall mit der Stimme hat offenbahret . . . Dann an der äusserlichen Gestaltnüss aller Creaturen / an ihrem Trieb und Begierde / item, an ihrem aussgehenden Hall / Stimm oder Sprache / kennet man den verborgenen Geist . . . Ein jedes Ding hat seinen Mund zur Offenbahrung. Und das ist die Natur-sprache / daraus jedes Ding aus seiner Eigenschafft redet / und sich immer selber offenbahret.'⁵⁸† Spoken language is thus the domain of the free, spontaneous utterance of the creature, whereas the written language of allegory enslaves objects in the eccentric embrace of meaning. This language, for Böhme the language of the blessed creature, in the verse of the *Trauerspiel* the language of the fallen creature, is accounted natural not only by virtue of its expression, but rather by its very origin. 'Von den Wörtern ist diese alte Streitfrage / ob dieselbige [sic] / als äusserliche Anzeigungen unsers inwendigen Sinnbegriffs / weren von Natur oder Chur / natürlich oder willkührlich / φύσει oder θέσει Und wird von den Gelahrten / was die Wörter in den Hauptsprachen

---

* The Eternal Word, or Divine Sound or Voice, which is a Spirit, has introduced itself with the Generation of the great Mystery into Formings, *viz.* into an expressed Word or Sound: And as the joyful Melody is in itself in the Spirit of the eternal Generation, so likewise is the Instrument, *viz.* the expressed Form in itself, which the living Eternal Voice guides, and strikes with his own Eternal Will-Spirit, that it sounds and melodizes; as an Organ of divers and various Sounds or Notes is moved with one only Air, so that each Note, yea every Pipe has its peculiar Tune.

† All whatever is spoken, written, or taught of God, without the Knowledge of the Signature is dumb and void of Understanding; for it proceeds only from an historical Conjecture, from the Mouth of another, wherein the Spirit without Knowledge is dumb; but if the Spirit opens to him the *Signature*, then he understands the Speech of another; and further he understands how the Spirit has manifested and revealed itself . . . in the Sound with the Voice . . . For by the external Form of all Creatures, by their Instigation, Inclination and Desire, also by their Sound, Voice and Speech which they utter, the hidden Spirit is known . . . Every Thing has its Mouth to Manifestation; and this is the Language of Nature, whence every Thing speaks out of its Property, and continually manifests itself.

betrifft / dieses einer sonderbaren natürlichen Wirckung zugeschrieben.'⁵⁹* Naturally enough the first place among the 'major languages' was occupied by the 'deutsche Haupt- und Heldensprache' [German chief and heroic language] – an expression which first occurs in Fischart's *Geschichtsklitterung* of 1575. The theory that it was directly descended from Hebrew was widespread, and it was not the most radical theory. There were others which actually traced Hebrew, Greek, and Latin back to German. According to Borinski, 'in Germany it was proved historically, from the Bible, that the whole world, including classical antiquity, was originally German'.⁶⁰ And so, on the one hand, attempts were made to lay claim to the most remote cultural materials, and on the other hand, the aim was to conceal the artificiality of this attitude in an extreme foreshortening of the historical perspective. Everything is placed in the same rarified atmosphere. As for the complete assimilation of all oral manifestations to a single primeval linguistic state, this sometimes took a spiritualist, sometimes a naturalist direction. The extremes are represented by the theory of Böhme and the practice of the Nuremberg school. Scaliger provided a starting-point for both, but only in the sense of a subject. The passage of the *Poetics* in question sounds remarkable enough. 'In A, latitudo. In I, longitudo. In E, profunditas. In O, coarctatio . . . Multum potest ad animi suspensionem, quae in Voto, in Religione: praesertim cum producitur, vt dij. etiam cum corripitur: Pij. Et ad tractum omnen denique designandum, Littora, Lites, Lituus, It, Ira, Mitis, Diues, Ciere, Dicere, Diripiunt . . . Dij, Pij, Iit: non sine manifestissima spiritus profectione. Lituus non sine soni, quem significat, similitudine . . . P, tamen quandam quaerit firmitatem. Agnosco enim in Piget, pudet, poenitet, pax, pugna, pes, paruus, pono, pauor, piger, aliquam fictionem. Parce metu, constantiam quandam insinuat. Et Pastor plenius, quam Castor. sic Plenum ipsum, et Purum, Posco, et alia eiusmodi. T, vero plurimum sese ostentat: Est enim litera sonitus explicatrix, fit namque sonus aut per S, aut per R, aut per T. Tuba, tonitru, tundo. Sed in fine

---

* There is a long-standing controversy about words: whether, as external indications of our inner sense of meaning, they derive from nature or nuture, necessarily or arbitrarily, φύσει or θέσει : and as far as the words of the major languages are concerned, do scholars ascribe this to a particular natural effect.

tametsi maximam verborum claudit apud Latinos partem, tamen in iis, quae sonum afferunt, affert ipsum quoque soni non minus. Rupit enim plus rumpit, quam Rumpo.'[61]* Analogously, but clearly independently of Scaliger, Böhme pursued his own speculations on speech. He thinks of the language of creatures 'not as a realm of words but ... as something resolved into its sounds and noises'.[62] 'In his view A was the first letter which forces its way from the heart, I the centre of the highest love, R possessed the character of the source of fire because it "schnarrt, prasselt und rasselt" [rasps, crackles, and rattles], and S was sacred fire.'[63] It can be assumed that the obviousness which such descriptions then possessed partly derived from the vitality of the dialects which still flourished universally. For the attempts of the linguistic societies to standardize the language were confined to written German. On the other hand creaturely language was naturalistically described as an onomatopoeic structure. A typical example is provided by the poetics of Buchner, which only carry through the opinions of his teacher Opitz.[64] It is true that, according to Buchner himself, genuine onomatopoeia is not permissible in the

---

* The letter A has a suggestion of breadth about it, the letter I suggests length, while about the letter E there is a hint of depth. The letter O indicates a certain degree of concentration ... The vowel combination figuring in the word 'voto' and in the word 'religione' contributes in an abundant manner to a heightening of the sensibilities. This is especially true of a word which is dragged out, like 'dii',† but is no less true of a word uttered rapidly, like 'pii'. Finally, to indicate every sort of lengthening taking place within a word, there are words like 'Littora, Lites, Lituus, It, Ira, Mitis, Dives, Ciere, Dicere, Diripiunt ... Dii, Pii, Iit', all of them words which cannot be spoken without a marked exhalation of breath. The word 'Lituus' carries a sound not unlike the thing it signifies ... The letter P, however, is lacking, to some degree, in firmness. For in words like 'piget, pudet, poenitet, pax, pugna, pes, paruus, pono, pavor' and 'piger' I recognize a certain onomatopoeic quality. The word 'parce', however, through fear does succeed in introducing an element of toughness. And 'pastor' exhibits this firmness much more than the word 'Castor'. The same is true of the word 'plenum' and 'purum, posco' and other examples of this kind. But the letter T is that letter which makes its mark most of all. For it is a letter which seems to proclaim its own sound. You could say that a very definite kind of sound is produced by the letter S, or R or T. 'Tuba, tonitru' and 'tundo' are examples in which the last letter figures. But in the last analysis, even though it ends the majority of Latin verbs, nevertheless, in the case of those verbs which are onomatopoeic, whatever their inflexions, the addition of the letter T contributes its own special kind of sound. Thus the word 'rupit' has within it a greater sense of 'breaking' than the word 'rumpo'.

† N.B. The word 'dii' is a biform of the word 'di', and thus is 'dragged out' in pronunciation in a way in which the word 'pii' is not. *Translator's note.*

Trauerspiel.[65] But is not pathos to some extent the regal natural sound of the *Trauerspiel*? The Nuremberg school goes furthest here. Klajus declares: 'there is no word in the German language which does not express its meaning in a "sonderliches Gleichniss".'[66]* Harsdörffer inverts the statement. 'Die Natur redet in allen Dingen / welche ein Getön von sich geben / unsere Teutsche Sprache / und daher haben etliche wähnen wollen / der erste Mensch Adam habe das Geflügel und alle Thier auf Erden nicht anderst als mit unseren Worten nennen können / weil er jedes eingeborne selbstlautende Eigenschafft Natur-mässig ausgedruket; und ist sich deswegen nicht zu verwundern / dass unsere Stammwörter meinsten Theils mit der heiligen Sprache gleich-stimmig sind.'[67]† He deduced from this that the task of German lyric poetry was 'to grasp the language of nature, so to speak, in words and rhythms. For him as for Birken such lyric poetry was actually required by religion, because it is God who is revealed in the rustling of the forests . . . and the roar of the storm.'[68] Something similar is again evident in the *Sturm und Drang*. 'Tears and sighs are the common language of the nations; I can understand even the helpless Hottentots, and will not be dumb before God, although I am from Tarent! . . . Dust possesses will-power, that is the sublimest thought I have for the creator, and I value the all-powerful impulse to freedom even in the struggling fly.'[69] This is the philosophy of the creature and its language, removed from the context of allegory.

The explanation of the status of the alexandrine as the verse-form of the baroque *Trauerspiel*, with reference to that strict division into two halves which frequently leads to antithesis, is not an entirely satisfactory one.

---

*peculiar analogy.

† In all things which utter sounds, nature speaks in the German language, and so some have wished to presume that Adam, the first man, cannot but have used our words to name the fowls of the air and the beasts of the earth, because he expressed every original, self-sounding property in a natural way; and it is therefore not surprising that our root-words are for the most part similar in sound to those of the holy language.

Every bit as characteristic of this verse is the contrast between the logical
– if one will, the classicistic – structure of the façade, and the phonetic
violence within. For, in the words of Omeis, the 'tragische *Stilus* . . . [ist]
mit prächtigen, langtönenden Wörtern angefüllt'.[70]* If, in the fact of the
colossal proportions of baroque architecture and baroque painting, it has
been permissible to emphasize the 'tendency to simulate the occupation
of space'[71] that is common to both, then the language of the *Trauerspiel*,
which expands in painterly fashion in the alexandrine, has the same function. The sententious maxim – even if the action with which it deals
becomes quite static – must at least give the impression of movement;
this made pathos a technical necessity. The violence which is a characteristic of maxims, as indeed of all verse, is made clearly visible by
Harsdörffer. 'Warum solche Spiele meistentheils in gebundner Rede
geschrieben werden? Antwort: weil die Gemüter eifferigst sollen bewegt
werden / ist zu den Trauer- und Hirtenspielen das Reimgebäud bräuch-
lich / welches gleich einer Trompeten die Wort / und Stimme einzwenget
/ dass sie so viel grössern Nachdruk haben.'[72]† And since the maxim,
which often adheres involuntarily to the stock imagery, is prone to push
thought along in well-worn grooves, the phonetic aspect is all the more
noteworthy. It was inevitable that, in its treatment of the alexandrine,
stylistic criticism also fell into the general error of the older school of
philology in accepting the ancient stimuli to, or pretexts for, its formation
as evidence of its real essence. Although very perceptive in its first part,
the following comment from Richter's study, *Liebeskampf 1630 und
Schaubühne 1670*, is typical: 'The special artistic merit of the great
dramatists of the seventeenth century is closely connected with the creative
distinction of their verbal style. It is not so much by its characterization or
its composition . . . as by what it achieves with rhetorical artistic means,
which in the last analysis are always derived from antiquity, that the high
tragedy of the seventeenth century affirms its unique stature. But not only

---

* the tragic style is full of grand, resonant words.

† Why are such plays usually written in metrical language? Answer: because the feelings
must be most keenly moved, *Trauerspiele* and pastoral plays are best served by the system of
rhyming, which compresses words and voice like a trumpet so that they have a much greater
emphasis.

did the image-packed concentration and taut structure of the periods and stylistic figures create difficulties for the actors who had to memorize them, they were so deeply rooted in the completely heterogeneous formal world of antiquity that their remoteness from the language of the people was infinite . . . It is a matter for regret that we . . . possess no evidence as to what the average man made of it.'[73] Even if the language of these dramas had been exclusively a matter for scholars, the uneducated would still have derived enjoyment from the element of spectacle. But the bombast corresponded to the expressive impulses of the age, and these impulses are usually immeasurably stronger than the intellectual interest in the transparent details of plot. The Jesuits, who had a masterly understanding of the public, could scarcely have had, at their performances, an audience consisting entirely of people who understood Latin.[74] They probably felt convinced of the ancient truth that the authority of a statement depends so little on its comprehensibility that it can actually be increased by obscurity.

The practices of these writers combine with the principles of their linguistic theories to bring out a basic motif of the allegorical approach in a most surprising place. In the anagrams, the onomatopoeic phrases, and many other examples of linguistic virtuosity, word, syllable, and sound are emancipated from any context of traditional meaning and are flaunted as objects which can be exploited for allegorical purposes. The language of the baroque is constantly convulsed by rebellion on the part of the elements which make it up. It is only in its greater plasticity, which derives from its greater artistry, that the following passage from the Herod-drama of Calderón is superior to similar passages, particularly in Gryphius. By chance, Mariamne, the wife of Herod, catches sight of the fragments of a letter in which her husband orders that, in the event of his own death, she should be killed in order to preserve his supposedly threatened honour. She picks up these fragments from the ground and gives an account of their content in extremely evocative lines. 'What do they contain? I Death is the very first word I which I encounter; here is

the word honour, I And there I see Mariamne. I What does this mean?
Heaven help me! I For much is said in the three words I Mariamne, death,
and honour. I Here it says: secretly; here: I dignity; here: commands; and
here: ambition; I And here, it continues: if I die. I But what doubt can
there be? I am already informed I By the folds of the paper, I Which are
related I to the crime they enfold. I O field, on your green carpet I Let me
piece them together!'[75] Even in their isolation the words reveal themselves as fateful. Indeed, one is tempted to say that the very fact that they
still have a meaning in their isolation lends a threatening quality to this
remnant of meaning they have kept. In this way language is broken up so
as to acquire a changed and intensified meaning in its fragments. With
the baroque the place of the capital letter was established in German
orthography. It is not only the aspiration to pomp, but at the same time
the disjunctive, atomizing principle of the allegorical approach which is
asserted here. Without any doubt many of the words written with an
initial capital at first acquired for the reader an element of the allegorical.
In its individual parts fragmented language has ceased merely to serve
the process of communication, and as a new-born object acquires a
dignity equal to that of gods, rivers, virtues and similar natural forms
which fuse into the allegorical. As has already been said, the work of the
young Gryphius provides particularly extreme examples of this. And if it
is not possible, either here or elsewhere in German literature, to find a
counterpart to the incomparable passage from Calderón, the vigour of
Andreas Gryphius is, in comparison with the refinement of the Spaniard,
by no means to be despised. For he possesses a quite astonishing mastery
of the art of allowing characters to answer each other in debate with, so to
speak, independent fragments of speech. In the second act of *Leo Armenius*, for instance. 'Leo: Diss hauss wird stehn, dafern des hauses feinde
fallen. I Theodosia: Wo nicht ihr fall verletzt, die dieses hauss umwallen. I
Leo: Umwallen mit den schwerdt. Theodosia: Mit dem sie uns beschützt.
I Leo: Das sie auf uns gezuckt. Theodosia: Die unsern stuhl gestützt.'[76]*

---

* Leo: This house will stand if the enemies of the house fall. Theodosia: If their fall does
not harm those who ring round this house. Leo: Ring it round with the sword. Theodosia:
With which they have defended us. Leo: With which they have threatened us. Theodosia:
Who have supported our throne.

When the exchanges become angry and violent there is an evident preference for accumulations of fragmentary passages of dialogue. They are more numerous in Gryphius than in the later writers,[77] and, along with the abrupt laconisms, they fit very well into the overall stylistic fabric of his dramas: for both produce an impression of the fragmentary and chaotic. However useful this technique of presentation is for the creation of theatrical excitement, it is by no means dependent on the dramatic genre. In the following utterance from the work of Schiebel it is a consciously pastoral device: 'Noch heutiges Tages bekömmt manchmal ein andächtiger Christ ein Tröpfflein Trostes / (auch wohl ein Wörtgen nur / aus einem geistreichen Liede oder erbaulichen Predigt /) das schlingt er (gleichsam) so appetitlich hinunter / dass es ihm wohl gedeyet / inniglich afficiret / und dermassen erquicket / dass er bekennen muss / es stecke was Göttliches darunter.'[78]* It is no accident that, in such a figurative turn of speech, the reception of words is, as it were, attributed to the sense of taste. For the baroque sound is and remains something purely sensuous; meaning has its home in written language. And the spoken word is only afflicted by meaning, so to speak, as if by an inescapable disease; it breaks off in the middle of the process of resounding, and the damming up of the feeling, which was ready to pour forth, provokes mourning. Here meaning is encountered, and will continue to be encountered as the reason for mournfulness. The antithesis of sound and meaning could not but be at its most intense where both could be successfully combined in *one*, without their actually cohering in the sense of forming an organic linguistic structure. This task, a deducible one, is accomplished in a scene which stands out as a masterpiece in an otherwise uninteresting Viennese *Haupt- und Staatsaktion*. In *Die Glorreiche Marter Joannes von Nepomuck* the fourteenth scene of the first act shows one of the intriguers (Zytho) acting as an echo to the mythological speeches of his victim (Quido), and answering them with ominous intimations.[79] The conversion of the pure sound of creaturely language into the richly significant irony which re-

---

* Even today a devout Christian sometimes receives a crumb of comfort (be it only a word from an intelligent song or an edifying sermon), and this he swallows (as it were) so hungrily that it does him good, inwardly stirs him and refreshes him so much that he has to confess that it contains something divine.

echoes from the mouth of the intriguer, is highly indicative of the relationship of this character to language. The intriguer is the master of meanings. In the harmless effusion of an onomatopoeic natural language they are the obstacle, and so the origin of a mourning for which the intriguer is responsible along with them. If the echo, the true domain of the free play of sound, is now, so to speak, taken over by meaning, then it must prove to be entirely a manifestation of the linguistic, as the age understood it. And a form was indeed provided for it. 'The echo, which repeats the last two or three syllables of a strophe, often omitting a letter so that it sounds like an answer, a warning, or a prophecy, is something very "pleasing" and very popular.' This game, like other similar ones, which were so readily taken for foolish trifles, brings us to the heart of the matter. In them the linguistic attitude of bombast is so far from being denied that they could very well serve as illustrations of its formula. Language which, on the one hand, seeks, in the fullness of sound, to assert its creaturely rights, is, on the other hand, in the pattern of the alexandrine, unremittingly bound to a forced logicality. This is the stylistic law of bombast, the formula for the 'Asiatische Worte'[80]* of the *Trauerspiel*. The gesture, which thereby seeks to incorporate meaning, is of a piece with the violent distortion of history. In language, as in life, to adopt only the typical movement of the creature and yet to express the whole of the cultural world from antiquity to Christian Europe – such is the remarkable mental attitude which is never renounced even in the *Trauerspiel*. The enormous artificiality of its mode of expression thus has its roots in that same extreme yearning for nature as the pastoral plays. On the other hand, this very mode of expression, which only represents – that is to say represents the nature of language – and as far as possible avoids profane communication, is courtly and refined. One cannot perhaps speak of a genuine transcendence of the baroque, a reconciliation of sound and meaning, before Klopstock, thanks to what A. W. Schlegel called the 'grammatical' tendency of his odes. His bombast depends much less on sound and image than on the arrangement of words, the word-order.

---

* Asiatic words

The phonetic tension in the language of the seventeenth century leads directly to music, the opposite of meaning-laden speech. Like all the other roots of the *Trauerspiel*, this one too is entwined with those of the pastoral. That which is initially present in the *Trauerspiel* as a dancing chorus, and with the passage of time tends increasingly to become a spoken, oratorical chorus, openly displays its operatic character in the pastoral play. The 'passion for the organic',[81] which has long had a place in the discussion of the visual art of the baroque, is not so easy to describe in literary terms. And it must always be borne in mind that such words refer not so much to the external form as to the mysterious interiors of the organic. The voice emerges from out of these interiors and, properly speaking, its dominion extends in fact to what might be called an organic impulse in poetry, such as can be studied in the oratorio-like intermezzi, in the work of Hallmann especially. He writes: 'Palladius: Der zuckersüsse Tantz ist Göttern selbst geweiht! I Antonius: Der zuckersüsse Tantz verzuckert alles Leid! I Svetonius: Der zuckersüsse Tantz beweget Stein' und Eisen! I Julianius: Den zuckersüssen Tantz muss Plato selber preisen! I Septitius: Der zuckersüsse Tantz besieget alle Lust! I Honorius: Der zuckersüsse Tantz erquicket Seel' und Brust!'[82]* On stylistic grounds it may be supposed that such passages were spoken in the chorus.[83] Flemming says the same with reference to Gryphius: 'Too much could not be expected of the subsidiary roles. He therefore gives them little to say, preferring to combine them in the chorus, and in so doing he achieves significant artistic effects which could never have been attained through naturalistic speech on the part of individuals. In this way the artist effectively turns the constraints of the material to artistic account.'[84] Here one should think of the judges, the conspirators, and the underlings in *Leo Armenius*, the courtiers of Catharina, the maidens of Julia. A further operatic impulse was the musical overture, which preceded the plays of both the Jesuits and the protestants. Nor do the choreographical interludes and the – in a deeper

---

* Palladius: The sugar-sweet dance is dedicated to the gods themselves! Antonius: The sugar-sweet dance sweetens all pain! Suetonius: The sugar-sweet dance moves stone and iron! Julianus: The sugar-sweet dance must Plato himself praise! Septitius: The sugar-sweet dance is victorious over all pleasure! Honorius: The sugar-sweet dance refreshes soul and breast!

sense – choreographical style of the intrigue run counter to this development which, at the end of the century brought about the dissolution of the *Trauerspiel* into opera. The related ideas which it is the purpose of these observations to call to mind have been developed by Nietzsche in *The Birth of Tragedy*. His concern was to make a proper distinction between Wagner's 'tragic' *Gesamtkunstwerk* and the frivolous opera, which had its preparatory stages in the baroque. He threw down the gauntlet with his condemnation of recitative. And in so doing he proclaimed his adherence to that form which so completely corresponded to the fashionable tendency to re-awaken the primal voice of all creatures. 'They could abandon themselves to the dream of having descended once more into the paradisiacal beginnings of mankind, where music also must have had that unsurpassed purity, power, and innocence of which the poets, in their pastoral plays, could give such touching accounts . . . The recitative was regarded as the rediscovered language of this primitive man; opera as the rediscovered country of this idyllically or heroically good creature, who simultaneously with every action follows a natural artistic impulse, who accomplishes his speech with a little singing, in order that he may immediately break forth into full song at the slightest emotional excitement . . . The man incapable of art creates for himself a kind of art precisely because he is the inartistic man as such. Because he does not sense the Dionysian depth of music, he changes his musical taste into an appreciation of the understandable word-and-tone-rhetoric of the passions in the *stilo rappresentativo*, and into the voluptuousness of the arts of the song. Because he is unable to behold a vision, he forces the machinist and the decorative artist into his service. Because he cannot comprehend the true nature of the artist, he conjures up the "artistic primitive man" to suit his taste, that is, the man who sings and recites verses under the influence of passion.'[85] Just as every comparison with tragedy – not to mention musical tragedy – is of no value for the understanding of opera, so it is that from the point of view of literature, and especially the *Trauerspiel*, opera must seem unmistakably to be a product of decadence. The obstacle of meaning and intrigue loses its weight, and both operatic plot and operatic language follow their course without encountering any resistance, issuing finally into banality. With the disappearance of the obstacle the soul of the work, mourning, also disappears, and just as the dramatic structure is emptied, so too is the scenic structure, which looks elsewhere for its justification, now that allegory, where it is not omitted, has become a hollow façade.

The self-indulgent delight in sheer sound played its part in the decline of the *Trauerspiel*. Nonetheless, music – by virtue of its own essence rather than the favour of the authors – is something with which the allegorical drama is intimately familiar. This, at least, is the lesson to be derived from the musical philosophy of the romantic writers, who have an elective affinity with the baroque, and whose voice ought to be heeded here. This, and this alone, would, at least yield a synthesis of the antitheses deliberately opened up by the baroque, and only through it would the full justification of the antitheses be clear. Such a romantic approach to the *Trauerspiel* does at least raise the question of how far music has a more than functional, theatrical role in the work of Shakespeare and Calderón. For it surely does. And so the following account by the brilliant Johann Wilhelm Ritter may be presumed to open up a perspective, the penetration of which we must ourselves forego, for it would be irresponsible improvisation. It could only be accomplished by a fundamental discussion of language, music, and script. What follow are passages from a long and, if one may say so, monologue-like essay in which, perhaps almost involuntarily, in the course of a letter which the scholar is writing about Chladni's figures, ideas arise which embrace many things, either powerfully or more tentatively: 'It would be beautiful,' he remarks about those lines which form different patterns on a glass plate strewn with sand at the touch of different notes, 'if what became externally clear here were also exactly what the sound pattern is for us inwardly: a light pattern, firewriting... Every sound would then have its own letter directly to hand... That inward connection of word and script – so powerful that we write when we speak... has long interested me. Tell me: how do we transform the thought, the idea, into the word; and do we ever have a thought or an idea without its hieroglyph, its letter, its script? Truly, it is so: but we do not usually think of it. But once, when human nature was more powerful, it really was more extensively thought about; and this is proved by the existence of word and script. Their original, and absolute, simultaneity was rooted in the fact that the organ of speech itself writes in order to speak. The letter alone speaks, or rather: word and script are, at source, one, and neither is possible without the other . . . Every sound pattern is an electric pattern, and every electric pattern is a sound pattern.'[86] 'My aim . . . was therefore to re-discover, or else to find the primeval or natural script by means of electricity.'[87] 'In reality the whole of creation is language, and so is literally created by the word, the created and creating word itself . . . But the letter is inextricably bound up with this word both in general and in particular.'[88] 'All the plastic arts: architecture, sculpture, painting, etc. belong pre-eminently among such script, and developments and derivations of it.'[89] With these comments the virtual romantic theory of allegory concludes, on a question as it were. Any answer would have to find a place for this divination of Ritter's among the concepts proper to it; it would have to bring oral and written language together, by whatever means possible, which can only mean identifying them dialectically as thesis and antithesis; to secure for music, the antithetical mediating link, and the last remaining universal language since the tower of Babel, its rightful central position as antithesis; and it would have to investigate how written language grows out of music and not directly from the sounds of the spoken word. These are tasks which lie far outside the domain of both romantic intuitions and non-theological philosophy. This romantic theory of allegory remains only virtual, but it is nonetheless an unmistakable monument to the affinity of baroque and romanticism. There is no need to add that actual discussions of allegory, such as that in Friedrich Schlegel's *Gespräch über die Poesie*,[90] do not possess the same profundity as Ritter's exposition; indeed, following the example of Friedrich Schlegel's imprecise use of language, they probably mean, with the statement that all beauty is allegory, nothing more than the classicistic commonplace that it is a symbol. Not so Ritter. With the theory that every image is only a form of writing, he gets to the very heart of the allegorical attitude. In the context of allegory the image is only a signature, only the monogram of essence, not the essence itself in a mask.

But there is nothing subordinate about written script; it is not cast away in reading, like dross. It is absorbed along with what is read, as its 'pattern'. The printers, and indeed the writers of the baroque, paid the closest possible attention to the pattern of the words on the page. It is known that Lohenstein practised 'the inscription of the engraving 'Castus amor Cygnis vehitur, Venus improba corvis' [Chaste love is expressed by swans, base Venus by crows], in its printed form, on the paper with his own hand'.[91] Herder finds – and this is still valid today – that the baroque literature is 'almost unsurpassed . . . in printing and decoration'.[92] And so the age was not entirely without some sense of those comprehensive relationships between spoken language and script, which provide the philosophical basis of the allegorical, and which contain within them the resolution of their true tension. If, that is, Strich's ingenious and illuminating hypothesis about the pictorial poems is correct, namely that 'the underlying idea may have been that the changing length of the lines, if it imitates an organic form, must also yield an organically rising and falling rhythm'.[93] The opinion of Birken – expressed through the mouth of Floridan in the *Dannebergische Helden-Blut* – points very much in the same direction: 'every natural occurrence in this world could be the effect of the materialization of a cosmic reverberation or sound, even the movement of the stars'.[94] This finally establishes the unity, in terms of theory of language, between the verbal and the visual manifestations of the baroque.

> Ja / wenn der Höchste wird vom Kirch-Hof erndten
> ein / So werd ich Todten-Kopff ein Englisch Antlitz
> seyn.
> Daniel Casper von Lohenstein: *Redender Todten-Kopff*
> *Herrn Matthäus Machners**

All the material, with its far-reaching implications, which it has been possible to uncover by a method which occasionally seemed vague, occa-

---

* Yea, when the Highest comes to bring in the harvest from the graveyard, so will I, a death's-head, become an angel's countenance.

sionally reminiscent of cultural history, forms a whole when seen in relation to allegory, comes together in the idea of the *Trauerspiel*. Our account may, indeed must, linger so insistently over the allegorical structure of this form for the simple reason that it is only thanks to this structure that the *Trauerspiel* can assimilate as its content the subjects which contemporary conditions provide it. Moreover this assimilated content cannot be elucidated without the aid of the theological concepts, which were indispensable even to its exposition. If, in the concluding part of this study, we do not hesitate to use such concepts, this is no μετάβασις εἰς ἄλλο γένος [transition to a different subject]. For a critical understanding of the *Trauerspiel*, in its extreme, allegorical form, is possible only from the higher domain of theology; so long as the approach is an aesthetic one, paradox must have the last word. Such a resolution, like the resolution of anything profane into the sacred, can only be accomplished historically, in terms of a theology of history, and only dynamically, not statically in the sense of a guaranteed economics of salvation; that would be clear even if the baroque *Trauerspiel* were less obviously related to the *Sturm und Drang* and romanticism, and even if its – probably vain – hopes for the rehabilitation of what is best in it by current dramatic experiments were less intense. The long-overdue interpretation of its content will – this much is obvious – have to get especially seriously to grips with those awkward motifs with which it does not seem possible to do anything except establish their material content. Above all: what is the significance of those scenes of cruelty and anguish in which the baroque drama revels? It is of a piece with the un-self-conscious and unreflective attitude of baroque art-criticism that there is not a torrent of direct replies. A concealed but valuable one is contained in the statement that: 'Integrum humanum corpus symbolicam iconem nigredi non posse, partem tamen corporis ei constituendae non esse ineptam.'[1]* This occurs in the account of a controversy about the norms of emblematics. The orthodox emblematist could not think differently: the human body could be no exception to the commandment which ordered the destruction of the organic so that the true meaning, as it was written and ordained, might be picked up from

---

*The whole human body cannot enter a symbolical icon, but it is not inappropriate for part of the body to constitute it.

its fragments. Where, indeed, could this law be more triumphantly displayed than in the man who abandons his conventional, conscious physis in order to scatter it to the manifold regions of meaning? Emblematics and heraldry have not always unreservedly complied with this. In the *Ars heraldica*, to which we have already referred, it says only: 'Die Haar bedeuten die vielfältigen Gedancken',[2]* while 'die Herolden' [the heralds] cut the lion right in two: 'Das Haupt / die Brust / und das gantze vordere Theil bedeutet Grossmüthigkeit und Dapfferkeit / das hintere aber / die Stärcke / Grimm und Zorn / so dem Brüllen folget.'[3]† Transferred to the sphere of a quality which still affects the body, this emblematic division is the inspiration of Opitz's exquisite phrase, 'Handhabung der Keuschheit',[4]‡ which he claims to have learned from Judith. It is the same in Hallmann, as he illustrates this virtue in the chaste Ägytha, whose 'Geburts-Glied'§ is said to have been found still undecayed in her grave many years after her burial.[5] If martyrdom thus prepares the body of the living person for emblematic purposes, it is not without significance that physical pain as such was ever present for the dramatist to use as an element in the action. It is not only the dualism of Descartes that is baroque; as a consequence of the doctrine of psycho-physical determination, the theory of the passions also deserves the closest consideration. Since, in fact, the spirit is in itself pure reason, true to itself, and it is physical influences alone which bring it into contact with the world, the torture which it endures was a more immediate basis of violent emotions than so-called tragic conflicts. And if it is in death that the spirit becomes free, in the manner of spirits, it is not until then that the body too comes properly into its own. For this much is self-evident: the allegorization of the physis can only be carried through in all its vigour in respect of the corpse. And the characters of the *Trauerspiel* die, because it is only thus, as corpses, that they can enter into the homeland of allegory. It is not for the sake of immortality that they meet their end, but for the sake of the

---

* Hair signifies many and varied thoughts
† The head, the breast, and the whole front part signify magnanimity and courage, but the hind part signifies the strength, rage, and anger, which follow the roar.
‡ use of chastity
§ Birth-member (i.e. womb)

corpse. 'Er lässt uns seine leichen | Zum pfande letzter gunst',[6]* says the daughter of Charles Stuart about her father, who, for his part, did not forget to request that it be embalmed. Seen from the point of view of death, the product of the corpse is life. It is not only in the loss of limbs, not only in the changes of the aging body, but in all the processes of elimination and purification that everything corpse-like falls away from the body piece by piece. It is no accident that precisely nails and hair, which are cut away as dead matter from the living body, continue to grow on the corpse. There is in the physis, in the memory itself, a *memento mori*; the obsession of the men of the middle ages and the baroque with death would be quite unthinkable if it were only a question of reflection about the end of their lives. The corpse-poetry of a writer like Lohenstein is, in essence, not mannerism, although it would not be wrong to recognise this element in it. Among the earliest works of Lohenstein there are remarkable experiments in this lyric theme. While still at school he had had the task of celebrating 'the passion of Christ in alternate Latin and German poems, arranged like the limbs of the human body',[7] in accordance with a traditional scheme. The *Denck- und Danck-Altar* [Altar of memory and gratitude], which he dedicated to his dead mother, is an example of the same type. The parts of the body are described in the state of putrefaction in nine unrelenting strophes. Such themes must have had similar relevance for Gryphius, and his study of anatomy, which he never abandoned, was doubtless influenced by these strange emblematic interests as well as by scientific ones. Sources for corresponding descriptions in drama were found in Seneca's *Hercules Oetaeüs* in particular, but also in his *Phaedra*, *Troades*, and elsewhere. 'In the manner of anatomical dissection, and with an unmistakable delight in cruelty, the parts of the body are individually enumerated.'[8] It is well known that Seneca was, in other respects as well, a respected authority for the baroque theatre of cruelty, and it would be worth investigating how far analogous assumptions provide the basis for those motifs in his dramas which were influential at that time. In the *Trauerspiel* of the seventeenth century the corpse becomes quite simply the pre-eminent emblematic property. The apotheoses are

* He leaves us his body as a pledge of final goodwill

barely conceivable without it. 'Mit blassen Leichen prangen [sie]';[9]* and it is the function of the tyrant to provide the *Trauerspiel* with them. Thus the conclusion of *Papinian*, in which there are traces of the influence of the troupe-play on the late Gryphius, shows what Bassianus Caracalla has done to the family of Papinian. The father and two sons are killed. 'Beyde leichen werden auf zweyen trauerbetten von Papiniani dienern auf den schauplatz getragen und einander gegenüber gestellet. Plautia redet nichts ferner, sondern gehet höchst-traurig von einer leiche zu der andern, küsset zuweilen die häupter und hände, bis sie zuletzt auf Papiniani leichnam ohnmächtig sincket und durch ihre statsjungfern den leichen nachgetragen wird.'[10]† At the conclusion of Hallmann's *Sophia*, after the execution of every kind of torture on the constant Christian and her daughters, the inner stage opens, 'in welchem die Todtenmahlzeit gezeiget wird / nehmlich die drey Köpfe der Kinder mit drey Gläsern Blut'.[11]‡ The 'Todtenmahlzeit' [banquet of death] was held in high regard. In Gryphius it is not yet shown, but reported. 'Fürst Meurab, blind von hass, getrotzt durch so viel leiden, | Liess der entleibten schaar die bleichen köpff abschneiden, | Und als der häupter reyh, die ihn so hoch verletzt, | Zu einem schaugericht auf seinen tisch gesetzt, | Nam er, schier ausser sich, den dargereichten becher | Und schrie: diss ist der kelch, den ich, der meinen rächer, | Nu nicht mehr sclav, erwisch!'[12]§ In later works such banquets came to be seen on stage, the dramatists availing themselves of an Italian trick, which is recommended by Harsdörffer and Birken. Through a hole in the top of a table, the cloth of which hung down to the ground, there appeared the head of an actor. Occasionally these displays of the dead body occur at the beginning of the

---

* They are resplendent with pale corpses

† The two bodies are borne onto the stage on biers by servants of Papinian, and placed on opposite sides. Plantia speaks no more but goes most mournfully from one corpse to the other, kisses the heads and the hands, until she finally sinks down unconscious over the body of Papinian, and is carried off after the bodies by her ladies-in-waiting.

‡ and the banquet of death is revealed: the heads of the three children with three glasses of blood.

§ Prince Meurab, blind with hatred, obstinate through so much suffering, had the pallid heads cut off from the dead men, and when the row of heads, which had so injured him, had been served up as a feast on his table, quite beside himself, he took the proffered cup and cried: this is the cup which I, the avenger of my own, a slave no longer, now take hold of!

Trauerspiel. The introductory stage direction to *Catharina von Georgien*[13] provides one example of this, as does the curious set in the first act of *Heraclius*: 'Ein grosses Feld / erfüllet mit sehr vielen Leichen des geschlagenen Krieges-Heeres des Keisers Mauritii nebst etlichen aus dem benachbarten Gebirge entspringenden Wässerbächlein.'[14]*

It is not antiquarian interest which enjoins us to follow the tracks which lead from here, more clearly than from anywhere else, back into the middle ages. For it is not possible to overestimate the importance for the baroque of the knowledge of the Christian origin of the allegorical outlook. And these tracks, although they have been left by so many and so different spirits, are the signposts on a road followed by the genius of allegorical vision even in its changing intentions. The writers of the seventeenth century have often re-assured themselves with a backward glance at this trail. In connection with his *Leidender Christus* [Christ in agony] Harsdörffer referred his pupil Klai to the Passion-poetry of Gregory of Nazianzus.[15] Gryphius, too, 'translated almost twenty early mediaeval hymns . . . into his own language, which was well suited to their solemn but vigorous style; he particularly favours the greatest of all the hymn-writers, Prudentius'.[16] There is a threefold material affinity between baroque and mediaeval Christianity. The struggle against the pagan gods, the triumph of allegory, the torment of the flesh, are equally essential to both. These motifs are most intimately connected. In terms of the history of religion – so it becomes clear – they are one and the same. And it is only in these terms that the origin of allegory can be illuminated. If the dissolution of the pantheon of antiquity has a decisive role in this origin, it is exceedingly instructive that its reinvigoration in humanism arouses the seventeenth century to protest. Rist, Moscherosch, Zesen, Harsdörffer, Birken, raise their voices against mythologically embellished literature as, before them, only the old Christian Latin authors had done;

---

* A large field, filled with very many bodies, soldiers in the defeated army of the Emperor Mauritius, as well as several rivulets flowing from the nearby mountains.

and then Prudentius, Juvencus, Venantius Fortunatus, are cited as praiseworthy examples of a chaste muse. 'Wahre Teufel'* is how Birken describes the pagan gods,[17] and there is a passage in Hallmann in which the attitude of a thousand years earlier is quite strikingly re-echoed; and this is clearly not the result of any concern for historical colour. In the religious dispute between Sophia and the Emperor Honorius the following question is asked: 'Beschützt nicht Jupiter den Kaiserlichen Thron?' And Sophia replies: 'Vielmehr als Jupiter ist Gottes wahrer Sohn!'[18]† This archaic swiftness in response derives directly from the baroque attitude. For once again antiquity was threateningly close to Christianity, in that form in which it made a final, and not unsuccessful attempt to impose itself upon the new teaching: gnosticism. With the Renaissance, occultist tendencies gained in strength, being particularly favoured by neo-Platonic studies. Rosicrucianism and alchemy took their places alongside astrology, the ancient occidental residue of oriental paganism. European antiquity was divided and its obscure after-effects in the middle-ages drew inspiration from its radiant after-image in humanism. Out of deep spiritual kinship Warburg has given a fascinating explanation of how, in the Renaissance 'heavenly manifestations were conceived in human terms, so that their demonic power might be at least visually contained'.[19] The Renaissance stimulates the visual memory – how much, can be seen from the conjuration scenes in the *Trauerspiel* – but at the same time it awakens a visual speculation which is perhaps of greater import for the formation of style. And the emblematics of this speculation are bound up with the world of the middle ages. There is no product of allegorical fantasy, however baroque, which is without a counterpart in this world. The allegorists among the mythographers, who had already been a subject of interest in early Christian apologetics, are resurrected. At the age of sixteen, Grotius edits Martianus Capella. Entirely in the early Christian manner, the ancient Gods and the allegories are on one and the same level in the chorus of the *Trauerspiel*. And because the fear

---

* veritable devils

† Does not Jupiter protect the imperial throne? . . . The true son of God is much more than Jupiter!

of demons cannot but make the flesh, suspect as it already is, seem particularly oppressive, the middle ages saw the beginnings of a radical attempt at its subjection in emblematics. 'Nakedness as an emblem' – this could well be used as a title for the following account by Bezold. 'Only in the beyond were the blessed supposed to enjoy an incorruptible corporeality and a reciprocal pleasure in each other's beauty in complete purity (Augustine: *De Civitate dei*, xxii, 24). Until then nakedness remained a sign of impurity, and as such it was, at most, appropriate for Greek gods, or infernal demons. Accordingly, whenever mediaeval scholarship came across unclothed figures, it sought to explain this impropriety with reference to a symbolism which was frequently far-fetched, and generally hostile. It is only necessary to read the explanations of Fulgentius and his followers as to why Venus, Cupid, and Bacchus are painted naked; Venus, for instance, because she sends her admirers away stripped bare, or because the crime of lust cannot be concealed; Bacchus, because drinkers throw away all their possessions, or because the drunkard cannot keep his most secret thoughts to himself . . . The implications which a Carolingian writer, Walahfrid Strabo, seeks to discover in his extremely obscure description of a naked sculpture are ingenious to a wearisome degree. In question is a subordinate figure in the gilded equestrian statue of Theodoric . . . The fact that . . . the black, ungilded "attendant" shows his naked flesh, leads the poet to the conceit that the naked man brings particular discredit upon the other, who is also naked, that is to say the Arian tyrant, naked of all virtue.'[20] As can be seen, allegorical exegesis tended above all in two directions: it was designed to establish, from a Christian point of view, the true, demonic nature of the ancient gods, and it also served the pious mortification of the flesh. It is therefore no accident that the middle ages and the baroque took pleasure in the meaningful juxtaposition of statues of idols and the bones of the dead. In the *Vita Constantini* Eusebius can write of skulls and bones in the statues of the gods, and Männling asserts that the 'Egyptier [hätten] in höltzernen Bildern Leichen begraben'.*

---

* the Egyptians buried bodies in wooden images

The concept of the allegorical can do justice to the *Trauerspiel* only in the particular form in which it is distinguished, not just from the theological symbol, but equally from the mere decorative epithet. Allegory did not originate as a scholastic arabesque to the ancient conception of the gods. Originally it had none of that playfulness, detachment, and superiority which, with an eye to its latest products, it has been customary to attribute to it; quite the contrary. If the church had not been able quite simply to banish the gods from the memory of the faithful, allegorical language would never have come into being. For it is not an epigonal victory monument; but rather the word which is intended to exorcise a surviving remnant of antique life. It is, of course, true that in the first centuries of the Christian era the gods themselves very frequently took on an element of the abstract. Usener writes: 'To the extent that the belief in the gods of the classical age lost its strength, the ideas of the gods, as shaped by art and literature, were released and became available as suitable means of poetic representation. This process can be traced from the writers of Nero's age, indeed from Horace and Ovid, to its peak in the later Alexandrian school; its most important, and, for the subsequent period, most influential representative is Nonnos; in Latin literature, Claudius Claudianus of Alexandria. In their work everything, every action, every event, is transformed into an interaction of divine powers. Small wonder that with these writers there is more room even for abstract concepts; for them the personified gods have no greater significance than these concepts; they have both become very flexible forms for the ideas of the poetic imagination.'[21] All this is, of course, part of an intensive preparation for allegory. But, if allegory itself is more than the 'vaporization' – however abstract – of theological essences, their survival in an unsuitable, indeed hostile, environment, then this late-Roman version is not the truly allegorical way of looking at things. In the course of such a literature the world of the ancient gods would have had to die out, and it is precisely allegory which preserved it. For an appreciation of the transience of things, and the concern to rescue them for eternity, is one of the strongest impulses in allegory. In the middle ages there was nothing, either in art, or science, or the state, which could stand alongside the legacy of antiquity in all these domains. At that time the knowledge of the impermanence of things was inescapably derived from observation; just as, several centuries later, at the time of the Thirty Years War, the same knowledge stared European humanity in the face. Here it is worth noting that the most obvious catastrophes did not perhaps impress this experience on men any more bitterly than the changes in legal norms, with their claims to eternal validity, which were particularly evident at those historical turning-points. Allegory established itself most permanently where transitoriness and eternity confronted each other most closely. In his *Götternamen* [The names of the gods] Usener himself has provided the means with which to draw accurately the historico-philosophical line of demarcation between the only 'apparently abstract' nature of certain antique divinities and allegorical abstraction. 'We must therefore reconcile ourselves to the fact that the excitable religious sensibility of antiquity could unhesitatingly elevate even abstract concepts to divine status. The reason why, almost without exception, they remained shadowy and bloodless is none other than the reason why the particular gods [*sondergötter*] also could not but pale before the personal [*persönlich*] gods: the transparency of the word.'[22] It may well be that the ground of antiquity was prepared for the reception of allegory by these religious improvizations; but allegory itself was sown by Christianity. For it was absolutely decisive for the development of this mode of thought that not only transitoriness, but also guilt should seem evidently to have its home in the province of idols and of the flesh. The allegorically significant is prevented by guilt from finding fulfilment of its meaning in itself. Guilt is not confined to the allegorical observer, who betrays the world for the sake of knowledge, but it also attaches to the object of his contemplation. This view, rooted in the doctrine of the fall of the creature, which brought down nature with it, is responsible for the ferment which distinguishes the profundity of western allegory from the oriental rhetoric of this form of expression. Because it is mute, fallen nature mourns. But the converse of this statement leads even deeper into the essence of nature: its mournfulness makes it become mute. In all mourning there is a tendency to silence, and this infinitely more than inability or reluctance to communicate. The mournful has the feeling that it is known comprehensively by the unknowable. To be named – even if the name-giver is god-like and saintly – perhaps always brings with it a presentiment of mourning. But how much more so not to be named, only to be read, to be read uncertainly by the allegorist, and to have become highly significant thanks only to him. On the other hand, the more nature and antiquity were felt to be guilt-laden, the more necessary was their allegorical interpretation, as their only conceivable salvation. For in the midst of the conscious degradation of the object the melancholic intention keeps faith with its own quality as a thing in an incomparable way. But even after twelve hundred years the prophecy of Prudentius: 'Cleansed of all blood, the marble will ultimately gleam; the bronzes, which are now regarded as idols, will stand innocent',[23] had still not been fulfilled. For the Baroque, even for the Renaissance, the marble and the bronzes of antiquity still preserved something of the horror with which Augustine had recognized in them 'the bodies of the gods so to speak'. 'Certain spirits have been induced to take up their abode in them, and they have the power either to do harm or to satisfy many of the wants of those who offer them divine honours and obedient worship.'[24] Or, as Warburg puts it, with reference to the Renaissance: 'The formal beauty of the figures of the gods, and the tasteful reconciliation of Christian and pagan beliefs should not blind us to the fact that even in Italy around 1520, that is at the time of the most free and creative artistic activity, antiquity was venerated, as it were, in a double herma, which had one dark, demonic countenance, that called for a superstitious cult, and another, serene Olympian one, which demanded aesthetic veneration.'[25] The three most important impulses in the origin of western allegory are non-antique, anti-antique: the gods project into the alien world, they become evil, and they become creatures. The attire of the Olympians is left behind, and in the course of time the emblems collect around it. And this attire is as creaturely as a devil's body. In this sense the enlightened Hellenistic theology of Euhemeros incorporates, curiously enough, in its share, an element of the nascent popular belief. For 'the reduction of the gods to mere mortals was bound ever closer to the idea that evil magic powers continued to be effective in the remnants of their cult, above all in their images. But the proof of their complete impotence was weakened again by the fact that the powers which had been stripped from them were taken over by satanic substitutes.'[26] On the other hand, alongside the emblems and the attire, the words and the names remain behind, and, as the living contexts of their birth disappear, so they become the origins of concepts, in which these words acquire a new content, which is predisposed to allegorical representation; such is the case with Fortuna, Venus (as Dame World) and so on. The deadness of the figures and the abstraction of the concepts are therefore the precondition for the allegorical metamorphosis of the pantheon into a world of magical, conceptual creatures. This is the basis of the representation of Cupid by Giotto, 'as a demon of wantonness with a bat's wings and claws'; and it is the basis for the survival of fabulous creatures like the faun, centaur, siren and harpy as allegorical figures in the circle of Christian hell. 'The classically refined world of the ancient divinities has, of course, been impressed upon us so deeply since the time of Winckelmann, that we entirely forget that it is a new creation of scholarly humanist culture; this "Olympic" aspect of antiquity had first to be wrested from the traditional "demonic" side; for the ancient divinities had, as cosmic demons, belonged among the religious powers of Christian Europe uninterruptedly since the end of antiquity, and in practice they influenced its way of life so decisively that it is not possible to deny the existence of an alternative government of pagan cosmology, in particular astrology, tacitly accepted by the Christian church.'[27] Allegory corresponds to the ancient gods in the deadness of its concrete tangibility. There is, then, a profounder truth than is generally believed in the statement: 'The proximity of the gods is indeed one of the most important prerequisites for the vigorous development of allegory.'[28]

The allegorical outlook has its origin in the conflict between the guilt-laden physis, held up as an example by Christianity and a purer *natura deorum* [nature of the gods], embodied in the pantheon. With the revival of paganism in the Renaissance, and Christianity in the Counter-Reformation, allegory, the form of their conflict, also had to be renewed. The importance of this for the *Trauerspiel* is that, in the figure of Satan, the middle ages had bound the material and the demonic inextricably together. Above all, the concentration of the numerous pagan powers into *one*, theologically rigorously defined, Antichrist meant that this supreme manifestation of darkness was imposed upon matter more unambiguously than in a number of demons. And not only did the middle ages come thus to impose strict limits on the scientific study of nature; even mathematicians were rendered suspect by this devilish essence of matter. The schoolman, Henry of Ghent, explains: 'Whatever they think, it is something spatial *(quantum)*, or else it is located in space like a point. Such people are therefore melancholic, and make the best mathematicians, but the worst metaphysicians.'[29] If it is the creaturely world of things, the dead, or at best the half–living, that is the object of the allegorical intention, then man does not enter its field of vision. If it sticks exclusively to emblems, then revolution, salvation is not inconceivable. But scorning all emblematic disguise, the undisguised visage of the devil can raise itself up from out of the depths of the earth into the view of the allegorist, in triumphant vitality and nakedness. It was only in the middle ages that these sharp, angular features were etched in the originally greater demonic head of antiquity. According to gnostic-manichaean doctrine, matter was created to bring about the 'de-Tartarization' of the world, and was destined to absorb everything devilish, so that with its elimination the world might display itself in its purity; but in the devil it calls to mind its Tartarean nature, scorns its allegorical 'significance', and mocks anyone who believes he can pursue it into the depths with impunity. Just as earthly mournfulness is of a piece with allegorical interpretation, so is devilish mirth with its frustration in the triumph of matter. This explains the devilish jocularity of the intriguer, his intellectuality, his knowledge of significance. The mute creature is able to hope for salvation through that which is signified. The clever versatility of man expresses itself, and, in a most basely calculating act, lends its material aspect an almost human self-confidence, so that the allegorist is countered by the scornful laughter of hell. Here, of course, the muteness of matter is overcome. In laughter, above all, mind is enthusiastically embraced by matter, in highly eccentric disguise. Indeed it becomes so spiritual that it far outstrips language. It is aiming higher, and ends in shrill laughter. However brutish the external effect may be, the inner madness is conscious of it only as spirituality. There is no jesting with 'Lucifer / Fürst der finsternis /

regierer der tiefen trawrigkeit / keiser des Hellischen Spuls / Hertzog des
Schwebelwassers / König des abgrunds'.[30]* Julius Leopold Klein rightly
calls him the 'original allegorical figure'. Indeed, one of the most powerful
of Shakespeare's characters is, as this literary historian has suggested in
some excellent observations, to be understood only in terms of allegory,
with reference to the figure of Satan. 'Shakespeare's Richard III . . . relates
himself to the iniquity role of Vice, Vice swollen into the historical
buffoon–devil, and so he reveals, in a highly remarkable way, his development and descent, in terms of the history of the theatre, from the Devil
of the mystery-plays and from the deceitfully "moralizing" Vice of the
"morality play", as the legitimate, historical, flesh-and-blood descendant
of both: the devil and Vice.' This is illustrated in a footnote: '"Gloster
(aside): Thus, like the formal Vice, Iniquity, I I moralize two meanings
in one word." In the character of Richard III, Devil and Vice appear,
according to his own confessional aside, fused into a warlike hero of
tragedy with a historical pedigree.'[31] But precisely not a hero of tragedy.
Rather may we point out once again – and this is the justification for this
digression – that for *Richard III*, for *Hamlet*, as indeed for all Shakespearian 'tragedies', the theory of the *Trauerspiel* is predestined to contain the prolegomena of interpretation. For in Shakespeare allegory
reaches much deeper than the metaphorical forms where Goethe noticed
it: 'Shakespeare is rich in wonderful figures of speech, which arise from
personified concepts and which would not be at all suitable nowadays, but
which are entirely in place in his work because in his day all art was
dominated by allegory.'[32] Novalis is more emphatic: 'In a Shakespearian
play it is possible to find an arbitrary idea, allegory, etc.'[33] But the *Sturm
und Drang*, which discovered Shakespeare for Germany, had eyes only
for the elemental aspect of his work, not the allegorical. And yet what is
characteristic of Shakespeare is precisely that both aspects are equally
essential. Every elemental utterance of the creature acquires significance
from its allegorical existence, and everything allegorical acquires emphasis from the elemental aspect of the world of the senses. With the

---

* Lucifer, prince of darkness, ruler of deep mournfulness, emperor of the hellish cesspit,
duke of sulphurous water, king of the abyss

extinction of the allegorical impetus the elemental power is also lost to the drama until, in the *Sturm und Drang*, it is revived – in the form of the *Trauerspiel*. Romanticism subsequently regained a glimpse of the allegorical. But so long as romanticism adhered to Shakespeare, it was no more than a glimpse. For in Shakespeare the elemental takes pride of place, in Calderón, the allegorical. Before causing terror in mourning, Satan tempts. He initiates men in knowledge, which forms the basis of culpable behaviour. If the lesson of Socrates, that knowledge of good makes for good actions, may be wrong, this is far more true of knowledge about evil. And it is not as an inner light, a *lumen naturale*, that this knowledge shines forth in the night of mournfulness, but a subterranean phosphorescence glimmers from the depths of the earth. It kindles the rebellious, penetrating gaze of Satan in the contemplative man. This confirms once again the significance of baroque polymathy for the *Trauerspiel*. For something can take on allegorical form only for the man who has knowledge. But on the other hand, if contemplation is not so much patiently devoted to truth, as unconditionally and compulsively, in direct meditation, bent on absolute knowledge, then it is eluded by things, in the simplicity of their essence, and they lie before it as enigmatic allegorical references, they continue to be dust. The intention which underlies allegory is so opposed to that which is concerned with the discovery of truth that it reveals more clearly than anything else the identity of the pure curiosity which is aimed at mere knowledge with the proud isolation of man. 'Der greuliche Alchimist der erschreckliche Todt'[34]* – Hallmann's profound metaphor is not based only on the process of decay. Magical knowledge, which includes alchemy, threatens the adept with isolation and spiritual death. As alchemy and rosicrucianism, and the conjuration-scenes in the *Trauerspiel* prove, this age was no less devoted to magic than the renaissance. Whatever it picks up, its Midas-touch turns it into something endowed with significance. Its element was transformation of every sort; and allegory was its scheme. Because this passion did not remain confined to the age of the baroque, it is all the more suitable as an unambiguous

---

* That cruel alchemist, horrible death.

indication of baroque qualities in later periods. It justifies a more recent linguistic practice, whereby baroque features are recognized in the late Goethe or the late Hölderlin. Knowledge, not action, is the most characteristic mode of existence of evil. Accordingly, physical temptation conceived in sensual terms, as lechery, gluttony, and sloth, is far from being the sole basis of its existence; indeed, strictly speaking, it is ultimately and precisely not basic to it at all. Rather is the basis of its existence revealed in the *fata morgana* of a realm of absolute, that is to say godless, spirituality, bound to the material as its counterpart, such as can only be concretely experienced through evil. Its dominant mood is that of mourning, which is at once the mother of the allegories and their content. And from it three original satanic promises are born. They are spiritual in kind. The *Trauerspiel* continually shows them at work, now in the figure of the tyrant, now in that of the intriguer. What tempts is the illusion of freedom – in the exploration of what is forbidden; the illusion of independence – in the secession from the community of the pious; the illusion of infinity – in the empty abyss of evil. For it is characteristic of all virtue to have an end before it: namely its model, in God; just as all infamy opens up an infinite progression into the depths. The theology of evil can therefore be derived much more readily from the fall of Satan, in which the above-mentioned motifs are confirmed, than from the warnings in which ecclesiastical doctrine tends to represent the snarer of souls. The absolute spirituality, which is what Satan means, destroys itself in its emancipation from what is sacred. Materiality – but here soulless materiality – becomes its home. The purely material and this absolute spiritual are the poles of the satanic realm; and the consciousness is their illusory synthesis, in which the genuine synthesis, that of life, is imitated. However, the speculation of the consciousness, which clings to the object-world of emblems, ultimately, in its remoteness from life, discovers the knowledge of the demons. According to Augustine's *The City of God*, 'The word Δαίμονες is Greek; and demons are so called because of their knowledge.'[35] The verdict of fanatic spirituality was most spiritedly uttered by St Francis of Assisi. It points out the true path to a disciple who shut himself up all too deeply in study: 'Unus solus daimon plus scit quam tu.'*

---

* One single demon knows more than you

In the form of knowledge instinct leads down into the empty abyss of evil in order to make sure of infinity. But this is also the bottomless pit of contemplation. Its data are not capable of being incorporated in philosophical constellations. They are therefore to be found in the emblem-books of the baroque as the stock requisites of gloomy spectacle. More than any other form, the *Trauerspiel* operates with this stock of requisites. Tirelessly transforming, interpreting, and deepening, it rings the changes on its images. Above all it is contrast which is dominant. And yet it would be mistaken, or, at least, it would be superficial, to attribute to delight in antithesis for its own sake those numerous effects in which, visually or only verbally, the throne room is transformed into the dungeon, the pleasure-chamber into a tomb, the crown into a wreath of bloody cypress. Even the contrast of being and appearance does not accurately describe this technique of metaphors and apotheoses. Its basis is the emblematic schema from which, by means of an artifice whose effect always had to be overwhelming, that which is signified springs obviously into view. The crown – that means the wreath of cypress. Among the countless documents of this rash of emblems – examples have long since been assembled[36] – one that is not to be surpassed in its unashamed crudity is Hallmann's transformation of a harp into a 'Mordbeil . . . wann der Politische Himmel blitzet'.[37]* In much the same style is the following exposition from his *Leich-Reden*: 'Denn betrachtet man die unzählbahren Leichen / womit theils die raasende Pest / theils die Kriegerischen Waffen nicht nur unser Teutschland / sondern fast gantz Europam erfüllet / so müssen wir bekennen / dass unsere Rosen in Dornen / unsre Lilgen in Nesseln / unsre Paradise in Kirchhöfe / ja unser gantzes Wesen in ein Bildnüss dess Todes verwandelt worden. Dannenhero wird mir hoffentlich nicht ungütig gedeutet werden / dass ich auf dieser allgemeinen Schaubühne dess Todes auch meinen papirenen Kirchhoff zu eröffnen mich unterwunden.'[38]† Such metamorphoses also occur in the choruses.[39]

---

* executioner's axe . . . when lightning flashes in the political firmament

† For if we consider the innumerable corpses with which, partly, the ravages of the plague and, partly, weapons of war, have filled not only our Germany, but almost the whole of Europe, then we must admit that our roses have been transformed into thorns, our lilies into nettles, our paradises into cemeteries, indeed our whole being into an image of death. It is therefore my hope that it will not be held against me that in this general theatre of death I have not foreborne to set up my own paper graveyard.

As those who lose their footing turn somersaults in their fall, so would the allegorical intention fall from emblem to emblem down into the dizziness of its bottomless depths, were it not that, even in the most extreme of them, it had so to turn about that all its darkness, vainglory, and godlessness seems to be nothing but self-delusion. For it is to misunderstand the allegorical entirely if we make a distinction between the store of images, in which this about-turn into salvation and redemption takes place, and that grim store which signifies death and damnation. For it is precisely visions of the frenzy of destruction, in which all earthly things collapse into a heap of ruins, which reveal the limit set upon allegorical contemplation, rather than its ideal quality. The bleak confusion of Golgotha, which can be recognized as the schema underlying the allegorical figures in hundreds of the engravings and descriptions of the period, is not just a symbol of the desolation of human existence. In it transitoriness is not signified or allegorically represented, so much as, in its own significance, displayed as allegory. As the allegory of resurrection. Ultimately in the death-signs of the baroque the direction of allegorical reflection is reversed; on the second part of its wide arc it returns, to redeem. The seven years of its immersion are but a day. For even this time of hell is secularized in space, and that world, which abandoned itself to the deep spirit of Satan and betrayed itself, is God's world. In God's world the allegorist awakens. 'Ja / wenn der Höchste wird vom Kirch-Hof erndten ein / I So werd ich Todten-Kopff ein Englisch Antlitz seyn.'[40]* This solves the riddle of the most fragmented, the most defunct, the most dispersed. Allegory, of course, thereby loses everything that was most peculiar to it: the secret, privileged knowledge, the arbitrary rule in the realm of dead objects, the supposed infinity of a world without hope. All this vanishes with this *one* about-turn, in which the immersion of allegory has to clear away the final phantasmagoria of the objective and, left entirely to its own devices, re-discovers itself, not playfully in the earthly world of things, but seriously under the eyes of heaven. And this is the essence of melancholy immersion: that its ultimate objects, in which it believes it can most

---

* Yea, when the Highest comes to reap the harvest from the graveyard, then I, a death's head, will be an angel's countenance.

fully secure for itself that which is vile, turn into allegories, and that these allegories fill out and deny the void in which they are represented, just as, ultimately, the intention does not faithfully rest in the contemplation of bones, but faithlessly leaps forward to the idea of resurrection.

'Mit Weinen streuten wir den Samen in die Brachen I und giegen traurig aus.'[41]* Allegory goes away empty-handed. Evil as such, which it cherished as enduring profundity, exists only in allegory, is nothing other than allegory, and means something different from what it is. It means precisely the non-existence of what it presents. The absolute vices, as exemplified by tyrants and intriguers, are allegories. They are not real, and that which they represent, they possess only in the subjective view of melancholy; they are this view, which is destroyed by its own offspring because they only signify its blindness. They point to the absolutely subjective pensiveness, to which alone they owe their existence. By its allegorical form evil as such reveals itself to be a subjective phenomenon. The enormous, anti-artistic subjectivity of the baroque converges here with the theological essence of the subjective. The Bible introduces evil in the concept of knowledge. The serpent's promise to the first men was to make them 'knowing both good and evil'.[42] But it is said of God after the creation: 'And God saw everything that he had made, and, behold it was very good.'[43] Knowledge of evil therefore has no object. There is no evil in the world. It arises in man himself, with the desire for knowledge, or rather for judgment. Knowledge of good, as knowledge, is secondary. It ensues from practice. Knowledge of evil – as knowledge this is primary. It ensues from contemplation. Knowledge of good and evil is, then, the opposite of all factual knowledge. Related as it is to the depths of the subjective, it is basically only knowledge of evil. It is 'nonsense' [*Geschwätz*] in the profound sense in which Kierkegaard conceived the word. This knowledge, the triumph of subjectivity and the onset of an arbitrary rule over things, is the origin of all allegorical contemplation. In the very fall

---

* Weeping we scattered the seed on the fallow ground and sadly we went away.

of man the unity of guilt and signifying emerges as an abstraction. The allegorical has its existence in abstractions; as an abstraction, as a faculty of the spirit of language itself, it is at home in the Fall. For good and evil are unnameable, they are nameless entities, outside the language of names, in which man, in paradise, named things, and which he forsakes in the abyss of that problem. For languages the name is only a base in which the concrete elements have their roots. The abstract elements of language, however, have their roots in the evaluative word, the judgment. And while, in the earthly court, the uncertain subjectivity of judgment is firmly anchored in reality, with punishments, in the heavenly court the illusion of evil comes entirely into its own. Here the unconcealed subjectivity triumphs over every deceptive objectivity of justice, and is incorporated into divine omnipotence as a 'work of supreme wisdom and primial love', [44] as hell. It is not appearance, and, equally, it is not satiated being, but it is the reflection in reality of empty subjectivity in the good. In evil as such subjectivity grasps what is real in it, and sees it simply as its own reflection in God. In the allegorical image of the world, therefore, the subjective perspective is entirely absorbed in the economy of the whole. Thus it is that the pillars of a baroque balcony in Bamberg are in reality arrayed in exactly the way in which, in a regular construction, they would appear from below. And thus it is that the fire of ecstasy is preserved, without a single spark being lost, secularized in the prosaic, as is necessary: in a hallucination, St Theresa sees the Virgin strewing roses on her bed; she tells her confessor. 'I see none', he replies. 'Our Lady brought them to *me*', answers the Saint. In this way the display of manifest subjectivity becomes a formal guarantee of the miracle, because it proclaims the divine action itself. And 'there is no turn of events which the baroque style would not conclude with a miracle'.[45] 'The Aristotelian idea of θαυμαστόν [wonder], the artistic expression of the miracle (the Biblical σημεῖα [sign]), is what dominates [art and architecture too] in the period after the counter-reformation, most especially after the Council of Trent ... The impression of supernatural forces is supposed to be aroused in the powerfully projecting and apparently self-supporting structures precisely in the upper regions, interpreted and accentuated by the perilously soaring angels of the sculptural decoration ... With the sole purpose of intensifying this impression, the reality of these laws is, on the other hand – in the lower regions – recalled in an exaggerated fashion. What else can be the purpose of the constant references to the violence of the supporting and supported forces, the enormous pedestals, the doubly and triply augmented projecting columns and pilasters, the strengthening and reinforcement of their interconnecting elements, all bearing – a balcony? What other function have they than to emphasize the soaring miracle above, by drawing attention to the difficulties of supporting it from below. The *ponderación misteriosa*, the intervention of God in the work of art, is assumed to be possible.'[46] Subjectivity, like an angel falling into the depths, is brought back by allegories, and is held fast in heaven, in God, by *ponderación misteriosa*. But with the banal equipment of the theatre – chorus, interlude, and dumbshow – it is not possible to realize the transfigured apotheosis familiar from Calderón. This takes shape and acquires conviction from a meaningful arrangement of the whole, which only emphasizes it more strongly, but less enduringly. The inadequacy of the German *Trauerspiel* is rooted in the deficient development of the intrigue, which seldom even remotely approaches that of the Spanish dramatist. The intrigue alone would have been able to bring about that allegorical totality of scenic organization, thanks to which one of the images of the sequence stands out, in the image of the apotheosis, as different in kind, and gives mourning at one and the same time the cue for its entry and its exit. The powerful design of this form should be thought through to its conclusion; only under this condition is it possible to discuss the idea of the German *Trauerspiel*. In the ruins of great buildings the idea of the plan speaks more impressively than in lesser buildings, however well preserved they are; and for this reason the German *Trauerspiel* merits interpretation. In the spirit of allegory it is conceived from the outset as a ruin, a fragment. Others may shine resplendently as on the first day; this form preserves the image of beauty to the very last.

Notes

References are as given in *Gesammelte Schriften*, I, (i), pp. 410–30.

Epistemo-Critical prologue

Motto – Goethe, *Sämtliche Werke*. Jubiläums-Ausgabe. In Verbindung mit Konrad Burdach [et al.] hrsg. von Eduard von der Hellen, Stuttgart, Berlin, n.d. [1907 ff.], XL, Schriften zur Naturwissenschaft, 2, pp. 140/141.

1   cf. Emile Meyerson, *De l'explication dans les sciences*. 2 vols, Paris, 1921, passim.

2   Hermann Güntert, *Von der Sprache der Götter und Geister. Bedeutungsgeschichtliche Untersuchungen zur homerischen und eddischen Göttersprache*, Halle a.d.S., 1921, p. 49. – cf. Hermann Usener, *Götternamen. Versuch einer Lehre von der religiösen Begriffsbildung*, Bonn, 1896, p. 321.

3   Jean Hering, 'Bemerkungen über das Wesen, die Wesenheit und die Idee', *Jahrbuch für Philosophie und phänomenologische Forschung*, IV (1921), p. 522.

4   Max Scheler, *Vom Umsturz der Werte. Der Abhandlungen und Aufsätze* 2., durchges. Aufl., I, Leipzig, 1919, p. 241.

5   Konrad Burdach, *Reformation, Renaissance, Humanismus. Zwei Abhandlungen über die Grundlage moderner Bildung und Sprachkunst*, Berlin, 1918, pp. 100 ff.

6   Burdach, op. cit., p. 213 (fn.).

7   Fritz Strich, 'Der lyrische Stil des siebzehnten Jahrhunderts', *Abhandlungen zur deutschen Literaturgeschichte. Franz Muncker zum 60. Geburtstage*, dargebracht von Eduard Berend [et al.], Munich, 1916, p. 52.

8   Richard M. Meyer, 'Über das Verständnis von Kunstwerken', *Neue Jahrbücher für das klassische Altertum, Geschichte und deutsche Literatur*, IV (1901), (= *Neue Jahrbücher für das klassische Altertum, Geschichte und deutsche Literatur und für Pädagogik*, VII), p. 378.

9   Meyer, op. cit., p. 372.

10   Benedetto Croce, *Grundriss der Asthetik. Vier Vorlesungen*. Autorisierte deutsche Ausg. von Theodor Poppe, Leipzig, 1913 (Wissen und Forschen, 5), p. 43. [*The Essence of Aesthetic*, trans. by Douglas Ainslie, London, 1921, pp. 53 f.]

11   Croce, op. cit., p. 46 [p. 57.]

12   Croce, op. cit., p. 48. [p. 59.]

13   cf. Hermann Cohen, *Logik der reinen Erkenntnis* (System der Philosophie, I), Berlin, 1914², pp. 35/36.

14   cf. Walter Benjamin, 'Die Aufgabe des Übersetzers', *Charles Baudelaire: Tableaux parisiens*. Deutsche Übertragung mit einem Vorwort von Walter Benjamin, Heidelberg,

1923, (Die Drucke des Argonautenkreises, 5), pp. VIII/IX. ['The Task of the Translator', *Illuminations*, edited and with an introduction by Hannah Arendt, trans. by Harry Zohn, London, 1970, pp. 71 ff.]

15 Strich, op. cit., p. 21.

16 cf. August Wilhelm von Schlegel, *Sämmtliche Werke*, hrsg. von Eduard Böcking, VI, Vorlesungen über dramatische Kunst und Litteratur, 3. Ausg., 2. Theil, Leipzig, 1846, p. 403. – Also A. W. Schlegel, *Vorlesungen über schöne Litteratur und Kunst*, hrsg. von J. Minor, 3. Teil (1803–1804), Geschichte der romantischen Litteratur, Heilbronn, 1884 (Deutsche Litteraturdenkmale des 18. und 19. Jahrhunderts, 19), p. 72. [*A Course of Lectures on Dramatic Art and Literature*, trans. John Black, revised by A. J. W. Morrison, London, 1846, p. 508.]

17 cf. Karl Lamprecht, *Deutsche Geschichte*, 2. Abt., Neuere Zeit. Zeitalter des individuellen Seelenlebens, III, (i) (= VII, i, of the complete series), 3. unveränd. Aufl., Berlin, 1912, p. 267.

18 cf. Hans Heinrich Borcherdt, *Augustus Buchner und seine Bedeutung für die deutsche Literatur des siebzehnten Jahrhunderts*, Munich, 1919, p. 58.

19 Conrad Müller, *Beiträge zum Leben und Dichten Daniel Caspers von Lohenstein*, Breslau, 1882 (Germanistische Abhandlungen, 1), pp. 72/73.

20 Goethe, *Werke*, hrsg. im Auftrage der Grossherzogin Sophie von Sachsen (= Weimarer Ausgabe), 4. Abt., Briefe, XLII (Jan.–Jul., 1827), Weimar, 1907, p. 104.

21 Ulrich von Wilamowitz-Moellendorff, *Einleitung in die griechische Tragödie*. Unveränd. Abdr. aus der 1. Aufl. von Euripides Herakles I, chap. I–IV, Berlin, 1907, p. 109.

22 Herbert Cysarz, *Deutsche Barockdichtung. Renaissance, Barock, Rokoko*, Leipzig, 1924, p. 299.

23 cf. J. Petersen, 'Der Aufbau der Literaturgeschichte', *Germanisch-romanische Monatsschrift*, VI (1914), 1–16 and 129–152; esp. pp. 149 and 151.

24 Louis G. Wysocki, *Andreas Gryphius et la tragédie allemande au XVIIe siècle* (Thèse de doctorat), Paris, 1892, p. 14.

25 Petersen, op. cit., p. 13.

26 cf. Christian Hofman von Hofmanswaldau, *Auserlesene Gedichte*. Mit einer Einleitung hrsg. von Felix Paul Greve, Leipzig, 1907, p. 8.

27 But cf. Arthur Hübscher, 'Barock als Gestaltung antithetischen Lebensgefühls. Grundlegung einer Phaseologie der Geistesgeschichte', *Euphorion*, XXIV (1922), 517–562 and 759–805.

28 Victor Manheimer, *Die Lyrik des Andreas Gryphius. Studien und Materialien*, Berlin, 1904, p. XIII.

29 Wilhelm Hausenstein, *Vom Geist des Barock*, 3.–5. Aufl., Munich, 1921, p. 28.

Trauerspiel and tragedy (Part 1)

Motto – *Filidors* [Caspar Stieler?] *Trauer- Lust- und Misch-Spiele*. Erster Theil, Jena, 1665, p. 1 [of the pagination of *Ernelinde Oder Die Viermal Braut*. *Mischspiel*, Rudolstadt, n.d. (I, i)].

1 Cysarz, op. cit., p. 72.

2 cf. Alois Riegl, *Die Entstehung der Barockkunst* in Rom. Aus seinem Nachlass hrsg. von Arthur Burda und Max Dvorák, Vienna, 1923[2], p. 147.

3 Paul Stachel, *Seneca und das deutsche Renaissancedrama. Studien zur Literatur- und Stilgeschichte des 16. und 17. Jahrhunderts*, Berlin, 1907 (Palaestra, 46), p. 326.

4 cf. Lamprecht, op. cit., p. 265.

5 *Teusche Rede-bind- und Dicht-Kunst | verfasset durch Den Erwachsenen* [Sigmund von Birken], Nuremberg, 1679, p. 336.

6 cf. Wilhelm Dilthey, *Weltanschauung und Analyse des Menschen seit Renaissance und Reformation. Abhandlungen zur Geschichte der Philosophie und Religion* (Gesammelte Schriften, II), Leipzig, Berlin, 1923, p. 445.

7 Martin Opitz, *Prosodia Germanica, Oder Buch von der Deudschen Poeterey.* Nunmehr zum siebenden mal correct gedruckt, Frankfurt a.M., n.d. [ca 1650], pp. 30/31.

8 *Die Aller Edelste Belustigung Kunst- und Tugendliebender Gemühter* [April-gesprach]/ beschrieben und fürgestellt von Dem Rüstigen [Johann Rist], Frankfurt, 1666, pp. 241/242.

9 A[ugust] A[dolf] von H[augwitz], *Prodomus Poeticus, Oder: Poetischer Vortrab*, Dresden, 1684, p. 78 [of the pagination of *Schuldige Unschuld Oder Maria Stuarda* (fn.)].

10 Andreas Gryphius, *Trauerspiele*, hrsg. von Hermann Palm, Tübingen, 1882 (Bibliothek des litterarischen Vereins in Stuttgart, 162), p. 635 (*Amilius Paulus Papinianus*, fn.).

11 Bernhard Erdmannsdorffer, *Deutsche Geschichte vom Westfälischen Frieden bis zum Regierungsantritt Friedrich's des Grossen.* 1648–1740, I, Berlin, 1892 (Allgemeine Geschichte in Einzeldarstellungen, 3, 7), p. 102.

12 Martin Opitz, *L. Annaei Senecae Trojanerinnen*, Wittenberg, 1625, p. 1 (of the unpaginated preface).

13 Johann Klai; quoted from: Karl Weiss, *Die Wiener Haupt / und Staatsactionen. Ein Beitrag zur Geschichte des deutschen Theaters*, Vienna, 1854, p. 14.

14 cf. Carl Schmitt, *Politische Theologie. Vier Kapitel zur Lehre von der Souverenatität*, Munich, Leipzig, 1922, pp. 11/12.

15 cf. August Koberstein, *Geschichte der deutschen Nationalliteratur vom Anfang des siebzehnten bis zum zweiten Viertel des achtzehnten Jahrhunderts.* 5., umgearb. Aufl. von Karl Bartsch, Leipzig, 1872 (Grundriss der Geschichte der deutschen Nationalliteratur, 2), p. 15.

16 Schmitt, op. cit., p. 14.

17 Schmitt, op. cit., p. 14.

18 Hauoonotein, op. oit., p. 40.

19 [Christian Hofmann von Hofmannswaldau], *Helden-Briefe*, Leipzig, Breslau, 1680, pp. 8/9 (of the unpaginated preface).

20 Birken, *Deutsche Redebind- und Dichtkunst*, ed. cit., p. 242.

21 Gryphius, op. cit., p. 61 (*Leo Armenius* II, 433 ff.).

22 Johann Christian Hallmann, *Trauer- Freuden- und Schäffer-Spiele*, Breslau, n.d. [1684], p. 17 (of the pagination of *Die beleidigte Liebe oder die grossmütige Mariamne* [I, 477/478]). – cf. ibid., p. 12 (I, 355).

23 [Diego Saavedra Fajardo], *Abris Eines Christlich-Politischen Printzens / In CI Sinn-Bildern / Zuvor auss dem spanischen ins Lateinisch: Nun in Teutsch versetzet*, Coloniae, 1674, p. 897. [Don Diego Saavedra Faxardo, *The Royal Politician represented in one hundred emblems*, done into English by Sir Ja. Astry, London, 1700, II, 210.]

24 Karl Krumbacher, 'Die griechische Literatur des Mittelalters', *Die Kultur der Gegenwart. Ihre Entwicklung und ihre Ziele*, hrsg. von Paul Hinneberg, Teil I, Abt. 8, Die griechische und lateinische Literatur und Sprache. Von U. v. Wilamowitz-Moellendorff [et al.], Leipzig, Berlin, 1912³, p. 367.

25 [Anon], *Die Glorreiche Marter Joannes von Nepomuck*; quoted from Weiss, op. cit., p. 154.

26 *Die Glorreiche Marter Joannes von Nepomuck*; quoted from Weiss, op. cit., p. 120.

27 Joseph [Felix] Kurz, *Prinzessin Pumphia*, Vienna, 1883 (Wiener Neudrucke, 2) p. 1 (reproduction of the old title-page).

28 *Lorentz Gratians Staats-kluger Catholischer Ferdinand /* aus dem Spanischen übersetzet von Daniel Caspern von Lohenstein, Breslau, 1676, p. 123.

29 cf. Willi Flemming, *Andreas Gryphius und die Bühne*, Halle a.d.S., 1921, p. 386.

30 Gryphius, ed. cit., p. 212 (*Catharina von Georgien*, III, 438).

31 cf. Marcus Landau, 'Die Dramen von Herodes und Mariamne', *Zeitschrift für ver-*

gleichende Literaturgeschichte, NF VIII (1895), pp. 175–212 and pp. 279–317, and NF IX (1896), pp. 185–223.

32   cf. Hausenstein, op. cit., p. 94.

33   Cysarz, op. cit., p. 31.

34   Daniel Casper von Lohenstein, *Sophonisbe*, Frankfurt, Leipzig, 1724, p. 73 (IV, 504 ff.).

35   Gryphius, ed. cit., p. 213 (*Catharina von Georgien*, III, 457 ff.). – cf. Hallmann, *Trauer-, Freuden- und Schäferspiele*, ed. cit., *Mariamne*, p. 86 (V, 351).

36   [Josef Anton Stranitzky], *Wiener Haupt- und Staatsaktionen*. Eingeleitet und hrsg. von Rudolf Payer von Thurn, I, Vienna, 1908 (Schriften des Literarischen Vereins in Wien, 10), p. 301 (*Die Gestürzte Tyrannay in der Person dess Messinischen Wüttrichs* Pelifonte, II, 8).

37   [Georg Philipp Harsdörffer], *Poetischen Trichters zweyter Theil*, Nuremberg, 1648, p. 84.

38   Julius Wilhelm Zincgref, *Emblematum Ethico-Politicorum Centuria*. Editio secunda, Frankfurt, 1624, Embl. 71.

39   [Claudius Salmasius], *Königliche Verthätigung für Carl den I. geschrieben an den durchläuchtigsten König von Grossbritannien Carl den Andern*, 1650.

40   cf. Stachel, op. cit., p. 29.

41   cf. Gotthold Ephraim Lessing, *Sämtliche Schriften*. Neue rechtmässige Ausg., hrsg von Karl Lachmann, VII, Berlin, 1839, pp. 7 ff. (*Hamburgische Dramaturgie*, 1. und 2. Stück).

42   Hallmann, *Trauer-, Freuden- und Schäferspiele*, ed. cit., *Mariamne*, p. 27 (II, 263/264).

43   Hallmann, *Trauer-, Freuden- und Schäferspiele*, ed. cit., *Mariamne*, p. 112 (fn.).

44   Birken, *Deutsche Redebind- und Dichtkunst*, ed. cit., p. 323.

45   Georg Gottfried Gervinus, *Geschichte der Deutschen Dichtung*, III, hrsg. von Karl Bartsch, Leipzig, 1872[5], p. 553.

46   cf. Alfred von Martin, *Coluccio Salutati's Traktat 'Vom Tyrannen'. Eine kulturgeschichtliche Untersuchung nebst Textedition*. Mit einer Einleitung über Salutati's Leben und Schriften und einem Exkurs über seine philologisch-historische Methode, Berlin, Leipzig, 1913 (Abhandlungen zur Mittleren und Neueren Geschichte, 47), p. 48.

47   Flemming, *Andreas Gryphius und die Bühne*, p. 79.

48   cf. Burdach, op. cit., pp. 135/136, and p. 215 (fn.).

49   Georg Popp, 'Über den Begriff des Dramas in den deutschen Poetiken des 17. Jahrhunderts' (doctoral dissertation), Leipzig, 1895, p. 80.

50   cf. Julius Caesar Scaliger, *Poetices libri septem*. Editio quinta [Geneva], 1617, pp. 333/334 (III, 96).

51   Vinzenz von Beauvais, *Bibliotheca mundi seu speculi majoris*. Tomus secundus, qui speculum doctrinale inscribitur, Duaci, 1624, column 287.

52   *Schauspiele des Mittelalters*. Aus den Handschriften hrsg. und erklärt von Franz Joseph Mone, I, Karlsruhe, 1846, p. 336.

53   Claude de Saumaise, *Apologie royale pour Charles I. roy d'Angleterre*, Paris, 1650, pp. 642/643.

54   Willi Flemming, *Geschichte des Jesuitentheaters in den Landen deutscher Zunge*, Berlin, 1923 (Schriften der Gesellschaft für Theatergeschichte, 32), pp. 3/4.

55   Don Pedro Calderón de la Barca, *Schauspiele*, übers. von Johann Diederich Gries, I, Berlin, 1815, p. 295 (*Das Leben ein Traum*, III). [*Life's a dream*, trans. Kathleen Raine and R. M. Nadal, London, 1968, p. 87.]

56   Lohenstein, *Sophonisbe*, ed. cit., pp. 13/14 (of the unpaginated dedication).

57   Lohenstein, *Sophonisbe*, pp. 8/9 (of the unpaginated dedication).

58   Don Pedro Calderón de la Barca, *Schauspiele*, übers. von August Wilhelm Schlegel. Zweyter Theil, Vienna, 1813, pp. 88/89; cf. also p. 90 (Der standhafte Prinz, III). [*The steadfast Prince*, *Dramas of Calderon, Tragic, Comic and Legendary*, trans Denis Florence M'Carthy, London, 1853, I, 95/96.]

59 Hans Georg Schmidt, *Die Lehre vom Tyrannenmord. Ein Kapitel aus der Rechtsphiloso-phie*, Tübingen, Leipzig, 1901, p. 92.

60 Johann Christian Hallmann, *Leich-Reden / Todten-Gedichte und Aus dem Italiänischen übersetzte Grab-Schrifften*, Frankfurt, Leipzig, 1682, p. 88.

61 cf. Hans Heinrich Borchardt, *Andreas Tscherning. Ein Beitrag zur Literatur- und Kultur-Geschichte des 17. Jahrhunderts*, Munich, Leipzig, 1912, pp. 90/91.

62 August Buchner, *Poetik*, hrsg. von Othone Prätorio, Wittenberg, 1665, p. 5.

63 Samuel von Butschky, *Wohl-Bebauter Rosen-Thal*, Nuremberg, 1679, p. 761.

64 Gryphius, ed. cit., p. 109 (Leo Armenius IV, 387 ff.).

65 cf. Hallmann, *Trauer-, Freuden- und Schäferspiele*, 'Die göttliche Rache oder der verführte Theodoricus Veronensis', p. 104 (V, 364 ff.).

66 *Theatralische / Galante Und Geistliche Gedichte / Von Menantes* [Christian Friedrich Hunold], Hamburg, 1706, p. 181 (Of the special pagination of the Theatralische Gedichte) (Nebucadnezar, III, 3; stage direction).

67 Georg Wilhelm Friedrich Hegel, *Werke*. Vollständige Ausgabe durch einen Verein von Freunden des Verewigten: Philipp Marheineke [et al.], X, ii, Vorlesungen über die Asthetik, hrsg. von Heinrich Gustav Hotho, II, Berlin, 1837, p. 176. [*The Philosophy of Fine Art*, trans. with notes by F. P. B. Osmaston, London, 1920, II, 335.]

68 Hegel, op. cit., p. 167. [*The Philosophy of Fine Art*, II, 327.]

69 Arthur Schopenhauer, *Sämmtliche Werke*, hrsg. von Eduard Grisebach, II, Die Welt als Wille und Vorstellung, II, Leipzig, n.d. [1891], pp. 505/506. [*The World as Will and Representation*, trans. E. F. J. Payne, Indian Hills, Colorado, 1958, II, 431.]

70 Wilhelm Wackernagel, *Über die dramatische Poesie. Academische Gelegenheitsschrift*, Basel, 1838, pp. 34/35.

71 cf. Johann Jacob Breitinger, *Critische Abhandlung Von der Natur den Absichten und dem Gebrauche der Gleichnisse*, Zürich, 1740, p. 489.

72 Daniel Casper von Lohenstein, *Agrippina. Trauer-Spiel*, Leipzig, 1724, p. 78 (V, 118).

73 Breitinger, op. cit., p. 467, p. 470.

74 cf. Erich Schmidt, [review of] Felix Bobertag, *Geschichte des Romans und der ihm verwandten Dichtungsgattungen in Deutschland*, 1. Abt., 2 Bd., 1. Hälfte, Breslau, 1879, *Archiv für Litteraturgeschichte*, IX (1880), p. 411.

75 cf. Hallmann, *Leichreden*, p. 115, p. 299.

76 cf. Hallmann, *Leichreden*, p. 64, p. 212.

77 Daniel Casper von Lohenstein, *Blumen*, Breslau, 1708, p. 27 (of the pagination of 'Hyacinthen' [Die Höhe Des Menschlichen Geistes über das Absterben Herrn Andreae Gryphii]).

78 Hübscher, op. cit., p. 542.

79 Julius Tittmann, *Die Nürnberger Dichterschule. Harsdörffer, Klaj, Birken. Beitrag zur deutschen Literatur- und Kulturgeschichte des siebzehnten Jahrhunderts* (Kleine Schriften zur deutschen Literatur- und Kulturgeschichte, I), Göttingen, 1847, p. 148.

80 Cysarz, op. cit., p. 27 (fn.).

81 Cysarz, op. cit., p. 108 (fn.); cf. also pp. 107/108.

82 cf. Harsdörffer, *Poetischen Trichters Dritter Theil*, Nuremberg, 1653, pp. 265–272.

83 Lohenstein, *Sophonisbe*, p. 10 (of the unpaginated dedication).

84 Gryphius, ed. cit., p. 437 (Carolus Stuardus, IV, 47).

85 Harsdörffer, *Vom Theatrum oder Schawplatz*. Für die Gesellschaft für Theatergeschichte aufs Newe in Truck gegeben, Berlin, 1914, p. 6.

86 August Wilhelm Schlegel, *Sämtliche Werke*, VI, 397. [*A Course of Lectures on Dramatic Art and Literature*, p. 504.]

87 Calderón, *Schauspiele* (trans. Gries), I, 206 (Das Leben ein Traum, I). [*Life's a dream*, ed. cit., p. 24.]

88 Calderón, *Schauspiele* (trans. Gries), III, Berlin, 1818, p. 236 (Eifersucht das grösste Scheusal, I).

89 cf. Gryphius, ed. cit., pp. 756 ff. (Die sieben Brüder, II, 343 ff.).

90 cf. Lohenstein, *Epicharis. Trauer-Spiel*, Leipzig, 1724, pp. 74/75 (III, 721 ff.).

91 cf. Lohenstein, *Agrippina*, pp. 53 ff. (III, 497 ff.).

92 cf. Haugwitz, ed. cit., 'Maria Stuarda', p. 50 (III, 237 ff.).

93 Hallmann, *Trauer-, Freuden- und Schäferspiele*, 'Mariamne', p. 2 (I, 40 ff.).

94 Kurt Kolitz, *Johann Christian Hallmanns Dramen. Ein Beitrag zur Geschichte des deutschen Dramas in der Barockzeit*, Berlin, 1911, pp. 158/159.

95 Tittmann, op. cit., p. 212.

96 cf. Hunold, op. cit., passim.

97 Birken, *Deutsche Redebind- und Dichtkunst*, pp. 329/330.

98 cf. Erich Schmidt, op. cit., p. 412.

99 Dilthey, op. cit., pp. 439/440.

100 Johann Christoph Mennling [Männling], *Schaubühne des Todes / Oder Leich-Reden*, Wittenberg, 1692, p. 367.

101 Hallmann, *Trauer-, Freuden- und Schäferspiele*, 'Mariamne', p. 34 (II, 493/494).

102 Hallmann, *Trauer-, Freuden- und Schäferspiele*, 'Mariamne', p. 44 (III, 194 ff.).

103 Lohenstein, *Agrippina*, p. 79 (V, 160 ff.).

104 cf. Henri Bergson, *Zeit und Freiheit. Eine Abhandlung über die unmittelbaren Bewusstseinstatsachen*, Jena, 1911, pp. 84/85. [*Time and Free Will. An Essay on the Immediate Data of Consciousness*, trans. F. L. Pogson, London, 1910, pp. 107 f.]

105 Frédéric Atger, *Essai sur l'histoire des doctrines du contrat social* (doctoral dissertation), Nimes, 1906, p. 136.

106 Rochus Freiherr von Liliencron, introduction to: Aegidius Albertinus, *Lucifers Königreich und Seelengejaidt*, hrsg. von Rochus Freiherrn von Liliencron, Berlin, Stuttgart, n.d. [1884], (Deutsche National-Litteratur, 26), p. xi.

107 Gryphius, ed. cit., p. 20 (Leo Armenius, I, 23/24).

108 Lohenstein, *Ibrahim Bassa. Trauer-Spiel*, Breslau, 1709, pp. 3/4 (of the unpaginated dedication). cf. Johann Elias Schlegel, *Ästhetische und dramaturgische Schriften*, hrsg. von Johann von Antoniewicz, Heilbronn, 1887 (Deutsche Litteraturdenkmale des 18. u. 19. Jahrhunderts, 26), p. 8.

109 Hallmann, *Leichreden*, p. 133.

110 Cysarz, op. cit., p. 248.

111 cf. Egon Cohn, *Gesellschaftsideale und Gesellschaftsroman des 17. Jahrhunderts. Studien zur deutschen Bildungsgeschichte*, Berlin, 1921 (Germanische Studien, 13), p. 11.

112 Scaliger, op. cit., p. 832 (VII, 3). [*Select translations from Scaliger's Poetics*, by Frederick Morgan Padelford (Yale Studies in English, 26), New York, 1904–5, p. 83.]

113 cf. Riegl, op. cit., p. 33.

114 Hübscher, op. cit., p. 546.

Trauerspiel and tragedy (Part 2)

Motto – Johann Georg Schiebel, *Neu-erbauter Schausaal*, Nuremberg, 1684, p. 127.

1 Johannes Volkelt, *Ästhetik des Tragischen*, 3., neu bearbeitete Aufl., Munich, 1917, pp. 469/470.

2 Volkelt, op. cit., p. 469.

3 Volkelt, op. cit., p. 450.

4 Volkelt, op. cit., p. 447.

5 Georg von Lukács, *Die Seele und die Formen. Essays*, Berlin, 1911, pp. 370/371.

6 Friedrich Nietzsche, *Werke* [2. Gesamtausg.], 1 Abt., I, Die Geburt der Tragödie, hrsg.

von Fritz Koegel, Leipzig, 1895, p. 155. [*Basic writings of Nietzsche*, translated and edited by Walter Kaufmann, New York, 1971, pp. 131/132.]

7 Nietzsche, op. cit., pp. 44/45. [*Basic writings*, p. 52.]

8 Nietzsche, op. cit., p. 171. [*Basic writings*, p. 143.]

9 Nietzsche, op. cit., p. 41. [*Basic writings*, p. 50.]

10 Nietzsche, op. cit., pp. 58/59. [*Basic writings*, pp. 62 f.]

11 Wilamowitz-Moellendorff, op. cit., p. 59.

12 cf. Walter Benjamin, 'Goethes Wahlverwandtschaften', *Neue Deutsche Beiträge*, 2. Folge, Heft 1 (April, 1924), pp. 83 ff.

13 cf. Croce, op. cit., p. 12. [*The Essence of Aesthetic*, pp. 13 f.]

14 cf. Carl Wilhelm Ferdinand Solger, *Nachgelassene Schriften und Briefwechsel*, hrsg. von Ludwig Tieck und Friedrich von Rauner, II, Leipzig, 1826, pp. 445 ff.

15 Wilamowitz-Moellendorff, op. cit., p. 107.

16 Wilamowitz-Moellendorff, op. cit., p. 119.

17 cf. Max Wundt, *Geschichte der griechischen Ethik*, I, Die Entstehung der griechischen Ethik, Leipzig, 1908, pp. 178/179.

18 cf. Wackernagel, op. cit., p. 39.

19 cf. Scheler, op. cit., pp. 266 ff.

20 Franz Rosenzweig, *Der Stern der Erlösung*, Frankfurt a.M., 1921, pp. 98/99. – cf. Walter Benjamin, 'Schicksal und Charakter', *Die Argonauten*, 1. Folge (1914 ff.), II (1915 ff.), H. 10–12 (1921), pp. 187–196.

21 Lukács, op. cit., p. 336.

22 Nietzsche, op. cit., p. 118. [*Basic writings*, p. 105.]

23 Hölderlin, *Sämtliche Werke*. Historisch-kritische Ausgabe. Unter Mitarbeit von Friedrich Seebass besorgt durch Norbert von Hellingrath, IV, Gedichte 1800–1806, Munich, Leipzig, 1916, p. 193. (Patmos, first draft, 144/145.)

24 cf. Wundt, op. cit., pp. 193 ff.

25 Benjamin, 'Schicksal und Charakter', p. 191.

26 Schopenhauer, *Sämtliche Werke*, II, 513/514. [*The World as Will etc.* II, 437.]

27 Karl Borinski, *Die Antike in Poetik und Kunsttheorie von Ausgang des klassischen Altertums bis auf Goethe und Wilhelm von Humboldt*, II. Aus dem Nachlass hrsg. von Richard Newald, Leipzig, 1924 (Das Erbe der Alten. Schriften über Wesen und Wirkung der Antike, 10), p. 315.

28 Schopenhauer, *Sämtliche Werke*, II, 509/510. [*The World as Will etc.*, II, 433/434.]

29 Rosenzweig, op. cit., pp. 268/269.

30 Wilamowitz-Moellendorff, op. cit., p. 106.

31 Nietzsche, op. cit., p. 96. [*Basic writings*, p. 89.]

32 Leopold Ziegler, *Zur Metaphysik des Tragischen. Eine philosophische Studie*, Leipzig, 1902, p. 45.

33 Lukács, op. cit., p. 342.

34 cf. Jacob Burckhardt, *Griechische Kulturgeschichte*, hrsg. von Jakob Oeri, IV, Berlin, Stuttgart, 1902, pp. 89 ff.

35 Kurt Latte, *Heiliges Recht. Untersuchungen zur Geschichte der sakralen Rechtsformen in Griechenland*, Tübingen, 1920, pp. 2/3.

36 Rosenzweig, op. cit., pp. 99/100.

37 Rosenzweig, op. cit., p. 104.

38 Lukács, op. cit., p. 430.

39 Jean Paul [Friedrich Richter], *Sämmtliche Werke*, XVIII, Berlin, 1841, p. 82 (Vorschule der Asthetik, 1. Abt. §19).

40 cf. Werner Weisbach, *Trionfi*, Berlin, 1919, pp. 17/18.

41 Nietzsche, op. cit., p. 59. [*Basic writings*, p. 63.]

42 Theodor Heinsius, *Volksthümliches Wörterbuch der Deutschen Sprache mit Bezeichnung der Aussprache und Betonung für die Geschäfts- und Lesewelt* IV, i, S bis T, Hannover, 1822, p. 1050.

43 cf. Gryphius, ed. cit., p. 77 (Leo Armenius, III, 126).

44 Hallmann, *Trauer-, Freuden- und Schäferspiele*, 'Mariamne', p. 36.

45 cf. Jacob Minor, *Die Schicksals-Tragödie in ihren Hauptvertretern*, Frankfurt a.M., 1883, p. 44, p. 49.

46 Johann Anton Leisewitz, *Sämmtliche Schriften*. Zum erstenmale vollständig gesammelt und mit einer Lebensbeschreibung des Autors eingeleitet. Nebst Leisewitz' Portrait und einem Facsimile. Einzig rechtmässige Gesammtausgabe, Braunschweig, 1838, p. 88 (Julius von Tarent, V, 4).

47 Johann Gottfried Herder, *Werke*, hrsg. von Hans Lambel, 3. Teil, 2. Abt., Stuttgart, n.d. [c. 1890] (Deutsche National-Litteratur, 76), p. 19 (Kritische Wälder, I, 3).

48 cf. Lessing, ed. cit., p. 264 (Hamburgische Dramaturgie, 59. Stück).

49 Hans Ehrenberg, *Tragödie und Kreuz* (2 vols), Würzburg, 1920, I, Die Tragödie unter dem Olymp, pp. 112/113.

50 Franz Horn, *Die Poesie und Beredsamkeit der Deutschen, von Luthers Zeit bis zur Gegenwart*, II, Berlin, 1823, pp. 294 ff.

51 Flemming, *Andreas Gryphius und die Bühne*, p. 221.

52 Saumaise, *Apologie royale pour Charles I*, p. 25.

53 Lohenstein, *Sophonisbe*, p. 11 (I, 322/323).

54 Lohenstein, *Sophonisbe*, p. 4 (I, 89).

55 Haugwitz, ed. cit., 'Maria Stuarda', p. 63 (V, 75 ff.).

56 Birken, *Deutsche Redebind- und Dichtkunst*, p. 329.

57 *Die Glorreiche Marter Joannes von Nepomuck*; quoted from Weiss, op. cit., pp. 113/114.

58 Stranitzky, ed. cit., p. 276 (Die Gestürzte Tyrannay in der Person dess Messinischen Wüttrichs Pelifonte, I, 8).

59 Filidor, *Trauer- Lust- und Misch-Spiele*, title-page.

60 Mone, *Schauspiele des Mittelalters*, p. 136.

61 Weiss, op. cit., p. 48.

62 Lohenstein, *Blumen*, 'Hyacinthen', p. 47 (Redender. Todten-Kopff Herrn Matthäus Machners).

63 Novalis [Friedrich von Hardenberg], *Schriften*, hrsg. von J. Minor, Jena, 1907, III, 4.

64 Novalis, *Schriften*, III, 20.

65 Volkelt, op. cit., p. 460.

66 Goethe, *Sämtliche Werke*. Jubiläums Ausgabe, XXXIV, Schriften zur Kunst, 2, pp. 165/166 (Rameaus Neffe. Ein Dialog von Diderot, notes).

67 Volkelt, op. cit., p. 125.

68 Lohenstein, *Sophonisbe*, p. 65 (IV, 242).

69 cf. Lohenstein, *Blumen*, 'Rosen', pp. 130/131 (Vereinbarung Der Sterne und der Gemüther).

70 Karl Borinski, *Die Antike in Poetik und Kunsttheorie von Ausgang des klassischen Altertums bis auf Goethe und Wilhelm von Humboldt*, I, Mittelalter, Renaissance, Barock, Leipzig, 1914 (Das Erbe der Alten. Schriften über Wesen und Wirkung der Antike, 9), p. 21.

71 Lukács, op. cit., pp. 352/353.

72 Lukács, op. cit., pp. 355/356.

73 cf. Walter Benjamin, 'Zur Kritik der Gewalt', *Archiv für Sozialwissenschaft und Sozialpolitik*, XLVII (1920/21), p. 828 (Heft 3, Aug. '21).

74 Ehrenberg, op. cit., vol. II, Tragödie und Kreuz, p. 53.

75 Benjamin, 'Schicksal und Charakter', p. 92. – cf. also Benjamin, 'Goethes Wahlverwandtschaften', pp. 98 ff.; and Benjamin, 'Schicksal und Charakter', pp. 189–192.

76 Minor, op. cit., pp. 75/76.
77 August Wilhelm Schlegel, *Sämtliche Werke*, VI, 386. [*A Course of Lectures on Dramatic Art and Literature*, p. 496.]
78 Peter Berens, 'Calderóns Schicksalstragödien', *Romanische Forschungen*, XXXIX (1926), pp. 55/56.
79 Gryphius, ed. cit., p. 265 (Cardenio und Celinde, preface).
80 Kolitz, op. cit., p. 163.
81 cf. Benjamin, 'Schicksal und Charakter', p. 192.
82 Shakespeare, *Dramatische Werke* nach der Übers. von August Wilhelm Schlegel u. Ludwig Tieck, sorgfältig revidirt u. theilweise neu bearbeitet, mit Einleitungen u. Noten versehen, unter Redaction von Hermann Ulrici, hrsg. durch die Deutsche Shakespeare-Gesellschaft, VI, Berlin, 1877², p. 98 (Hamlet, III, 2).
83 Stranitzky, ed. cit., p. 322 (Die Gestürzte Tyrannay in der Person dess Messinischen Wüttrichs Pelifonte, III, 12).
84 Ehrenberg, op. cit., p. 46.
85 Lukács, op. cit., p. 345.
86 Friedrich Schlegel, *Alarcos. Ein Trauerspiel*, Berlin, 1802, p. 46 (II, 1).
87 Albert Ludwig, 'Fortsetzungen. Eine Studie zur Psychologie der Literatur', *Germanisch-romanische Monatsschrift*, VI (1914), p. 433.
88 Ziegler, op. cit., p. 52.
89 Ehrenberg, op. cit., II, 57.
90 Müller, op. cit., pp. 82/83.
91 cf. Conrad Höfer, *Die Rudolstädter Festspiele aus den Jahren 1665–67 und ihr Dichter. Eine literarhistorische Studie*, Leipzig, 1904 (Probefahrten, 1), p. 141.

Trauerspiel and tragedy (Part 3)

Motto – Andreas Tscherning, *Vortrab Des Sommers Deutscher Getichte*, Rostock, 1655 (unpaginated).

1 Shakespeare, *Dramatische Werke*, VI, 118/119 (Hamlet, IV, 4).
2 Samuel von Butschky, 'Parabeln und Aphorismen', *Monatsschrift von und für Schlesien*, hrsg. von Heinrich Hoffmann, Breslau, 1829, I, 330.
3 [Jakob] Ayrer, *Dramen*, hrsg. von Adelbert von Keller, I, Stuttgart, 1865 (Bibliothek des litterarischen Vereins in Stuttgart, 76), p. 4. – cf. also Butschky, *Wohlbebauter Rosental*, pp. 410/411.
4 Hübscher, op. cit., p. 552.
5 Pascal, *Pensées*. Edition de 1670. Avec une notice sur Blaise Pascal, un avant-propos et la préface d'Etienne Périer, Paris, n.d. [1905] (Les meilleurs auteurs classiques), pp. 211/212. [*Monsieur Pascall's Thoughts, Meditations, and Prayers, Touching Matters Moral and Divine . . . Done into English by Jos. Walker*, London, 1688, pp. 162/3.]
6 Pascal, op. cit., pp. 215/216. [*Monsieur Pascall's Thoughts*, pp. 165/166.]
7 Gryphius, ed. cit., p. 34 (Leo Armenius, I, 385 ff.).
8 Gryphius, ed. cit., p. 111 (Leo Armenius, V, 53).
9 Filidor, ed. cit., 'Ernelinde', p. 138.
10 cf. Aegidius Albertinus, *Lucifers Königreich und Seelengejaidt: Oder Narrenhatz*, Augsburg, 1617, p. 390.
11 Albertinus, op. cit., p. 411.
12 Harsdörffer, *Poetischer Trichter*, 3. Teil, p. 116.
13 cf. Lohenstein, *Sophonisbe*, pp. 52 ff. (III, 431 ff.).
14 Albertinus, op. cit., p. 414.
15 cf. Hunold, ed. cit., p. 180 (Nebucadnezar, III, 3).

16   Carl Giehlow, 'Dürers Stich "Melencolia I" und der maximilianische Humanisten-kreis', *Mitteilungen der Gesellschaft für vervielfältigende Kunst*, Beilage der *Graphischen Künste*, Vienna, XXVI (1903), p. 32 (Nr 2).

17   Wiener Hofbibliothek, *Codex 5486* (Sammelband medizinischer Manuskripte von 1471); quoted from Giehlow, op. cit., p. 34.

18   Gryphius, ed. cit., p. 91 (Leo Armenius, III, 406/407).

19   Cervantes, *Don Quixote* (Vollst. deutsche Taschenausg. in 2 Bänden besorgt von Konrad Thorer, eingel. von Felix Poppenberg), Leipzig, 1914, II, 106. [*The History of the Valorous and Witty Knight-Errant Don Quixote of the Mancha*, by Miguel de Cervantes, transl. by Thomas Shelton (Library of English Classics), London, 1900, II, 254 f.]

20   Theophrastus Paracelsus, *Erster Theil Der Bücher und Schriften*, Basel, 1589, pp. 363/364.

21   Giehlow, 'Dürers Stich "Melencolia I" etc.', *Mitteilungen der Gesellschaft für verviel-fältigende Kunst*, XXVII (1904), p. 72 (Nr 4).

22   Tscherning, ed. cit. (Melancholey Redet selber.)

23   Immanuel Kant, *Beobachtungen über das Gefühl des Schönen und Erhabenen*, Königs-berg, 1764, pp. 33/34.

24   cf. Paracelsus, op. cit., pp. 82/83, p. 86; *Ander Theil Der Bücher und Schrifften*, pp. 206/207; *Vierdter Theil etc.*, pp. 157/158. – On the other hand, see I, 44, and IV, 189/190.

25   Giehlow, 'Dürers Stich "Melencolia I" etc.', *Mitteilungen etc.*, XXVII, 14 (Nr 1/2).

26   Erwin Panofsky und Fritz Saxl, *Dürers 'Melencolia I'. Eine quellen- und typengeschicht-liche Untersuchung*, Leipzig, Berlin, 1923 (Studien der Bibliothek Warburg, 2), pp. 18/19.

27   Panofsky and Saxl, op. cit., p. 10.

28   Panofsky and Saxl, op. cit., p. 14.

29   Aby Warburg, *Heidnisch-antike Weissagung in Wort und Bild zu Luthers Zeiten*, Heidel-berg, 1920 (Sitzungsgerichte der Heidelberger Akademie der Wissenschaften. Philosophisch-historische Klasse, 1920 [1919], 26. Abhdlg), p. 24.

30   Warburg, op. cit., p. 25.

31   Philippus Melanchthon, *De anima*, Vitebergae, 1548, fol. 821°; quoted from Warburg, p. 61.

32   Melanchthon, op. cit., fol. 76v°; quoted from Warburg, p. 62.

33   Giehlow, op. cit., p. 78.

34   Giehlow, op. cit., p. 72.

35   Giehlow, op. cit., p. 72.

36   Quoted from Franz Boll, *Sternglaube und Sterndeutung. Die Geschichte und das Wesen der Astrologie* (Unter Mitwirkung von Carl Bezold dargestellt von Franz Boll), Leipzig, Berlin, 1918 (Aus Natur und Geisteswelt, 638), p. 46.

37   Tscherning, ed. cit. (Melancholey Redet selber).

38   Marsilius Ficinus, *De vita triplici* I (1482), 4 (*Marsilii Ficini opera*, Basileae, 1576, p. 496); quoted from Panofsky and Saxl, op. cit., p. 51 (fn. 2).

39   cf. Panofsky and Saxl, op. cit., p. 51 (fn. 2).

40   cf. Panofsky and Saxl, op. cit., p. 64 (fn. 3).

41   Warburg, op. cit., p. 54.

42   cf. Albertinus, op. cit., p. 406.

43   Hallmann, *Leichreden*, p. 137.

44   Filidor, ed. cit., 'Ernelinde', pp. 135/136.

45   Quoted from *Schauspiele des Mittelalters*, p. 329.

46   Albertinus, op. cit., p. 390.

47   Anton Hauber, *Planetenkinderbilder und Sternbilder. Zur Geschichte des menschlichen Glaubens und Irrens*, Strasbourg, 1916 (Studien zur deutschen Kunstgeschichte, 194), p. 126.

48   Daniel Halévy, *Charles Péguy et les Cahiers de la Quinzaine*, Paris, 1919, p. 230.

49 *Abû Ma'sar*, übers. nach dem Cod. Leid. Or. 47, p. 255; quoted from Panofsky and Saxl, op. cit., p. 5.
50 cf. Boll, op. cit., p. 46.
51 cf. Rochus Freiherr von Liliencron, *Wie man in Amwald Musik macht. Die siebente Todsünde.* Zwei Novellen, Leipzig, 1903.

Allegory and Trauerspiel (Part 1)

Motto – Männling, op. cit., pp. 86/87.

1 cf. Walter Benjamin, *Der Begriff der Kunstkritik in der deutschen Romantik*, Bern, 1920 (Neue Berner Abhandlungen zur Philosophie und ihrer Geschichte, 5), pp. 6/7 (fn. 3) and pp. 80/81.
2 Goethe, *Sämtliche Werke*, XXXVIII, Schriften zur Literatur, 3, p. 261 (Maximen und Reflexionen).
3 Schopenhauer, *Sämmtliche Werke*, I, 314 ff. [*The World as Will etc.*, I, 237.]
4 cf. William Butler Yeats, *Erzählungen und Essays*. Ubertr. und eingel. von Friedrich Eckstein, Leipzig, 1916, p. 114. ['William Blake and his Illustrations to the Divine Comedy', *Ideas of Good and Evil*, London, 1903, p. 176.]
5 Cysarz, op. cit., p. 40.
6 Cysarz, op. cit., p. 296.
7 Friedrich Creuzer, *Symbolik und Mythologie der alten Völker, besonders der Griechen*, 1. Theil, 2., völlig umgearb. Ausg., Leipzig, Darmstadt, 1819, p. 118.
8 Creuzer, op. cit., p. 64.
9 Creuzer, op. cit., pp. 59 ff.
10 Creuzer, op. cit., pp. 66/67.
11 Creuzer, op. cit., pp. 63/64.
12 Creuzer, op. cit., p. 68.
13 Creuzer, op. cit., pp. 70/71.
14 Creuzer, op. cit., p. 199.
15 Creuzer, op. cit., pp. 147/148.
16 Johann Heinrich Voss, *Antisymbolik*, II, Stuttgart, 1826, p. 223.
17 Johann Gottfried Herder, *Vermischte Schriften*, V, Zerstreute Blätter. Zweyte, neu durchges. Ausg., Vienna, 1801, p. 58.
18 Herder, op. cit., p. 194.
19 Creuzer, op. cit., pp. 227/228.
20 Karl Giehlow, *Die Hieroglyphenkunde des Humanismus in der Allegorie der Renaissance, besonders der Ehrenpforte Kaisers Maximilian I. Ein Versuch*. Mit einem Nachwort von Arpad Weixlgärtner, Vienna, Leipzig, 1915 (Jahrbuch der kunsthistorischen Sammlungen des allerhöchsten Kaiserhauses, XXXII, 1), p. 36.
21 cf. Cesare Ripa, *Iconologia*, Rome, 1609.
22 Giehlow, *Die Hieroglyphenkunde*, p. 34.
23 Giehlow, op. cit., p. 12.
24 Giehlow, op. cit., p. 31.
25 Giehlow, op. cit., p. 23.
26 *Hieroglyphica sive de sacris aegyptiorum literis commentarii*, Ioannis Pierii Valeriani Bolzanii Belluensis, Basileae, 1556, title-page.
27 Pierio Valeriano, op. cit., p. 4.
28 Borinski, *Die Antike*, I, 189.
29 Borinski, *Die Antike*, II, 208/209.
30 cf. Nicolaus Caussinus, *Polyhistor symbolicus, electorum symbolorum, et parabolarum historicarum stromata*, XII. libris complectens, Coloniae Agrippinae, 1623.

31 Opitz, *Prosodia Germanica, Oder Buch von der Deudschen Poeterey*, p. 2.
32 Anonymous review of Menestrier, *La philosophie des images*; *Acta eruditorum*. Anno MDCLXXXIII publicata, Lipsiae, 1683, p. 17.
33 cf. Claude François Menestrier, *La philosophie des images*, Paris, 1682; and Menestrier, *Devises des princes, cavaliers, dames, scavans, et autres personnages illustres de l'Europe*, Paris, 1683.
34 Anonymous review of Menestrier, *Devises des princes*; *Acta eruditorum*, 1683, p. 344.
35 Georg Andreas Böckler, *Ars Heraldica, Das ist: Die Hoch-Edle Teutsche Adels-Kunst*, Nuremberg, 1688, p. 131.
36 Böckler, op. cit., p. 140.
37 Böckler, op. cit., p. 109.
38 Böckler, op. cit., p. 81.
39 Böckler, op. cit., p. 82.
40 Böckler, op. cit., p. 83.
41 Giehlow, *Die Hieroglyphenkunde*, p. 127.
42 cf. Benjamin, *Der Begriff der Kunstkritik*, p. 105.
43 Johann Joachim Winckelmann, *Versuch einer Allegorie besonders für die Kunst*. Säcularausg. Aus des Verfassers Handexemplar mit vielen Zusätzen von seiner Hand, sowie mit inedirten Briefen Winckelmanns und gleichzeitigen Aufzeichnungen über seine letzten Stunden, hrsg. von Albert Dressel. Mit einer Vorbemerkung von Constantin Tischendorf, Leipzig, 1866, pp. 143 ff.
44 Hermann Cohen, *Ästhetik des reinen Gefühls*, II (System der Philosophie, 3), Berlin, 1912, p. 305.
45 Carl Horst, *Barockprobleme*, Munich, 1912, pp. 39/40; cf. also pp. 41/42.
46 Borinski, *Die Antike*, I, 193/194.
47 Borinski, op. cit., pp. 305/306 (fn.).
48 August Buchner, *Wegweiser zur deutschen Tichtkunst*, Jena, n.d. [1663], pp. 80 ff.; quoted from Borcherdt, *Augustus Buchner*, p. 81.
49 Paul Hankamer, *Die Sprache. Ihr Begriff und ihre Deutung im sechzehnten und siebzehnten Jahrhundert. Ein Beitrag zur Frage der literarhistorischen Gliederung des Zeitraums*, Bonn, 1927, p. 135.
50 Burdach, op. cit., p. 178.
51 Hallmann, *Trauer-, Freuden- und Schäferspiele*, 'Mariamne', p. 90.
52 Lohenstein, *Agrippina*, pp. 33/34 (II, 380 ff.).
53 cf. Kolitz, op. cit., pp. 166/167.
54 Winckelmann, op. cit., p. 19.
55 cf. Benjamin, *Der Begriff der Kunstkritik*, pp. 53 ff.
56 Petersen, op. cit., p. 12.
57 Strich, op. cit., p. 26.

58 Johann Heinrich Merck, *Ausgewählte Schriften zur schönen Literatur und Kunst. Ein Denkmal*, hrsg. von Adolf Stahr, Oldenburg, 1840, p. 308.
59 Strich, op. cit., p. 39.
60 Franz von Baader, *Sämmtliche Werke*, hrsg. durch einen Verein von Freunden des Verewigten: Franz Hoffmann [et al.], 1. Hauptabt., II, Leipzig, 1851, p. 129.
61 Baader, op. cit., p. 129.
62 Hübscher, op. cit., p. 560.
63 Hübscher, op. cit., p. 555.
64 Cohn, op. cit., p. 23.
65 Tittmann, op. cit., p. 94.
66 Winckelmann, op. cit., p. 27. cf. also Creuzer, op. cit., p. 67, pp. 109/110.

67 Creuzer, op. cit., p. 64.
68 Creuzer, op. cit., p. 147.
69 Cysarz, op. cit., p. 31.
70 Novalis, *Schriften*, III, 5.
71 Novalis, *Schriften*, II, 308.
72 Borinski, *Die Antike*, I, 192.

Allegory and Trauerspiel (Part 2)

Motto – *Dreyständige Sinnbilder zu fruchtbringendem Nutzen und beliebender ergetzlichkeit* ausgefertigt durch den Geheimen [Franz Julius von dem Knesebeck], Braunschweig, 1643, plate 5.

1 Wackernagel, op. cit., p. 11.
2 Lohenstein, *Sophonisbe*, pp. 75/76 (IV, 563 ff.).
3 Müller, op. cit., p. 94.
4 Novalis, *Schriften*, III, 71.
5 cf. Lohenstein, *Sophonisbe*, p. 76 (IV, 585 ff.).
6 Julius Leopold Klein, *Geschichte des englischen Dramas*, II, Leipzig, 1876 (Geschichte des Dramas, 13), p. 57.
7 cf. Hans Steinberg, Die Reyen in den Trauerspielen des Andreas Gryphius (doctoral dissertation), Göttingen, 1914, p. 107.
8 Kolitz, op. cit., p. 182.
9 cf. Kolitz, op. cit., p. 102, p. 168.
10 Kolitz, op. cit., p. 168.
11 Steinberg, op. cit., p. 76.
12 Hübscher, op. cit., p. 557.
13 Gryphius, ed. cit., p. 599 (Amilius Paulus Papinianus, IV, stage-direction).
14 Steinberg, op. cit., p. 76.
15 cf. Lohenstein, *Sophonisbe*, pp. 17 ff. (I, 513 ff.).
16 cf. Kolitz, op. cit., p. 133.
17 cf. Kolitz, op. cit., p. 111.
18 cf. Gryphius, ed. cit., pp. 310 ff. (Cardenio und Celinde, IV, 1 ff.).
19 August Kerckhoffs, *Daniel Casper von Lohensteins Trauerspiele mit besonderer Berücksichtigung der Cleopatra. Ein Beitrag zur Geschichte des Dramas im XVII Jahrhundert*, Paderborn, 1877, p. 52.
20 Hallmann, *Trauer-, Freuden- und Schäferspiele*, 'Die himmlische Liebe oder die beständige Märterin Sophia', p. 69 (stage-direction).
21 cf. *Emblemata selectiora*, Amstelaedami, 1704, Tab. 15.
22 Hausenstein, op. cit., p. 9.
23 Flemming, *Andreas Gryphius und die Bühne*, p. 131.
24 cf. Hausenstein, op. cit., p. 71.
25 Tittmann, op. cit., p. 184.
26 Gryphius, ed. cit., p. 269 (Cardenio und Celinde, Table of contents).
27 Hallmann, *Trauer-, Freuden- und Schäferspiele*, p. 3 (of the unpaginated preface).
28 cf. Petrarca, *Sechs Triumphi oder Siegesprachten. In Deutsche Reime übergesetzt*, Cöthen, 1643.
29 Hallmann, *Leichreden*, p. 124.
30 *Herodes der Kindermörder, Nach Art eines Trauerspiels ausgebildet und In Nürnberg Einer Teutschliebenden Gemeine vorgestellet durch Johan Klaj*, Nuremberg, 1645; quoted from Tittmann, op. cit., p. 156.
31 Harsdörffer, *Poetischer Trichter*, II, 81.

32 cf. Hallmann, *Leichreden*, p. 7.
33 Gryphius, ed. cit., p. 512 (Aemilius Paulus Papinianus, I, 1 ff.).
34 Ernst Wilken, *Über die kritische Behandlung der geistlichen Spiele*, Halle, 1873, p. 10.
35 Meyer, op. cit., p. 367.
36 Wysocki, op. cit., p. 61.
37 cf. Erich Schmidt, op. cit., p. 414.
38 Kerckhoffs, op. cit., p. 89.
39 Fritz Schramm, *Schlagworte der Alamodezeit*, Strasbourg, 1914 (*Zeitschrift für deutsche Wortforschung*, Beiheft zum 15. Bd), p. 2; cf. also pp. 31/32.
40 Hallmann, *Trauer-, Freuden- und Schäferspiele*, 'Mariamne', p. 41 (III, 103).
41 Hallmann, 'Mariamne', p. 42 (III, 155).
42 Hallmann, 'Mariamne', p. 44 (III, 207).
43 Hallmann, 'Mariamne', p. 45 (III, 226).
44 Hallmann, 'Mariamne', p. 5 (I, 126/127).
45 Hallmann, *Trauer-, Freuden und Schäferspiele*, 'Theodoricus Veronensis', p. 102 (V, 285 ff.).
46 Hallmann, 'Mariamne', p. 65 (397/398).
47 cf. Hallmann, 'Mariamne', p. 57 (IV, 132 ff.).
48 cf. Stachel, op. cit., pp. 336 ff.
49 Hallmann, *Trauer-, Freuden- und Schäferspiele*, 'Mariamne', p. 42 (III, 160/161).
50 Hallman, 'Mariamne', p. 101 (V, 826/827).
51 Hallmann, 'Mariamne', p. 76 (V, 78).
52 Hallmann, 'Mariamne', p. 62 (IV, 296); cf. 'Mariamne', p. 12 (I, 351), pp. 38/39 (III, 32 and 59), p. 76 (V, 83), and p. 91 (V, 516); 'Sophia', p. 9 (I, 260); Hallmann, *Leichreden*, p. 497.
53 Hallmann, *Trauer-, Freuden- und Schäferspiele*, 'Mariamne', p. 16 (I, 449 ff.).
54 Haugwitz, ed. cit., 'Maria Stuarda', p. 35 (II, 125 ff.).
55 Breitinger, op. cit., p. 224; cf. p. 462, and Johann Jacob Bodmer, *Critische Betrachtungen über die Poetischen Gemählde Der Dichter*, Zürich, Leipzig, 1741, p. 107, pp. 425 ff.
56 J. J. Bodmer, *Gedichte in gereimten Versen*, Zürich, 1754[2], p. 32.
57 Jacob Böhme, *De signatura rerum*, Amsterdam, 1682, p. 208.
58 Böhme, op. cit., p. 5, pp. 8/9.
59 Knesebeck, op. cit., 'Kurtzer Vorbericht An den Teutschliebenden und geneigten Leser', aa/bb.
60 Borinski, *Die Antike*, II, 18.
61 Scaliger, op. cit., p. 478, p. 481 (IV, 47).
62 Hankamer, op. cit., p. 159.
63 Josef Nadler, *Literaturgeschichte der Deutschen Stämme und Landschaften*, II, Die Neustämme von 1300, die Altstämme von 1600–1780, Regensburg, 1913, p. 78.
64 cf. also Schutzschrift / für Die Teutsche Spracharbeit / und Derselben Beflissene, durch den Spielenden [Georg Philipp Harsdörffer], *Frauenzimmer Gesprechspiele*. Erster Theil, Nuremberg, 1644, p. 12 (of the separate pagination).
65 cf. Borcherdt, *Augustus Buchner*, pp. 84/85.
66 Tittmann, op. cit., p. 228.
67 Harsdörffer, *Schutzschrift*, p. 14.
68 Strich, op. cit., pp. 45/46.
69 Leisewitz, ed. cit., pp. 45/46 (Julius von Tarent, II, 5).
70 Magnus Daniel Omeis, *Gründliche Anleitung zur Teutschen accuraten Reim- und Dichtkunst*, Nuremberg, 1704; quoted from Popp, op. cit., p. 45.
71 Borinski, *Die Antike*, I, 190.
72 Harsdörffer, *Poetischer Trichter*, II, 78/79.

73 Werner Richter, *Liebeskampf 1630 und Schaubühne 1670. Ein Beitrag zur deutschen Theatergeschichte des siebzehnten Jahrhunderts*, Berlin, 1910 (Palaestra, 78), pp. 170/171.

74 cf. Flemming, *Geschichte des Jesuitentheaters*, pp. 270 ff.

75 Calderón, *Schauspiele* (trans, Gries), III, 316 (Eifersucht das grosse Scheusal, II).

76 Gryphius, ed. cit., p. 62 (Leo Armenius, II, 455 ff.).

77 cf. Stachel, op. cit., p. 261.

78 Schiebel, op. cit., p. 358.

79 cf. *Die Glorreiche Marter Joannes von Nepomuck*; quoted from Weiss, op. cit., pp. 148 ff.

80 Hallmann, *Trauer-, Freuden- und Schäferspiele*, op. cit., p. 1 (of the unpaginated preface).

81 Hausenstein, op. cit., p. 14.

82 Hallmann, *Trauer-, Freuden- und Schäferspiele*, 'Sophia', p. 70 (V, 185 ff.); cf. p. 4 (I, 108 ff.).

83 cf. Richard Maria Werner, 'Johann Christian Hallmann als Dramatiker', *Zeitschrift für die österreichischen Gymnasien*, L (1899), p. 691. But see Horst Steger, 'Johann Christian Hallmann. Sein Leben und seine Werke' (doctoral dissertation), Leipzig (publ. Weida i. Th.), 1909, p. 89.

84 Flemming, *Andreas Gryphius und die Bühne*, p. 401.

85 Nietzsche, *Die Geburt der Tragödie*, ed. cit., pp. 132ff. [*Basic Writings*, pp. 115 ff.].

86 (Johann Wilhelm Ritter), *Fragmente aus dem Nachlasse eines jungen Physikers. Ein Taschenbuch für Freunde der Natur*, hrsg von J. W. Ritter [editorship fictional]. Zweytes Bändchen, Heidelberg, 1810, pp. 227 ff.

87 Ritter, op. cit., p. 230.

88 Ritter, op. cit., p. 242.

89 Ritter, op. cit., p. 246.

90 cf. Friedrich Schlegel, *Seine prosaischen Jugendschriften*, hrsg. von J. Minor, II, Zur deutschen Literatur und Philosophie, Vienna, 1906², p. 364.

91 Müller, op. cit., p. 71 (fn.).

92 Herder, *Vermischte Schriften*, pp. 193/194.

93 Strich, op. cit., p. 42.

94 Cysarz, op. cit., p. 114.

Allegory and Trauerspiel (Part 3)

Motto – Lohenstein, *Blumen*, 'Hyacinthen', p. 50.

1 Anon., review of Menestrier, *La philosophie des images*, *Acta eruditorum 1683*, pp. 17/18.

2 Böckler, op. cit., p. 102.

3 Böckler, op. cit., p. 104.

4 Martin Opitz, *Judith*, Breslau, 1635, sheet Aij. v⁰.

5 cf. Hallmann, *Leichreden*, p. 377.

6 Gryphius, ed. cit., p. 390 (Carolus Stuardus, II, 389/390).

7 Müller, op. cit., p. 15.

8 Stachel, op. cit., p. 25.

9 Hallmann, *Trauer-, Freuden- und Schäferspiele*, 'Sophia', p. 68 (stage-direction).

10 Gryphius, ed. cit., p. 614 (Aemilius Paulus Papinianus, V, stage-direction).

11 Hallmann, *Trauer-, Freuden- und Schäferspiele*, 'Sophia', p. 68 (stage-direction).

12 Gryphius, ed. cit., p. 172 (Catharina von Georgien, I, 649 ff.).

13 cf. Gryphius, ed. cit., p. 149 (Catharina von Georgien, I, stage-direction).

14 Hallmann, *Trauer-, Freuden- und Schäferspiele*, 'Die listige Rache oder der tapfere Heraklius', p. 10 (stage-direction).

15 cf. Tittmann, op. cit., p. 175.
16 Mannheimer, op. cit., p. 139.
17 cf. Tittmann, op. cit., p. 46.
18 Hallmann, *Trauer-, Freuden- und Schäferspiele*, 'Sophia', p. 8 (I, 229/230).
19 Warburg, op. cit., p. 70.
20 Friedrich von Bezold, *Das Fortleben der antiken Götter im mittelalterlichen Humanismus*, Bonn, Leipzig, 1922, pp. 31/32. – cf. Vinzenz von Beauvais, op. cit., columns 295/296 (extracts from Fulgentius).
21 Usener, op. cit., p. 366.
22 Usener, op. cit., 368/369; cf. also pp. 316/317.
23 Aurelius P. Clemens Prudentius, *Contra Symmachum*, I, 501/502; quoted from Bezold, op. cit., p. 30.
24 *Des heiligen Augustinus zwey und zwanzig Bücher von der Stadt Gottes*. Aus dem Lateinischen der Mauriner Ausgabe übersetzt von J. P. Silbert, I, Vienna, 1826, p. 508 (VIII, 23). [Augustine of Hippo, *Concerning the City of God against Pagans*, trans. Henry Bettenson, ed. David Knowles, Harmondsworth, 1972, p. 331.]
25 Warburg, op. cit., p. 34.
26 Bezold, op. cit., p. 5.
27 Warburg, op. cit., p. 5.
28 Horst, op. cit., p. 42.
29 *Quodlibet Màgistri Henrici Goethals a Gandavo* [Heinrich von Gent], Parisiis, 1518, Fol. XXXIVr[0] (Quodl. II, Quaest. 9); quoted from the translation in Panofsky and Saxl, op. cit., p. 72.
30 From an anonymous Luciferan Letter of 1410 against John XXIII; quoted from Paul Lehmann, *Die Parodie im Mittelalter*, Munich, 1922, p. 97.
31 Klein, op. cit., pp. 3/4.
32 Goethe, *Sämtliche Werke*, XXXVIII, Schriften zur Literatur, 3, p. 258 (Maximen und Reflexionen).
33 Novalis, *Schriften*, III, 13.
34 Hallmann, *Leichreden*, p. 45.
35 Augustinus, op. cit., p. 564. [*Concerning the City of God*, p. 366.]
36 cf. Stachel, op. cit., pp. 336/337.
37 Hallmann, *Leichreden*, p. 9.
38 Hallmann, op. cit., p. 3 (of the unpaginated preface).
39 cf. Lohenstein, *Agrippina*, p. 74 (IV), and *Sophonisbe*, p. 75 (IV).
40 Lohenstein, *Blumen*, 'Hyacinthen', p. 50 (Redender Todten-Kopff Herrn Matthäus Machners).
41 *Die Fried-erfreute Teutonie*. Ausgefertigt von Sigismundo Betulio [Sigmund von Birken], Nuremberg, 1652, p. 114.
42 *Die vierundzwanzig Bücher der Heiligen Schrift*. Nach dem Masoretischen *Texte*, hrsg. von Leopold Zunz, Berlin, 1835, p. 3; I, 3, (v). [Genesis, III, 5.]
43 *Heilige Schrift*, p. 2; I, 1, (xxxi). [Genesis, I, 31.]
44 cf. Dante Allighieri, *La Divina Commedia*. Edizione minore fatta sul testo dell' edizione critica di Carlo Witte. Edizione seconda, Berlin, 1892, p. 13 (Inferno, III, 6). [*The Divine Comedy*, The Inferno, trans. John Aitken Carlyle (The Temple Classics), London, 1950, p. 27.]
45 Hausenstein, op. cit., p. 17.
46 Borinski, *Die Antike*, I, 193.

Index